S0-CFE-661

MORAL PHILOSOPHY IN BRITAIN

MORAL PHILOSOPHY IN BRITAIN

FROM BRADLEY TO WITTGENSTEIN

Cahal B. Daly

FOUR COURTS PRESS

Set in 11 on 12.5 point Ehrhardt
by Woodcote Typesetters for
FOUR COURTS PRESS
Kill Lane, Blackrock, Co. Dublin, Ireland
and in North America
FOUR COURTS PRESS
c/o ISBS, 5804 N.E. Hassalo Street, Portland, OR 97213.

A catalogue record for this title is
available from the British Library

ISBN 1-85182-227-5

Printed in Great Britain
by Antony Rowe Ltd, Chippenham, Wilts.

Contents

Preface

The research of which these pages are the fruit was undertaken in Paris during a sabbatical semester granted to me by Queen's University, Belfast, in 1960–1. It was unfortunately not completed before my return to resume my teaching duties in the Department of Scholastic Philosophy at the university at Easter 1961. My hope was that it could be completed in the summer of that year.

This hope was dashed by a series of events which followed. A dearly loved sister fell ill shortly after my return and died at an early age in September 1961. I became ill myself soon afterwards and had for some time to reduce my workload. The Second Vatican Council was convened in October 1962, and I was generously granted by my university a term's leave in each of the following years until the conclusion of the Council in 1965. In June 1967, I was appointed Bishop and left academic life.

For many years I retained the hope of finding time to return to my unfinished work and complete the study and publish it. The hope was unrealistic. The pastoral life of a bishop simply cannot be combined with academic study. However, I kept hoping that somehow before ending my days I could complete and publish this study, which I hoped and believed had retained some validity and relevance.

As the ending of my days loomed nearer, my desire to see it published grew stronger. At the same time, the hope of completing it as originally planned became quite unrealisable and had to be abandoned. I decided therefore to publish the chapters as I had left them, consoling myself that an *opus imperfectum* may still contribute to the *opus semper perfectibile* which philosophy in the Scholastic tradition was always held to be.

I feel chastened by a remark of Jean Paul Sartre that a person must not be allowed to plead that his or her book (or lecture) would have been better had he or she had more time to work on it. Such a person, Sartre contended, is in bad faith; indeed, this is for him a typical example of *mauvaise foi*. It is, nevertheless, in good faith that I offered these pages to the Four Courts Press for publication and that I now offer them to readers in the hope that they may be of some interest and may whet someone's appetite for further research.

7 April 1996, Easter Sunday

CHAPTER ONE

F.H. Bradley: Idealist Ethics

F.H. Bradley was born in 1846. In 1865, he went up to University College, Oxford. In 1870, he was awarded a fellowship at Merton College and he spent the rest of his life at Oxford. He was a sick and often suffering man during most of his life. His fellowship, however, entailed no teaching or lecturing duties and he was able to concentrate on his study and writing. He was much influenced by German philosophical thought. He read and admired Hegel, but was nevertheless not a Hegelian. He derived much of his ideas about religion from the Hegelianised Christianity of F.C. Baur and the Tübingen school of theology. He was a close student of Herbart. A magnificent stylist, he was in particular a master of scornful sarcasm. His most scathing paragraphs were reserved for British empiricists; his most cruel mockery for the British philosophical tradition, which he accused of dogmatism, insularity, smugness and ignorance of European, and especially German, philosophy. Bradley died in 1924.[1] Although in many ways a nineteenth-century rather than a twentieth-century figure, he remains important for the understanding of British philosophy in this century. Since Moore began to write, much of British philosophy has been a reaction against idealism, of which Bradley was one of the greatest British exponents. It has also been a reaction against 'metaphysics'; and when British philosophers use this word, if they are thinking of anything, and not just emitting a growling noise, it is often of Bradley they are thinking.

Bradley's only sustained work on ethics, the *Ethical Studies*, was published in 1876. It was soon out of print and was never republished. In the Preface, Bradley defined his purpose as being mainly critical.

[The writer] sees that ethical theories rest in the end on preconceptions metaphysical and psychological. He believes that many of the fundamental ideas now current, especially in England, are confused or even false; and he has endeavoured, by the correction of some of these, at least to remove what seem obstacles to the apprehension of moral facts.

---

1 See Richard Wollheim, *F. H. Bradley* (Penguin Books, 1959), pp. 13–15 (Biographical Note); and his "F. H. Bradley" in *The Revolution in Philosophy*, introd. by Gilbert Ryle (Macmillan, London, 1956), pp. 11–25. See also J.A. Passmore, *A Hundred Years of Philosophy* (Duckworth, London, 1957), pp. 59–70. On Bradley's ethical thought, see Wollheim, op.cit., pp. 233–76; Hastings Rasbdall, *The Theory of Good and Evil* (Oxford University Press, 1907), vol. II., pp. 60–106, 268–75, 419–27; Mary Warnock, *Ethics since 1900* (Home University Library, Oxford, 1960), pp. 1–15; Dorothea Krook, *Three Traditions of Moral Thought* (Cambridge University Press, 1959), pp. 226–53.

9

He granted that the Essays might seem 'dogmatic and one-sided'; but justified this by saying that he knew no English moral philosophy which was not 'at least as one-sided and even more dogmatic'.

Bradley in the main adhered throughout his life to his early views on ethics. In 1920, he was thinking about re-issuing the book. In 1924, he began to make rough notes for additional matter to be incorporated in a new edition; as well as inserting observations, sometimes sharply criticising points of detail in the argument of the first edition. This work was interrupted by his death. The additional matter and the foot-notes are incorporated in the Second Edition, posthumously published by the care of his brother and sister, who acknowledge their debt to Professor H.H. Joachim.[2]

Ethical Studies is an excellent example of Bradley's critical and dialectical method. His own thought is elaborated in opposition to theories which he criticises; and when he seems himself to have arrived at a firm personal position, he rounds on it in turn to show its inadequacies and the need to go forward to some higher synthesis. He is thus frequently misunderstood, being taken to stand over views which he modifies later in the book.

1 FREE WILL AND MORAL RESPONSIBILITY

The essence of morality, according to Bradley, is that it is not a collection of propositions, commands or appraisals, but is a life; an effort to give unity and meaning to one's life by a progressive realisation of one's true self. His constant criticism of existing theories is that they fail to do justice to the unity and wholeness of the moral life; they dissociate the moral person. This is already charged against both libertarianism and determinism in the first essay, 'The Vulgar Notion of Responsibility'. Here Bradley gives a remarkably balanced account of what the ordinary person means by responsibility. He shows that responsibility for the 'plain man' involves principally the notions of continuity of the moral person, accountability for one's actions and deservingness of punishment for one's wrong-doing.

In the first place, to feel responsible means to feel that my moral conscience has a right to judge *me now* for what I did *then*. This is not conceivable unless I am the same person now who acted in the past. My past actions are mine and I cannot disown them.[3] But when is an action *mine*? In an analysis which is very close to Aristotle (and hence to scholasticism), he shows that, if I am to be responsible for an action, the action must issue from my will, and I must act with knowledge of what I do and of the moral quality of what I do.[4]

2 Published at Oxford, at the Clarendon Press, 1927.   3 pp. 3–6.   4 pp. 6–9.

This ordinary notion of responsibility is not inconsistent with the predictability of my behaviour. So long as prediction is based on knowledge of my character, it traces my actions to me as their cause and in no way disturbs my sense of moral independence. The prediction which I would resent and repudiate would be one which purported to trace my actions to physical or mechanical causes outside my control; or to reduce my behaviour to causal uniformities or physical-science laws of which I as agent would be the effect. This would be incompatible with my feeling of responsibility; and it would be rejected by me as attempting to deduce the qualities of my being from that which is not myself. Such prediction-claims would amount to the depersonalising of the person, the annihilation of the self.[5]

Bradley contends that the unity of the moral person is shattered alike by libertarianism and by determinism. By libertarianism (he calls it simply 'the Free-will doctrine'), he means the theory that human acts issue from the pure indifference of a will which has no reason for acting, whose actions are therefore causeless, unpredictable, inexplicable. He rightly points out that this is the very opposite of responsible action; it makes human acts arbitrary and in a proper sense irresponsible.[6] This doctrine cuts a man's acts off from his self; for his self is nothing if not a permanent source of consistent activity. It also isolates the will from its acts and thus exempts it from moral responsibility. It is an abstract, acosmic, content-less and inefficacious will. It wills *nothing* and therefore is . . . nothing.[7]

---

5 pp. 14–24. 'If from given data and from universal rules, another man can work out the generation (of a man) like a sum, in arithmetic, where is his self gone to? It is invaded by another, broken up into selfless elements, put together again, mastered and handled just as a poor dead thing is mastered by man. And this being so, our man feels dimly that, if another can thus unmake and remake him, he himself might just as well have been anybody else from the start, since nothing remains which is especially his. The sanctum of his individuality is outraged and profaned: and with that profanation ends the existence that once seemed impenetrably sure. To explain the origin of a man is utterly to annihilate him' (p. 20). 6 pp. 11–14. 'Freedom means *chance*; you are free, because there is no reason which will account for your acts, because no one in the world not even yourself, can possibly say what you will and will not do next. You are "accountable", in short, because you are a wholly "unaccountable" creature' (p. 11). 7 pp. 10–11. The phrase, 'Indeterminism is a will which wills *nothing*' is taken by Bradley from Erdmarn. In idealist language, Bradley calls such a Will an 'abstract universal'. 'This I, in the act of "I will", is the self as pure I, which is superior to all its contents, desires etc. and descends into them only by its own *libertas arbitrii*'. (p. 11). Cf. *Appearance and Reality*, 2nd ed. (London, 1897), p. 435. This doctrine of Free-will, as Bradley represents it, has curious affinities with the concept of Will in Wittgenstein's *Tractatus*. There the will is separated from the world and can have no responsibility for what happens in the world; the goodness or badness of the will has nothing to do with 'changing the world' in the sense of placing acts or facts in the world (6.373–4, 6.43). In his later work, the *Philosophical Investigations*, Wittgenstein criticised his own earlier theory as being a typical example of false philosophical abstraction (611–46). What Wittgenstein says about the 'extensionless point . . . separate from all experience' of the pure 'I *do*' (in 620) is very like what Bradley says of the 'pure I' (on p. 11). What Wittgenstein says, in correction of this, about 'intention lying *also* in "What I did" (644) is comparable to Bradley's remarks about the solidarity of "I" and "will": 'In "I will" we write "I", and "will" in such a way that the notion of dividing them is absurd'. (p. 33). Muirhead (*Rule and End in Morals*, Oxford University Press, 1932, pp. 93, 95) refers to an article in *Mind*

Indeterminism, therefore, reduces the will to an 'extensionless point' by isolating it from the world. Determinism achieves the same result by merging the will into the non-human world. The effect of both doctrines is the same: the dismemberment of the moral personality. Bradley's rhetoric was never more devastating than when he criticises empiricistic mechanism and its related doctrine of the self, which he pillories in famous phrases as the 'onions-on-a-rope', 'grapes-in-a-bunch', 'marbles-in-a-bag' theory.[8] This thing-and-space-language has no application to what we know about ourselves as persons. It cannot account for the knowledge we have of the self as distinct from its desires, yet enclosing them in itself; capable of excluding them yet also of expressing itself in them, while remaining distinct from and responsible for them. Determinism deprives the words 'I will' of all meaning: it gives us a will which *wills* nothing and therefore is . . . nothing.[9] But the meaning and the truth of 'I will' resist all attempts to explain them away on the part of 'our "inductive" psychology, and our anti-metaphysical metaphysic and our all too metaphysical "Baconian" science'.[9A]

Similarly, indeterminism and determinism are alike irreconcilable with our ordinary moral convictions about punishment, which forbid us to isolate punishment from moral responsibility.[10] This requires personal identity, without which 'responsibility is sheer nonsense; and to the psychology of our Determinists personal identity . . . is a word without a vestige of meaning'.[11] For Determinism,

> a criminal is as 'responsible' for his acts of last year as the Thames at London is responsible for an accident on the Isis at Oxford, and he is no more responsible. And, to punish that criminal . . . is to repeat the story of Xerxes and the Hellespont.[12]

Bradley concludes

> that of 'the two great schools' which divide our philosophy, as the one, so the other, stands out of relation to vulgar morality; that for both alike responsibility (as we believe in it) is a word altogether devoid of signification and impossible of explanation.[13]

in which Bradley used different language for the relation of self to its desires, speaking of the power of the self to raise and suspend itself above different and conflicting elements in its physical nature, and to choose between them in accord or discord with its conception of the good life as a whole. 8 pp. 34–40. In mechanism and its parent empiricism (he refers to 'Locke and the friends of Locke'), 'we find every term and phrase has a meaning not until we import into the consideration of ourselves the coarsest and crassest mechanical metaphors of pulls and pushes, drawings and thrustings, which we believed to exist not anywhere except in the lowest phenomena of the natural world . . . We have nothing before our understanding, until, as it were, we call up before our eyes solid things in space, denting and punching and printing, another thing called a mind . . . a thing called a will pushed and pulled by things called motives . . .' (pp. 34–5). This doctrine breaks down the distinction between the natural and the non-natural world, between the physical and the mental'. (p. 25). 9 p. 26; cf. p. 12; as before, the phrase is from Erdman. 9a. p. 34. 10 p. 27: 'If punishment is inflicted for any other reason whatever than because it is merited by wrong, it is a gross immorality, a crying injustice, an abominable crime, and not what it pretends to be' (p. 27). 11 p. 36. 12 p. 40. 13 pp. 40–1.

We do not intend to pursue the problem of free will through the course of modern British moral philosophy, for this would require a volume by itself. We have felt, however, that Bradley's treatment of it should be expounded, because it is so closely integrated with the rest of his moral thinking, and because it is an approach which has been on the whole, and unfortunately, neglected by later philosophers. These have on the whole tended to see the free-will problem as a problem in scientific explanation of human conduct; they have taken the 'observer's' point of view, looking 'objectively' either on the conduct of others or on one's own past conduct. Bradley criticised this as ignoring the point of view of the moral subject, obliged to take to himself and assume responsiblity for his own present or past conduct. The existentialist doctrine of liberty is in this sense much closer to Bradley than to contemporary British writers.

Even when looking at the problem as a problem of explanation, rather than of moral action, modern writers frequently forget that there are many uses of the terms 'explanation', 'cause', 'reason'; and that one does not leave free human action inexplicable by refusing to 'explain' it in terms of physics. Bradley seems almost to anticipate Wittgenstein when he says:

> We may admit the 'because' (or rather, since our will is rational, we may demand it), but may say, there is more than one sort of 'because'. . . . And if we take this line, we may find that the 'because' which excludes accountability is only the 'because' which does not apply to mind, but to something else. If 'must' always means the 'must' of the falling stone, then 'must' is irreconcilable with 'ought' or 'can'.[14]

Bradley insists that explanation and even some degree of prediction of human behaviour is possible in terms of character and habit, but that this leaves freedom intact because character and habit are my-self-in-action. Bradley's type of approach to the free-will problem did not entirely disappear from subsequent British philosophy. A number of impressive philosophers—who are none the worse for being described as standing outside the main stream of contemporary British philosophy—continued to pose the problem in similar terms to his.[15] They seem to us to provide incomparably better discussions of the problem than most of the linguistic analysts do.

---

14 p. 56 (in an additional Note). Compare Wittgenstein, *Philosophical Investigations*, II xi (pp. 223–4). There is a Wittgensteinian ring also in Bradley's words: 'There is a view, which says to the necessitarian, "Are you not neglecting distinctions?"; to the believer in liberty, "Are you sure you *are* distinguishing?" Is there the smallest practical difference between external necessity and chance? . . . Is the opposite of a false view always true? Is it not much rather often (and always in some spheres) just *as* false?' (p. 56).
15 Compare, for example: C.A. Campbell, *In Defence of Free Will*, Inaugural Lecture (Jackson and Co., Glasgow, 1938); 'Self-activity and its modes', in *Contemporary British Philosophy*, ed. H.D. Lewis (Macmillan, London, 1957), pp. 85–115; *On Selfhood and Godhood*, (Allen and Unwin, London, 1957), pp. 130–57 (substantially a reproduction of the preceding), 158–79; J. Laird, *A Study in Moral Theory*, (Allen and Unwin, London, 1926), pp. 162–95; W. D. Lamont, *The Principles of Moral Judgment* (Oxford, 1946), pp. 194–218; A. Macbeath, *Experiments in Living* (Macmillan, London, 1952), pp. 33ff., 413ff.

2 SELF-REALISATION

Bradley's whole thought about ethics is, therefore, from the beginning suspended from the notion of the moral self. The last sentence of his additional Note to the first Essay is: '*What* is my true self?' This is the question which dominates also the second Essay: 'Why should I be moral?' To the question which gives its title to the essay, Bradley retorts that it is an illegitimate question. It insinuates that morality is a means to some end beyond itself, to some interest or advantage of man, the attainment of happiness, the avoidance of damnation; and Bradley protests that this destroys the nature of morality as an end in itself and the end of human existence.[16]

> We desert a moral point of view, we degrade and prostitute virtue, when to those who do not love her for herself we bring ourselves to recommend her for the sake of her pleasures.[17]

The only point of the question, therefore, is to make us realise that morality cannot be a means to any ulterior end, that it is itself the end for man; and then we shall be led to ask, 'In what way is morality an end?' Bradley replies that all action is a realisation or fulfilment of the self through an attainment of its ends; and that moral action can only be a realisation of the true self through an attainment of its whole and proper ends.[18] The crucial question for ethics is, therefore, 'What is the true self?' At the end of the additional Note to this Essay, Bradley wrote:

> If I am asked why I am to be moral, I can say no more than this, that what I cannot doubt is my own being now, and that since, in that being is involved a self, which is to be here and now, and yet in this here and now is not, I therefore cannot doubt that there is an end which I am to make real; and morality, if not equivalent to, is at all events included in this making real of myself.
>
> If it is absurd to ask for the further reason of my knowing and willing my own existence, then it is equally absurd to ask for the further reason of what is involved therein. The only rational question here is not Why? but What? What is the self that I know and will? What is its true nature and what is implied therein? What is the self that I am to make actual and how is the principle present, living and incarnate in its particular modes of realisation?[19]

---

16 He thinks that the Christian doctrine of reward and punishment in the next life destroys morality. He caustically calls it the 'do it or be damned' theory of morals. He declares: 'it seems to us to contain the essence of irreligion . . . it contributes nothing to moral philosophy, unless that has to do with the means whereby we are simply to get pleasure or avoid pain. (It) reduces (both morality and religion to deliberate selfishness' (p. 62n.). This is a view which is almost universal in modern British philosophy and we shall have to return to it later.   17 p. 63.   18 pp. 66–74.   19 p. 84.; cf. pp. 160–3.

The rest of Bradley's book is an attempt to answer this question by criticism of false views and amelioration of inadequate ones. Bradley is anxious to keep to the facts of moral experience;[20] but he is frequently carried into far-fetched abstractions by his idealist categories. In the present essay, he declares that ' "Realise yourself" does not mean merely "Be a whole" but "Be an *infinite* whole";' and argues that 'the mind is *not* finite just because it knows it *is* finite'.[21] Bradley contrasts the concrete infinite, which for him is the moral person, with the infinite of experience of the hedonists, which is only endlessly finite; and with the abstract infinite of Kantian Practical Reason, which is simply negation-of-finite and has no positive content or charactersitics of its own.[22] The concrete infinity of the self encounters limits and resistances within the living person. The facts of 'sensuous existence' oppose the ideal of my infinity. Self-realisation becomes a struggle 'to force the sensuous fact to correspond to the truth of ourselves . . . I alter and alter the sensuous facts, till I find nothing in them but myself carried out.' [23] Morality is a perpetual effort to realise my infinity in my finite situation.

I am both infinite *and* finite and that is why my moral life is a perpetual progress. I must progress, because I have an other which is to be, and yet never quite is myself, and so, as I am, I am in a state of contradiction.[24]

Morality is *becoming* what I *am*, infinite; it is realising an infinite whole in oneself, and making it and oneself truly infinite.[25] Morality is fulfilled by being surpassed; and by it, man is realised by being transcended and becoming . . . God.

It is obvious here that Bradley has wandered after words, leaving facts far behind. In his own terms, he has 'got rid of the facts by applying phrases to them'.[26] His 'infinite self' seems to have little to do with the self of flesh and blood. He speaks later of men as 'spiritualised animals';[27] but he never succeeds in giving 'body' to his 'self', or in giving a satisfactory account of what in detail the moral struggle is about. Bradley is always stronger in attack than in exposition, always happier in scepticism than in construction.

3 WHAT THE MORAL SELF IS NOT

Two false views of the moral self are eliminated, that of the Utilitarians and that of Kant. Among Bradley's best pieces of criticism is his essay on 'Pleasure for

---

20 See p. 74: 'A doctrine must not only hold together, but it must hold the facts together as well . . . The theory must take in the facts and an ultimate theory must take in all the facts'. Cf. p. 251: "what we most want . . . is to stand by *all* the facts. It is our duty to take them without picking and choosing them to suit our views, to explain them if we can, but not to explain them away; and to reason on them, and find the reason of them, but never to think ourselves rational when by the shortest cut to reason, we have reasoned ourselves out of them.' 21 pp. 74–5, 78. 22 pp. 76–8. 23 pp. 73–4. 24 p. 78. 25 pp. 79–80. 26 p. 320. 27 p. 139.

Pleasure's Sake'. In it we find some of his best prose. He straight-away attacks hedonism in its most plausible claim, which is that it proposes a palpable, attainable end to man and an indisputable criterion for morals, as contrasted with the 'transcendent longings' of other-worldly metaphysicians.[28] Bradley replies that there is no concept more vague than 'happiness', no state more uncertain or more unstable than pleasure.[29] Hedonism or utilitarianism in ethics, like impricism in epistemology, means the dissolution of the self. The psychology of utilitarianism 'stands upon uncriticised, violent and unreal metaphysical abstractions'.[30] Pleasures cannot form a sum or a whole; the pursuit of pleasure means a fragmented self.[31] It means also inevitable failure, for pleasure can be secured only by pursuing something else, that is by abandoning hedonism.[32]

From the moral point of view, utilitarianism stands condemned, because it can 'found no "ought" in the moral sense' and can provide no justification for passing from psychological descriptions to moral laws. It thus abolishes moral obligation and can only be called, as a theory, 'as grossly immoral a theory as ever was published'.[33] The argument of Mill ('our great modern logician', Bradley sarcastically calls him) that 'each person's happiness is a good to that person and the general happiness, therefore, a good to the aggregate of all persons', is tipped into a pig's trough.[34] Mill's attempt to distinguish higher from lower pleasures is equally trounced. Bradley argues that a criterion of pleasures must be quantitative, that is non-moral; and that to institute a qualitative criterion is to abandon the pleasure principle.[35]

With a calculated sigh, Bradley concludes: 'Hedonism *is* bankrupt; with weariness we have pursued it, as far as was necessary. . . .' In a fine peroration, he sums up:

> We agree that it is desirable to have a standard of virtue which is palpable and 'objective'; and therefore we refuse to place the end in what is most impalpable, what is absolutely and entirely 'subjective'. We agree that the end is not the

28 pp. 85–6. This claim is, of course, a constant with moralists of the empiricist tradition since Hume. 29 pp. 86–93. 'The name (of happiness) is a proverb for the visionary object of a universal and a fruitless search; of all the delusions which make a sport of our lives it is not one, but is a common title which covers and includes them all, which shows itself behind each in turn but to vanish and appear behind another'. (p. 86). He defines hedonism as the theory that 'the moral end for the individual and the race is the getting a maximim surplusage of pleasurable feeling and that there is nothing in the whole world which has the smallest moral value except this end and the means to it' (p. 88). 30 p. 116. 31 pp. 280, 304–5. Max Picard, in *L'homme du néant,*, trad. (Edits. du Seuil, Paris, 1947) and *La fuite devant Dieu*, trad. (P.U.F., Paris, 1956); and Gabriel Marcel in many of his works, somewhat similarly point out the fragmentation of personality, the option for discontinuity, the pursuit of timeless instants, which are involved in modern empiricism and hedonism. 32 pp. 90–104. In a memorable sentence at the end of the essay, he says: 'The end and standard is self-realisation, and is not the feeling of self-realisedness.' 33 pp. 109–23. 34 Bradley paraphrases it (noting that he takes the paraphrase from Kant and not from Carlyle): 'If many pigs are fed at one trough, each desires his own food, and somehow as a consequence does seem to desire the food of all; and by parity of reasoning it should follow that each pig desiring his own pleasure, desires also the pleasure of all' (p. 113). 35 pp. 116–20.

realisation of an abstract idea; and therefore we refuse to take as our end the greatest amount of pleasure; for that is an abstract idea, and it is altogether unrealizable. . . . We agree that happiness is the end; and therefore we say pleasure is not the end. . . .

We repeat the good old doctrine that the test of higher and lower cannot lie in a feeling which accompanies the exercise of every function, but is to be found in the quality of the function itself. To measure that, we are to go to the idea of man, and to his place in creation and his evolution in history.[36]

In a later essay, on 'Selfishness and Self-Sacrifice', he returns to the subject of hedonism in its egoistic form. The opening of the essay shows Bradley at his most mocking, mordant best. Unthinking persons, he says, will be shocked at the suggestion that all actions, including self-sacrifice, are equally selfish. But their reaction will only confirm the thinker in his view. 'For wonder, as he knows, is the beginning of philosophy: and a shudder comes over the not yet initiated, when the deeper mysteries are unveiled.'[37] The argument on which egoism rests is that, when I act, I do what I want, I seek what I like, I avoid what I dislike, I please myself, and that is selfish. 'If I were pleased to do otherwise, it would only be because I was otherwise pleased.'[38]

With an argument which linguistic analysts would be proud to own, but which they would hardly suspect to have belonged to Bradley, he retorts:

> That I do what I want to do is an idle proposition. That it should lead to a new result would be strange, unless truth were to be found in the barest tautologies . . . 'I know what I know', 'I experience what I experience', 'I want what I want', indeed 'here be truths'; . . . but it is a poor neighbourhood where such truths can be considered as making the fortune of a philosopher.[39]

There is a Wittgensteinian note about this argument; as there is about his summing up:

> Out of the present ideas of pleasures . . . to choose always what seems to me greatest is selfish; but to choose what pleases me most is not selfish or unselfish. It merely means *that* I choose, and says nothing whatever about *what* I choose.[40]

One is irresistibly reminded here of some contemporary 'right to choose' slogans!

---

36 pp. 124–5. He adds that pleasure is 'that element of the mind which is *least* distinctively human, and shared by us with the beasts that perish'; that it is unattainable, being 'a proverb for its fallaciousness'. Cf. p. 140: 'The practical man hears of the 'useful' and thinks he has got something solid, while really he is embracing . . . the cloud of a wild theoretical fiction. . . . The two words "useful" and "happiness" delude not only the public, but perhaps all Utilitarian writers.' 37 p. 251. 38 pp. 253 -4. 39 p. 254.
40 p. 261. The reasoning of egoism, he says, rests 'on the confusion between a pleasant thought and the thought of a pleasure; between the idea of an objective act or event, contemplation of which is pleasant, and of which I desire the realisation, and the idea of myself as the subject of a feeling of satisfaction which is to be' (p. 258; cf. pp. 259–61).

At the end of the essay on 'Pleasure for Pleasure's Sake', Bradley suggests that 'of all our Utilitarians there is perhaps not one who has not still a great deal to learn from Aristotle's Ethics'. But it seems that Bradley has much to learn too, from Aristotle or from some other; for, after having shown us that the moral self is not the self of hedonism, he leaves us *still* wondering what it positively *is*.

The fourth essay, 'Duty for Duty's Sake' is again critical, this time of Kantian ethics. Bradley likes to think of philosophical doctrines in terms of dialectic opposites, each erring by excess, both in fact finally coinciding in error; and of the true theory as a higher synthesis embracing the partial truths of both. Hedonism and Kantianism are for him such opposites; the former destroying the self by filling up its place with empirical contents, the latter destroying the self by emptying it of all empirical content. They both have a common vice, which he calls abstractness.[41] The danger of schematisms of this sort is that they tempt one to tailor the doctrine to make it fit the suit. Kant has had many ready-made suits pulled over him, but few more ill-fitting than Bradley's.[42] The doctrine which Bradley attributes to Kant is sheer travesty. He says Kant makes morality consist in realising non-contradiction; which in one sense is impossible (for 'non-contradiction' is empty form, and 'realisation' is 'giving content to'); and in another sense is mere tautology.[43] With lamentable injustice, he concludes that Kant's doctrine is tantamount to hedonism, or to the hypocritical maxim that 'before you do what you like, you should call it duty'.[44]

The irony of this essay is that the charge which Bradley makes against Kant is precisely the charge which modern philosophers would make—and with justice —against himself. It is the charge of idle abstractness, of vacuous generalisation. Kant, he says, does not tell us what right or good is;[45] but neither does Bradley. His criterion of self-realisation does not escape from the circularity he charges against Kant: good acts are those which realise the good self, and the good self is the self which is realised by good acts.[46]

4 WHAT ARE MY DUTIES?

Bradley's most determined effort to give content to his notion of the good self is his next essay, 'My Station and its Duties'. Self-realisation, he begins, must be the fulfilment of a will superior to ourselves, objective, universal and yet concrete.[47] This can only be the will of a community of which we are a part. Our place in the community will determine our duties and realise our selves.

---

41 p. 142. 42 Mary Warnock curiously writes: 'No doubt . . . he is not entirely fair to Kant, but all the same this seems to me one of the very best things ever written about Kant's moral philosophy' (*Ethics since 1900*, p. 10.) 43 pp. 148–56. 44 p. 156. 45 pp. 158–9. 46 Cf. Carritt, *The Theory of Morals* (Oxford University Press, 1928), 194–5, p. 50. 47 pp. 161–2.

We have found self-realisation, duty and happiness in one—yes, we have found ourselves, when we have found our station and its duties, our function as an organ in the social organism.[48]

He goes on to make a trenchant criticism of individualism and an eloquent exposé of the social nature of man. 'The individual apart from the community is', he argues, 'a false abstraction', and individualism rests, not on facts, but on the dogmatic metaphysics of empiricism. Man is what he is because of his insertion in 'human communities, the family, society and the state'.[49] Morality, too, must therefore be realisation of the social will. The good self is the social self; the bad self is the private or selfish self.[50]

It must be admitted that the insistence of Bradley and his fellow-idealists on the social nature of man is of prime importance for morals; and that its neglect by subsequent moralists, who have, on the whole, been strongly individualistic, has been a great weakness of British ethics. But when we look more closely at Bradley's 'social self', we find it a repellent sight. He begins by quoting Hegel:

In respect of morality the saying of the wisest men of antiquity is the only one which is true, that to be moral is to live in accordance with the moral tradition of one's country; and in respect of education, the one true answer is that which a Pythagorean gave to him who asked what was the best education for his son, If you make him the citizen of a people with good institutions.[51]

The communal smugness of this is surpassed by the individual smugness involved in what follows. Bradley presents the morality of 'my station and its duties' as offering deliverance from moral disquietude and from the sense of failure which is inevitable in Kantian morality. Kant's moral ideal is unattainable; it thus exacts from me 'the depressing perpetual confession that I am not what I ought to be in my inner heart, and that I never can be so'.[52] But in the duties of my station I am delivered from 'this peevish enemy'; I am made one with what I ought to be.

There I realise myself morally so that, not only what ought to be in the world is, but I am what I ought to be and so find my contentment and satisfaction.

We are exhorted not to 'look at our insides, but at our work and our life, and say to ourselves, Am I fulfilling my appointed function or not?' Perfect patriot, dependable clubman, irreproachable parent, man of honour and gentleman, I am immune from self-doubt and the feeling of unworthiness. Identifying ourselves with the will of society, which is the moral will, we are entitled to 'consider others

48 p. 163.   49 pp. 164–74.   50 pp. 174, 181–2.   51 p. 173.   52 p. 181.

and ourselves good too'; we are 'satisfied and have no right to be dissatisfied'.[53] 'The belief in this real moral organism is the one solution of ethical problems'.[54]

In fact, as there is no need in our disillusioned generation to point out, it is a blend of Bismarckian and Victorian priggishness; and in exposition of it Bradley's rhetoric becomes as hollow as that of Kipling at his most imperial.[55] It is imperialism and conservatism rationalised.[56] It is the perfect fulfilment of the descriptions Sartre offers of the 'middle-class morality' of the 'serious man'. Bradley's essay in fact is one of the best statements of the kind of morality against which Sartre's 'anti-moralist' ethics is worked out.

But what people have frequently not realised is that Bradley is only half convinced in defending it and that throughout most of his pleading for it he is already aware that it will not do.[57] In a contemporaneous post-script he more modestly remarks that 'it seems a great advance' on other theories and is 'in the main satisfactory'. But he notes also its defects. It does not secure that perfect identification of self with the good self which would eliminate the bad self and abolish moral discontent. A man cannot always be 'fully engaged in satisfactory work'. A man may be a citizen of a community which is 'in a confused or rotten condition'. Even in the best community, law and morals, or right and might, do not always coincide. There are afflictions in life for which no society has the remedy. The interest of the individual may clash with that of the community; it is hard to fit the requirement of self-sacrifice with that of the fulfilment of my social function. Man has duties to himself, to truth, to beauty, which do not come from his relation to society.[58]

Above all, Bradley has become partly and momentarily conscious of a vice which he shares with all British idealists, as of course with Hegel, the vice of applying Christian terminology to secular institutions, and thus of at once secularising Christianity and divinising the state. Bradley has been thinking of political society as if it were the Mystical Body of Christ or the Kingdom of God on earth.[59] He now realises that the 'visible community' of the state cannot realise

---

53 pp. 181–3. 54 p. 187. On p. 201, he says: 'There is nothing better than my station and its duties, nor anything higher nor more truly beautiful'. 55 Every cliché in the genre is deployed on pp. 184, 201–2, (even the 'heart of a nation rising high and beating in the breast of each one of her citizens'.) 56 pp. 199–201. 'If you could be as good as your world, you would be better than most likely you are and . . . to wish to be better than the world is to be already on the threshold of immorality'. 'Old people . . . are tolerant of new theories and youthful opinions that everything would be better upside down. . . . They are intolerant only of those who are old enough, and should be wise enough, to know better than that they know better than the world; for in such people they cannot help seeing the self-conceit which is pardonable only in youth'. Wollheim tells us that Bradley was 'deeply conservative or reactionary . . . the implacable enemy of all utilitarian or liberal teaching . . . , he could not abide pacifism or generalised humanitarian sentiment, and any belief in the natural equality of man or in the inviolability of life (whether political or religious in inspiration) he regarded as 'sentimental', 'degenerate' and 'disgusting' (op. cit., p. 14). 57 It is wrong to describe the concept of 'My Station and its Duties' as 'the core of Bradley's moral theory' (Mary Warnock, op. cit., p. 12). 58 pp. 203–5. 59 T.H. Green was an outstanding offender in this respect. For him the confusion of temporal with spiritual, state with (lay) Church, international community with 'the multitude of the redeemed' is complete. This partly explains the confusedness of

moral perfection, or abolish moral contradiction. Everything in time is relative and imperfect. Man, by the fact that he is conscious of different moral judgments in different communities, and of more and less perfect realisations of moral ideals in human affairs, is appealing to some standard beyond society and showing that he transcends his 'station and its duties'. He does not, he cannot 'take his morality simply from the moral world he is in'.[60]

In the sixth essay, on 'Ideal Morality', Bradley sets out to 'try to find a less one-sided solution'. Here he argues that the end of morality is the realisation of the good will or the ideal self; and that the means to this realisation are partly found in but also partly surpass the duties of my social station. But as to the content of the good will or the ideal self Bradley is far from satisfactory or convincing. He still thinks that

> the greater part of it consists in a man's loyally, and according to the spirit, performing his duties and filling his place as the member of a family, society and the state . . . The basis and foundation of the ideal self is the self which is true to my station and its duties.[61]

This latter is *real* morality. But beyond it is ideal morality, personal morality. 'Man is not man at all unless social', he writes; 'but man is not much above the beasts unless more than social'.[61A] But when we ask what this 'more than social' is, we find that it seems to be no other than the right of the individual to exempt himself from social or ordinary morality in the name of 'superior service' to science, art or . . . industry.

> Positive breaches of moral law (are) occasionally moral . . . The morality of the pushing man of business, and still more of the lawyer and the diplomatist in the exercise of their calling, is not measured by the standard of common life.[62]

Respectability is, however, preserved and the common people shielded from scandal. 'Some neglect' of 'common social morality' is unavoidable; but 'open and direct attack on the standing moral institutions . . . can be justified . . . only on the plea of overpowering moral necessity'.[63] Elsewhere, after declaring that 'it would be rash to say that any one act must be in all cases absolutely and unconditionally immoral', and that 'circumstances decide' moral cases, he goes on to observe that though this is a fact, it 'is a fact it would be well to keep in the background'.[64]

It is impossible not to be repelled by the smugness of this account of 'ideal

---

contemporary philosophers, both analysts and existentialists, who lump together idealist philosophy and Christianity and think that the refutation of the one is the destruction of the other. 60 pp. 203–6; cf. pp. 331–2 and the doubt expressed in a later footnote on p. 189. 61 p. 220. 61a p. 223. 62 pp. 226–7. 63 p. 227. 64 pp. 158–9. Suicide and 'excusable killing' are the examples he refers to. Cf. the quotation from Wollheim in n. 56 above.

morality', which rivals the smugness of the earlier description of the morality of our proper stations. But the important conclusion which emerges from it is that Bradley completely fails to give any content to the moral ideal or to provide any general criterion, of the morally good life. As the quotation we have just given shows, he does not believe that there is any act which is absolutely and unconditionally good or bad. 'There is no fixed code or rule of right.' Morality is unending progress from one stage of evolving civilisation to another, and is relative to the stage attained.

> The morality of every stage is justified for that stage; and the demand for a code of right in itself, apart from any stage, is . . . asking for an impossibility.[65]

Some of what Bradley says about the evolution and progress of morality is true. At every stage, he argues, there is 'the solid fact of the world so far moralised', which is handed on to the next generation of men 'as a sacred trust', as both a means and a challenge to the realisation of a higher and more complete moral truth.[66] But his thought is marked by the Victorian myth of inevitable moral progress. Above all, he seems to have forgotten the point he made against the utilitarians:

> Higher and lower . . . are 'relative': they are comparatives, and hence mean more or less of something. Higher means nearer some top, or it means nothing. Lower means nearer some bottom, or it means nothing. . . . When we talk of 'higher' and 'lower' . . . we ought to know what our top and our bottom are, or else we risk talking nonsense.[67]

But Bradley has not given any top or bottom or middle to his ideal self. He says that the business of ethics is 'not to make the world moral, but to reduce to theory the morality current in the world'.[68] But the result of the theory has been to show that the 'morality current in the world' may be over-ridden in deference to 'overpowering moral necessity'. 'Circumstances decide.' The final court of appeal in moral matters is not moral reasoning but 'moral art', the intuitive judgment, the moral 'seeing' and 'feeling' of the individual, who has 'imbibed the (moral) spirit of his *community*', but who also 'knows the heart and sees through moral illusion' and can judge when ordinary morality 'prevents us from performing our superior service'.[69]

65 pp. 189–92. 66 Ibid.; cf. p. 247. 67 p. 117. 68 p. 193; cf. p. 116, 156. 69 pp. 193–9, 225–8.

5 BEYOND 'MORALITY'?

In his chapter on 'Ideal Morality' and in his 'Concluding Remarks', Bradley argues that morality of its very nature tends towards the negation of itself, strives to surpass itself towards non-morality, or super-morality, that is to say, towards religion. For morality strives to annihilate the bad self; and if the bad self were annihilated, there would be no morality. Morality condemns us to discontent at our own imperfection; but to be conscious of imperfection is to desire and to envisage the possibility of perfection. This is how morality 'presses forward beyond itself' towards religion, in which the ideal and the real are made one.[70]

But the annihilation of the bad self and the making real of the ideal cannot be *really* or visibly real; for this would mean not only the abolition of morals but the destruction of religion; for the whole *content* of religion is moral.[71] It is therefore by *faith* that our bad self is annihilated and our ideal self made real. Faith is the will to believe that my bad acts and my bad self are not real—and this is forgiveness of sins and justification, as well as bliss. Faith is the will to believe that I am one with the Ideal—and this is Atonement.[72] Bradley claims that all this is the plain deliverance of the religious consciousness. He also claims that it is the doctrine of justification by faith alone and not by works, which is 'the eternal glory of Protestantism' and is 'the very centre of Christianity'.[73]

But we must remember, as Christians sometimes do not remember, that people who use Christian terms do not necessarily mean Christian things by them. Bradley's terms have nothing to do with Christian realities. His God is only a name for the ideal self within ourselves: 'God and man are identical in a subject.'[74] Religion is one element, with art and philosophy, of a single human-divine process, which is simply man's project to become God.[75] Thus, as always in Hegel and in idealism generally, we find that God is only the name for the highest in man apotheosised. Feuerbach and Marx, followed by Sartre, have only to say that God is the name for the highest in man 'alienated'; and the God of idealism will at once become the Man of Marxism or of atheistic existentialism.[76]

---

70 pp. 230–5, 243–4, 313–6, 320–2.   71 p. 333.   72 pp. 321–337. 'You must believe that you too really are one with the divine, and must act as if you believed it. In short, you must be justified not by works but solely by faith.'   73 pp. 325, 328, 338–9.   74 pp. 323–5. Bradley's Church, or 'whole body of Christ', is the whole of humanity. The Church, as distinct from churches, can have no hierarchy, no spiritual superiors, 'because the spirit of Christianity excludes such things'. 'You can have true religion without sacraments or public worship, and again both without clergymen.' 'For a large number of our clergy', Bradley assures us: 'I have a sincere personal respect'; and he holds no office higher in esteem than theirs. He also recognises 'the general necessity both for private devotion and public worship'. It is 'the abuse and the excess of them' against which he feels bound to protest (pp. 339–42).   75 pp. 320–1. 76 Father de Lubac quotes Gilson to the effect that 'to convict Voltaire of atheism is not, after all, to score a victory over Christian thought'; and he continues, '—any more than to show that the God of Fichte or Hegel turns without any trouble into the Man of Feuerbach' (*Les chemins de Dieu*, Aubier, Paris, 1956, p. 204). See Sartre, *Being and Nothingness*, E. trans. by Hazel E. Barnes (Philosophical Library, New York, 1956), p. 566: 'Man is the being whose project is to be God. . . . Man fundamentally is the desire to be

We have found in Bradley a complex of attitudes towards Christian concepts which is worth summarising because it recurs right through modern British ethics. There is his idea that the Christian doctrine of eternal rewards and punishments is sheer hedonism and is anti-moral. There is his notion that moral progress tends towards the surpassing of morality and that the moral 'hero' or the saint is 'beyond morality'. There is his notion of eternity as the cessation of activity in perfect immobilism. We shall meet each of these ideas again in later chapters.

6 THE MORAL PERSON AND THE MORAL LIFE

Bradley has failed to give us satisfaction on the question of what acts are moral and by what sort of conduct I shall become a moral person. But his ethics retains one great merit compared with that of most of his successors; it is that of seeing ethics as the vocation and continuing effort of a person to shape his own life according to moral ideals. Most of the later British moralists, whether of the inter-war or of the post-war schools, have seen ethics either as a collection of separate and unarguable intuitions; or as a succession of personal attitudes or decisions or persuasions; or as exercises in issuing commands, 'awarding marks' or addressing 'behests and re-proaches' to others.[77]

It is worth while, then, to bring together in conclusion some of Bradley's passages about the moral life and the moral person. Morality, he repeats, is imposed by the nature of man as a being who receives his nature and his place in the world as a task, and feels responsible for the way he moulds that nature and fills that place. Morality springs from the tension in man between what he is and what he knows he ought to be; between a self which seeks satisfaction and a self which refuses to be self-satisfied; between a self which chooses and a self which judges. Morality is a dualism which struggles to be one.[78] It is an effort to spiritualise the animal in us, to moralise the non-moral in us and in the world.[79] It is a lived contradiction because man is a living contradiction.[80] To understand morality, we must try to understand man.

This is an admirable statement of the programme of ethics; but Bradley leaves us with the programme unfulfilled. He does not face the question, 'What makes

---

God' (p. 615): 'The passion of man is the reverse of that of Christ, for man loses himself as man in order that God may be born'; cf. pp. 575, 591–2, 598–9, 623. Catholic idealists, such as Le Senne, Lavelle, Le Roy, have extreme difficulty in escaping from idealist immanence in order to affirm, as they wish to affirm, God as transcendent. See the writer's article, 'Idealism and Ethics: René Le Senne', *Irish Theological Quarterly*, April 1954, pp. 115–55.   77 Mary Warnock describes the contemporary British moralist as someone 'who neither acts nor feels but only awards marks' (*The Listener*, 8 January 1959). The 'behests and reproaches' piece, with other characteristic talk about 'warrants addressed to potential givers' of same, or 'impersonal injunction—tickets', is to be found in Ryle, *The Concept of Mind* (Hutchinson, London (1949) 1955), p. 128.   78 pp. 78, 84, 175, 205–6, 234–5, 309–310, 313.   79 pp. 73–4, 139, 190–2, 279.   80 pp. 78–9, 175, 231–2, 234–5.

the person thus contradictory and whence come its unattainable ideals'?[81] He does not face the implications of the fact that moral ideals are part of the nature and definition of human beings of flesh and blood, and that therefore the nature of the *ideal* and the way to its realisation must be revealed in the nature and 'quality of function' of the *real* in man.[82] Bradley's 'ideal' is supra-moral, his 'real' is infra-moral; and the moral struggle between them is a clash of ignorant armies by night, if not a 'useless passion'.

And yet, apart from some Christian philosophers and a group marked by the common influence of Professor C.A. Campbell,[83] we shall not find a better; indeed until very recent years we shall not find any description of the moral life and scarcely any recognition of morality as a life. Contemporary critics who urge British moralists to learn in this respect from Sartre, could just as well urge them to learn from Bradley. But we have seen that Bradley is not enough. It is important to define ethics as philosophical reflection on the moral life. But it is also important to realise how little is known about ethics when this programme has been stated.

81 He asks: 'How is it possible for the mind to frame an ideal; or, given as a fact a mind which idealises, what must be concluded as to its nature? Can anything idealise unless itself in some way *be* an ideal?' But for answer he merely remarks: 'This, we need not say, suggests serious problems which we cannot even touch upon here' (p. 221). On p. 75, he writes: 'The mind is not finite, just because it knows it is finite' (cf. pp. 78, 234). But he avoids any further discussion of the nature of mind here, doubtless on the ground that this would be to pass from ethics into metaphysics (see p. 247 and the Preface to the Second Edition). In *Appearance and Reality*, his thought about the mind and immortality is profoundly sceptical: here all reasoning is propelled inexorably forward towards the edge of the absolute, over which it must fall into the abyss of mindlessness. (See op.cit., pp. 501–10.)   82 Speaking of the distinction of higher and lower pleasures, he says: "We repeat the good old doctrine that the test of higher and lower . . . is to be found in the quality of the function itself. To measure that, we are to go to the idea of man and to his place in creation and his evolution in history' (p. 125). But this Bradley does not do.   83 e.g. A.E. Taylor, *The Faith of a Moralist* (Gifford Lectures, 1926–8), 2 vols. (Macmillan, London, 1931);W.G. de Burgh, *From Morality to Religion* (Evans, London, 1938; L.A. Reid, *Creative Morality* (Allen and Unwin, London, 1936). Among the other group, apart from C.A. Campbell himself, see Laird, Macbeath, Lamont already cited in connection with free-will.

CHAPTER TWO

G.E. Moore and Non-Naturalism

Professor George Edward Moore died in October 1958, at the age of 84. His whole life, from his undergraduate days, had been spent at Cambridge, where he was successively Lecturer in Moral Science (1911–1925) and Professor of Philosophy (1925–1939). His contemporaries, as undergraduate and as younger don, constituted as brilliant a generation as Cambridge ever knew, a generation who were to do more than perhaps any other single group of men to determine the pattern of thought and beliefs and attitudes in modern Britain. They included Bertrand Russell, A.N. Whitehead, Ludwig Wittgenstein, the 'Bloomsbury Group': John Maynard Keynes, Lytton Strachey, Leonard and Virginia Woolf, E.M. Forster, Roger Fry, Duncan Grant, Clive Bell, Desmond McCarthy. On many of these, the younger Moore exerted a dominating influence, both as philosopher and as friend. Through the non-philosophers, the influence of Moore's moral outlook spread widely through the cultural life of Britain. As a professional philosopher, throughout a long academic life, Moore had much to do with shaping the contemporary style and method of philosophising.[1]

In philosophy, Moore appeared first as leader of a revolution against idealism. Given the prestige and the redoubtable intellectual and controversial might of men like Bradley in Oxford and McTaggart in Cambridge, it took courage for a young man to challenge idealism. Moore had this courage. Russell followed him. These two men, in their different ways, and later Wittgenstein in his, contributed to make of British philosophy the protest against idealist metaphysics which it still largely remains. Yet Moore's rebellion was helped by weapons provided by

---

1 On biographical points, see 'An Autobiography', in *The Philosophy of G.E. Moore*, ed., P.A. Schilpp (New York, 1942); and 'My Mental Development', in *The Philosophy of Bertrand Russell*, ed. P.A. Schilpp, (New York, 1944); Bertrand Russell, *Portraits from Memory* (Allen and Unwin, London, 1956); *My Philosophical Development* (Allen and Unwin, London, 1959). See also a symposium of reminiscence on 'the influence and thought of G.E. Moore' by four of his friends, Bertrand Russell, Leonard Woolf, Professor Morton White (Harvard), Professor John Wisdom (Cambridge), broadcast by the BBC and printed in *The Listener*, 30 April 1959. On the philosophy and philosophical influence of Moore, see *The Philosophy of G.B. Moore*, cited above; J. Passmore, *A Hundred Years of Philosophy*, pp. 203–16; G.A. Paul, "G.B. Moore; Analysis Common Usage and Common Sense", in *The Revolution in Philosophy*, introd. by Gilbert Ryle, 1956; M.J. Charlesworth, *Philosophy and Linguistic Analysis*, pp. 11–46; John M. Keynes, 'My Early Beliefs', in *Two Memoirs*, ed. David Garnett (R. Hart-Davis, London, 1949). A useful short survey of "The Local Historical Background of Contemporary Cambridge Philosophy" is that given by the late C.D. Broad in *British Philosophy in the Mid-Century*, ed. C.A. Mace (Allen and Unwin, London, 1957) pp. 13–61. Of Moore, he says that he was the man 'who has undoubtedly had a greater influence than any one other man on English philosophy in general and Cambridge philosophy in particular during the last fifty years'.

26

the enemy. Bradley's criticisms of empiricism and 'psychologicism', his doctrine of the objective reference of the concept and the proposition, were turned by Moore against Bradley's own doctrine of the 'non-reality' of everyday experience and the 'error' of common-sense beliefs. Moore's philosophy remained anti-empiricist as much as it was anti-idealist. In moral philosophy, the same phenomenon is to be noted. Moore follows Bradley in his rejection of, and resembles Bradley in his criticism of, hedonism and utilitarianism. His ethics is anti-utilitarian as well as being anti-idealist and anti-metaphysical. This gives rise to the paradox that he lumps together the naturalist and anti-metaphysical ethics of hedonism and the metaphysical ethics of idealism, and finds them both guilty of the same fallacy which he calls the naturalistic fallacy.

Moore's moral philosophy is expounded chiefly in two books. The first and most influential of these, the *Principia Ethica*,[2] was published in 1903, when Moore was thirty years old. Before the end of his life, Moore had grave misgivings about many of its arguments and conclusions. But he never formulated an alternative theory of ethics, and seems to have been quite uncertain in later years as to where he stood in relation to current ethical controversy.[3] The smaller book, *Ethics*,[4] which he published in 1912, repeats substantially the same doctrine as that of *Principia Ethica*. Two papers, on 'The Conception of Intrinsic Value' and 'The Nature of Moral Philosophy',[5] complete Moore's writings on moral philosophy.

2 Cambridge, University Press (1903) 1948. 3 In "A Reply to my Critics", in *The Philosophy of G.E. Moore*, ed. P.A.. Schilpp, he discusses C.L. Stevenson's view that, to say, 'It was right of Brutus to stab Caesar', is not to assert anything that may be true or false, except that the speaker approves of Brutus' action and, possibly that Brutus did stab Caesar; furthermore, that someone who says, 'It was wrong of Brutus to stab Caesar', is not asserting anything which is logically incompatible with the former statement. Both of these views are totally opposed to Moore's earlier doctrines. But Moore's comment (1942) was: 'I have some inclination to think that in *any* "typically ethical" sense in which a man might assert that Brutus' action was right, he would be asserting nothing whatever which could conceivably be true or false, except, perhaps, that Brutus' action occurred—no more than if he had said, "Please shut the door." I certainly have *some* inclination to think all this, and that therefore not merely the contradictory, but the contrary, of my former view is true. But then, on the other hand, I also still have *some* inclination to think that my former view *is* true. And if you ask me to which of these incompatible views I have the *stronger* inclination, I can only answer that I simply do not know whether I am more strongly inclined to take the one than to take the other.—I think this is at least an honest statement of my present attitude . . . I feel some inclination to think that those two men are *not* making incompatible assertions: that their disagreement *is* merely a disagreement in attitude, like that between the man who says, "Let's play poker", and the other who says, "No; let's listen to a record": and I do not know that I am not as much inclined to think this as to think that they are making incompatible assertions. But I certainly still have *some* inclination to think that my old view was true and that they are making incompatible assertions.' 4. Home University Library, Williams and Norgate, London (1912) 1925. 5 Written sometime before 1921, and reprinted in G.E. Moore, *Philosophical Studies* (Kegan Paul, London, 1922).

I THE NATURALISTIC FALLACY

The detection and refutation of the 'naturalistic fallacy' is G.E. Moore's most characteristic contribution to ethics, and modern British ethics has been profoundly marked by it. It really is a way of asserting the autonomy of ethics, which had already been asserted in similar terms to Moore's by Hume and by Kant, as well as by Cudworth and the Cambridge Platonists and, just before Moore, by Sidgwick. But the argument assumes a peculiar form in Moore because of his distinctive philosophical position and method.

For Moore, the naturalistic fallacy is committed whenever 'good' is defined in terms of something other than 'good'. Definitions of 'good' usually try to reduce 'good' to terms of 'natural objects', such as 'pleasure', 'object of desire', 'direction of evolutionary progress'; and in these cases, the term 'naturalistic' is appropriate to describe the fallacy. But Moore holds that metaphysical definitions of 'good' in terms of 'non-natural objects', like 'the existent', 'the real', 'the eternal',[6] commit the same logical fallacy, and he inappropriately calls it also the 'naturalistic fallacy'.[7] It is important to note that the 'fallacy' is incurred by *any* attempt to define 'good' in terms which do not include 'good'; that is to say any attempt to define good at all.[8] It has been pointed out that the 'fallacy' is completely misnamed; and that a less misleading name for what Moore has in mind would be the 'definist fallacy'.[9] What is most paradoxical about this, is that it would exclude any definition of any 'simple' term. Moore has a quite peculiar notion of what it is to 'define'. It is to analyse a complex notion into the simple parts of which it is composed. He gives the example of a horse, which is defined when it is 'analysed' into 'parts' which are not further analysable, and when these parts are fully enumerated. It follows that only complex terms can be defined; and that all definition ends when we arrive at 'something which is simply different from anything else' and which can be understood only in terms of itself.[10] 'Good' in this respect is not unique; it shares its indefinability with a host of other 'simple notions' such as 'yellow'.[11]

---

6 Moore's use of the term 'object' is very peculiar. His definition of 'natural property' is curious too and seems at times circular: the term 'natural property' standing for any property that is not an ethical property. See A.N. Prior, *Logic and the Basis of Ethics* (Oxford, Clarendon Press, (1949) 1956), pp. 3–4. In "A Reply to my Critics", he says that the *Principia Ethica* notion of a natural property is 'utterly silly and preposterous'. See *The Philosophy of G.E. Moore*, p. 582.   7 He notes the inappropriateness on pp. 38–40, 110–2. Quite incongruously, C.D. Broad was later to speak of 'theological naturalism' (and also of 'theological hedonism'). See *Five Types of Ethical Theory* (Kegan Paul, London, 1944), pp. 160, 259. A.N. Prior, too, speaks of the 'theological naturalism' of Locke and Paley (*Logic and the Basis of Ethics*, pp. 96–100).   8 pp. 10–17, 21, 36–8, 46ff., 66ff., 113–14, 126–7.   9 See W.K. Frankena, 'The Naturalistic Fallacy', originally a paper published in *Mind*, 1939, reprinted in *Readings in Ethical Theory*, sel. and ed. by Wilfrid Sellars and John Hospers (Appleton-Century-Crofts, New York, 1952), pp. 103–14. Cf. G.C. Field, 'The Place of Definition in Ethics', in the same collection, pp. 100–2; see also A.C. Ewing, *The Definition of Good* (Macmillan, NY, 1947), pp. 41ff., 60–1; and the same author's 'Subjectivism and Naturalism in Ethics', a paper published in *Mind*, 1944, and reprinted in *Readings in Ethical Theory*, pp. 199–20.   10 pp. 7–9.   11 pp. 7, 8, 11, 14, 38.

This theory of definition is bound up with Moore's anti-idealist epistemology. The doctrine of a plural reality, composed of ultimate, simple indefinable 'objects', is Moore's alternative to the 'organic unities' and 'concrete universals' of idealist monism. To define one simple notion in terms of another, whether it be *esse* in terms of *percipi* or 'good' in terms of 'pleasure', is either a merely verbal statement; or is self-contradictory. If we say 'good' means 'pleasure' we are simply saying 'good is good', or 'pleasure is pleasure'—which is a barren and non-significant tautology. If we want our statement to be significant, we must give up the claim that we are defining 'good' or that our statement has any kind of necessity. In other words, statements about 'good' can never be necessary propositions asserting 'What good *is*'; but can only be synthetic propositions putting forward intuitive but challengeable claims as to '*What* is good'.[12]

This obviously amounts to the familiar claim, found in nearly all modern British philosophy, that all necessary propositions are analytic and tautologous; and that no synthetic or existential propositions can be necessary. This, if it were true, would exclude all metaphysical propositions. It would, however, also exclude, not only all definitions of, but all generalised statements, and indeed all reasoning, about 'simple objects'. The quotation from Bishop Butler, which Moore chose for his title page, 'Everything is what it is, and not another thing', would, if taken with Moore's literal-mindedness, make all reasoning impossible and reduce all speech to saying 'This is this.'[13] A.J. Ayer said, in praise of Moore, that 'when dealing with metaphysicians he employed the devastating technique of assuming that they meant exactly what they said, and then showing that their conclusions contradicted obvious facts'.[14] We shall be obliged, in examining Moore's ethics to do just that; to assume that he means exactly what he says. We shall then find that his conclusions contradict obvious facts, for they quite simply eliminate ethics. There is a fundamental ethical point involved in Moore's 'naturalistic fallacy' argument. But Moore confuses the issue by representing the fallacy as solely or primarily a *logical* one, and by tying his argument in with a fantastic and self-stultifying doctrine of definition and analysis. The 'fallacy' is not solely a logical one; it is a metaphysical fallacy—the confusing of whole categories of reality and of thought; the attempt to abolish moral reasoning and moral reality by merging ethics into natural science or psychology or the social

12 See Moore's paper, 'The Refutation of Idealism', published in the same year as *Principia Ethica*, and reprinted in *Philosophical Studies*, particularly pp. 5–17. The reasoning is exactly similar in *Principia Ethica*, pp. 6–17, 77, 148–9. Cf. M.J. Charlesworth, *Philosophy and Linguistic Analysis*, pp. 26–38.   13 Cf. W.K. Frankens, art. cit. pp. 109–11. A.N. Prior, in *Logic and the Basis of Ethics* (Oxford, Clarendon Press, 1956), pp. 4–5, quotes the whole passage of Butler from which the sentence of Moore's title-page is taken, and comments that Butler did not hold that 'good' is indefinable or that goodness is not determined by the qualities of objects; but was only maintaining that when we say, 'This act is good' we do not mean the same thing as when we say 'This act is disinterested' etc. (op. cit., pp. 4–6).   14 In an obituary appreciation, published in the *Sunday Times*, 26 October 1958.

sciences. The calamity of Moore's counter-argument is that his way of distinguishing ethics from natural science separates ethics from nature and from reality completely. He plunges from naturalistic fallacy into non-naturalist sophism. In fact, as we shall see, in order to have an ethics at all, he is himself obliged to commit again and again a 'naturalistic fallacy' quite similar to that of the utilitarians.

2 THE ANTI-NATURALISM OF 'PRINCIPIA ETHICA'

It is entirely typical of Moore that he should begin the Preface to his first book with this sentence:

> It appears to me that in Ethics as in all other philosophical studies the difficulties and disagreements, of which its history is full, are mainly due to a very simple cause: namely to the attempt to answer questions, without first discovering precisely *what* question it is which you desire to answer.

Failure to distinguish different questions has made previous ethics unscientific. Moore's book is, the Preface goes on, an endeavour to provide 'Prolegomena to any future ethics than can possibly pretend to be scientific' by discovering and establishing 'the fundamental principles of ethical reasoning'.

In ethics, he claims, there are two fundamental questions, which are generally confused with one another. These are, firstly: What kind of things ought to exist for their own sakes?; secondly: What kind of actions ought we to perform? Answers to the first question, he holds, cannot be argued about or proven; they can rest only on intuitions. Answers to the second question can be proven or disproven; because, besides intuitions of the first sort, they also contain causal statements bearing on the effectiveness of certain means to attain the ends intuitively seen to be good.[15]

The first question is equivalent to the question: What sort of things are good? And this in turn depends on the answer to the question: What is meant by 'good'? It follows that 'this question, how "good" is to be defined, is the most fundamental question in all Ethics'.[16] Indeed, 'that which is meant by "good" is . . . the *only* simple object of thought which is peculiar to ethics'.[17] On this depend both the intuitive judgments as to what things are good, and the causal judgments as to what actions are right, in other words, what actions will achieve good results. Moore's answer to this fundamental question is to say over and over again that 'good' is 'a simple, indefinable, unanalysable object of thought'.[18] 'Good is good and nothing else whatever.'[19]

15 Cf. pp. 25, 77,146ff., 223–4. 16 pp. 5–6. 17 p. 5; cfr. pp. 142–6. 18 p. 21; cf. pp. 7–8, 14, 173. On p. 37, he calls 'good', 'that peculiar predicate'; on p. 38, 'a certain simple quality'. 19 p. 144.

If I am asked 'What is good?', my answer is that good is good, and that is the end of the matter. Or if I am asked, 'How is good to be defined?', my answer is that it cannot be defined, and that is all I have to say about it.[20]

It is obvious, and we shall see more in detail later, that this amounts to the abolition of moral reasoning. Moore supports it by a critique of various types of naturalist and metaphysical ethics. He assumes that their basic error lies in the attempt to define 'good'. He assumes further that any definitions of good would commit the same error and this confirms his belief that nothing can be said about 'good' except that it is good.

He begins the critical part of his work by a general examination of naturalistic ethics. This is of course the defining case of the commission of the naturalistic fallacy. It purports to define good in terms of some natural property and is thus 'inconsistent with the possibility of any Ethics whatsoever . . . replacing Ethics by some one of the natural sciences' such as psychology, sociology, biology, physics.[21] By 'natural' and 'nature', Moore means 'all that has existed, does exist or will exist in time', all 'that which is the subject matter of the natural sciences or of psychology'.[22] Now neither nature as a whole, nor anything that is in nature, nor the nature of man, nor anything that is alleged to be natural to man, can be what is meant by 'good'. For of anything that is 'natural' it is always meaningful and necessary to ask 'Is it good?', and this shows that 'good' does not mean 'natural'.[23] Also many 'natural' things are evil; many good things, including the whole of civilised living, are 'unnatural', in the sense of being super-imposed by man on 'nature'; and virtue itself is 'unnatural' in the sense of being unusual and abnormal. Hence any ethical doctrine which recommends a 'life according to nature', any 'natural law' morality, stands convicted of fallacy.[24]

The same applies to evolutionistic ethics, of which Moore takes Spencer as typical representative. In Spencer, evolutionism is mixed up with hedonism, but in so far as his ethics rests on the theory of evolution, it holds

that we need only to consider the tendency of 'evolution' in order to discover the direction in which we *ought* to go . . . ; that we ought to move in the direction of evolution simply *because* it is the direction of evolution.[25]

---

20 pp. 6–7. 21 pp. 38–41. 22 pp. 40–1. 23 Moore often has recourse to this argument, which is a way of showing the irreducibility of moral to non-moral propositions, or the underivability of moral conclusions from non-moral premisses. He mixes it up with his thesis that good is indefinable; e.g. on p. 15 he writes: 'Whatever definition be offered, it may be always asked, with significance, of the complex so defined, whether it is itself good.' Cf. pp. 113–14, 118, 122, 126, 131–9; *Ethics*, 158–69; 'The Nature of Moral Philosophy', in *Philosophical Studies*, pp. 337–9. But the point, in itself, is valid and important. 24 pp. 41–6; cf. 11–17. 25 pp. 54, 56. The hedonistic part of Spencer's thought is dealt with in pp. 47–54.

This is a clear case of the naturalistic fallacy: it seeks to define 'good' by 'direction of evolution'; to substitute for an ethical statement about what ought to be the case, a non-ethical statement about what is the case. But the ethical question will not be silenced: we must always ask, 'Is the direction of evolution the *right* direction for us to follow; is the end it tends towards a *good* end?'[26]

Moore turns next to the critique of hedonism. In the case of the great majority of its defenders, hedonism has held that 'good' means 'pleasant'; in other words, it has rested on the naturalistic fallacy.[27] Moore begins with Mill as the ablest exponent of hedonism or utilitarianism. He quotes from *Utilitarianism* the famous passage beginning, 'The only proof capable of being given that a thing is visible is that people actually see it . . . '.[28] He breaks off to say:

> There, that is enough. . . . Mill has made as naïve and artless a use of the naturalistic fallacy as anybody could desire. . . . The fact is that 'desirable' does not mean 'able to be desired' as 'visible' means 'able to be seen'. The desirable means simply what *ought* to be desired or *deserves* to be desired; just as the detestable means not what can be but what ought to be detested and the damnable what deserves to be damned. Mill has, then, smuggled in, under cover of the word 'desirable', the very notion about which he ought to be quite clear. . . . If 'desirable' is to be identical with 'good' then it must bear one sense; and if it is to be identical with 'desired' then it must bear quite another sense.[29]

Later on, Moore continues:

> Mill tells us that we ought to desire something (an ethical proposition), because we actually do desire it; but if his contention that 'I ought to desire' means nothing but 'I do desire' were true, then he is only entitled to say, 'We do desire so and so, because we do desire it'; and that is not an ethical proposition at all; it is a mere tautology. The whole object of Mill's book is to help us to discover what we ought to do; but, in fact, by attempting to define

---

26 pp. 47–8, 57–8. He points out that biological evolution may be held to be tending towards the elimination of the human species as plausibly as to its survival; and that in Darwin's phrase, 'survival of the fittest', 'fittest' has no ethical significance—it means merely those creatures most fitted to survive in the conditions actually obtaining; and these, according to environmental conditions, need not be the best men, or good men, or even men at all, if ethical conclusions are to be drawn from evolutionary theory, ethical premisses must first be read into evolutionary theory, which would then cease to be scientific. 'The judgment that evolution has been a progress is itself an independent ethical judgment.' (p. 55). All these arguments of Moore had been anticipated by T.H. Huxley in his remarkable Romanes Lecture of 1893 on 'Evolution and Ethics' republished along with his grandson, Sir Julian Huxley's, 1943 Romanes Lecture on 'Evolutionary Ethics', in *Evolutionary Ethics* (Pilot Press, London, 1947). 27 pp. 59–64. 28 It is from the beginning of Chapter IV of *Utilitarianism;* see the Everyman edition (1948), p. 32. 29 pp. 66–7. Moore gives subsidiary reasons for rejecting the identification of 'good' and 'desired', namely that there can be bad desires as well as good desires; and, if 'good' meant 'desired' 'there can be no question of finding motives for doing it, as Mill is at such pains to do' (p. 67; cf. p. 95).

the meaning of this ought, he has completely debarred himself from ever fulfilling that object; he has confined himself to telling us what we do do.[30]

Moore finds the same fallacy in Mill's attempted distinction of quality between pleasures. The test of superior quality which Mill proposed was 'the preference of most people who have experienced both'. A pleasure so preferred is, he held, more desirable. But Mill has already defined 'desirable' as 'what is desired'. Hence 'the preference of experts merely proves that one pleasure is pleasanter than another'. So the alleged qualitative distinction between pleasures turns into a mere quantitative distinction; and we remain in the domain of psychology, not that of ethics. Mill wants his preferable or 'more desirable' to have ethical significance, to mean what 'ought to be preferred' or 'ought to be desired'. 'But, in that case, the basis of Mill's hedonism collapses, for he is admitting that one thing may be preferred over another, and thus proved more desirable, although it is not more desired.' In short, the hedonistic principle, 'Pleasure alone is good as an end' is inconsistent with the view that one pleasure may be of better quality than another. 'These two views are contradictory to one another. We must choose between them; and if we choose the latter, then we must give up the principle of Hedonism.'[31]

Moore uses hard words about Mill and hedonism: 'contemptible nonsense', 'obstinate belief in untruths', are among his phrases.[32] Both the language and the argument recall Bradley. There is really little in Moore's anti-hedonist case, save a difference of vocabulary, that was not already in Bradley. Moore refers to Bradley as the source of one of his arguments, namely that hedonism confuses 'a pleasant thought' with 'the thought of a pleasure'. The whole of Moore's section on the psychological and epistemological errors of hedonism is close to Bradley.[33]

Up to now, Moore's refutation of Mill's hedonism has rested mainly upon the 'naturalistic fallacy' argument. Mill has gone wrong, he holds, because he has

---

30 p. 73. Cf. pp. 11–12: '[One] may be trying to prove that the object of desire is not pleasure. But if this be all, where is his Ethics? The position he is maintaining is merely a psychological one. Desire is something which occurs in our minds, and pleasure is also something which so occurs; and our would be ethical philosopher is merely holding that the latter is not the object of the former. But what has that to do with the question in dispute? His opponent held the ethical proposition that pleasure was the good, and although he should prove a million times over the psychological proposition that pleasure is not the object of desire, he is no nearer proving his opponent to be wrong.' Moore goes on to say that each protagonist is simply defining 'good' dogmatically in his own way, and that no possibility is left for proving either right. He goes on: 'That is one alternative which any naturalistic Ethics has to face; if good is *defined* as something else, it is then impossible either to prove that any other definition is wrong or even to deny such definition. The other alternative will scarcely be more welcome. It is that the discussion is after all a verbal one. When A says "Good means pleasant" and B says "Good means desired" they may merely wish to assert that most people have used the word for what is pleasant and for what is desired respectively. And this is quite an interesting subject for discussion; only it is not a whit more an ethical discussion than the last was. . . . My dear sirs, what we want to know from you as ethical teachers, is not how people use a word; it is not even, what kind of actions they approve, which the use of this word "good" may certainly imply: what we want to know is simply what is good.' Cf. p. 139.   31 pp. 77–81; cf. *Ethics*, pp. 52–5.   32 pp. 72, 74. 33 pp. 67–72.

attempted to define 'good'. Like all attempts to define 'good', this has planted him on the sharp horns of a dilemma: it involves him either in a self-contradiction (saying that ' "good" = "pleasure" ', which latter is, *vi termini*, 'not-good'), or in a barren tautology (' "good" "pleasure" becoming ' "pleasure" = "pleasure" '). Moore holds that this part of Mill's doctrine is, therefore, capable of strict logical disproof. His own counter-argument is already becoming paradoxical, because of the epistemological preconceptions we have already noted. But at this point, the eccentricity of Moore's ethical thought gives his argument a still more peculiar twist.

He owns that naturalistic theories of 'good', though fallacious if they claim to be definitions or to rest on argument, *might* be valid as intuitions. It is perfectly open to someone to claim that he knows intuitively that 'pleasure *alone* is good as an end—good in and for itself'.[34] This would be, in fact, the only legitimate defence of hedonism. It was the merit of Sidgwick to see this; and it is Sidgwick's intuitionistic hedonism that is Moore's target in the second half of his chapter on hedonism.

Since Moore's own doctrine of the good is intuitionistic, he is not so far removed from the logic[35] of intuitionistic utilitarianism. He walks warily in criticising Sidgwick. He has to find a way of discriminating between intuitions; and this must be without recourse to proof. It is a matter of different intuitions 'to be submitted to our verdict'.[36] Here he introduces a technique of which he makes much use throughout his ethical writing—the 'method of absolute isolation'.[37] This consists in asking: 'What things are such that, if they existed *by themselves*, in absolute isolation, we should yet judge their existence to be good?'[38] In the controversy with Sidgwick, this takes the form of imagining two worlds, one exceedingly beautiful, and one unspeakably ugly; but both supposed to be such that no 'human being ever has or ever, by any possibility, *can*, live in either, can ever see and enjoy the beauty of the one or hate the foulness of the other'. Of these two 'absolutely isolated' worlds, Moore quite seriously asks:

> Well, even so, supposing them quite apart from any possible contemplation by human beings; still, is it irrational to hold that it is better that the beautiful world should exist, than the one which is ugly? 'Would it not be well, in any case, to do what we could to produce it rather than the other?'[39]

People have often spoken of the child-like innocence and literalness of Moore's mind. Russell used to say, as a joke, 'that Moore's philosophy had one fundamental premiss, namely that everything he was told before the age of six must be true'.[40] There certainly is a children's fairy-tale quality about these 'two worlds'.

---

34 p. 77.   **35** And even, as we shall see, from the substance.   **36** p. 77. He speaks (after Mill) of 'indirect proof', i.e. 'the hope of determining one another's intellect'.   **37** p. 188.   **38** p. 187; cf. *Ethics*, pp. 56–80 164–9; 'The Nature of Moral Philosophy' in *Philosophical Studies*, pp. 260, 326, 328.   **39** pp. 83–4. **40** See *The Listener*, 30 April 1959.

Philosophically, the idea is preposterous. It is exactly the kind of aberration which led Wittgenstein to liken philosophy to an illness.[41] It is just this sort of abstraction or isolation which Wittgenstein held 'only occurs in doing philosophy',[42] and is a sign of minds that have become so 'calloused by doing philosophy'[43] that they lose the feel of common sense. Somewhat similarly, Bradley, arguing against Sidgwick's 'intuition' of the hedonist Supreme Good, had said:

> Surely common sense must see that, to find what end we ought to pursue in the human life we live, by seeing what would be left to us to pursue in an unimaginable and inhuman predicament, is not common sense at all, but simply bad metaphysics.[44]

These seem hard words to say about the author of 'A Defence of Common Sense'. But we have only to look at the 'isolated worlds' argument to see that it is uncommon nonsense. What can it mean to call a world beautiful or ugly 'quite apart from its effects on any human feeling'? Since, by definition, no human beings can ever live in or see or know either of these 'worlds', and since we are human beings, how would it be *possible* for us to 'do what we could to produce' the beautiful one rather than the ugly one?[45] How would it be conceivably 'our positive duty to make the world more beautiful, so far as we were able'?[46] All this has as much sense as had the little girl, in the story to which Sartre somewhere refers, who rushed quickly and noisily out of the garden, and then tiptoed quietly back to see what the garden looked like when she was not looking at it!

Moore thinks that he has shown by this argument that 'we shall have to include in our ultimate end something beyond the limits of human existence'.[47] The same self-contradiction recurs here. 'Beyond', in Moore's context, means 'outside' or

---

41 *Philosophical Investigations*, 255; cf. 593.   42 Ibid. 38.   43 Ibid. 34–8; cf. 393.   44 *Ethical Studies*, p. 126; cf. pp. 164–8. The argument of Sidgwick to which he is referring is that, if there were 'only a single sentient conscious being in the universe', he could not but feel that the having of pleasure and the avoiding of pain were 'intrinsically and objectively desirable' or 'absolutely Good or Desirable'. Bradley drily retorts: 'So far as I can imagine myself absolutely alone in a material world, I do not think it would occur to me that I had anything to live for.'   45 Moore says: 'It is highly improbable, not to say impossible, we should ever have such a choice before us' (p. 84). The word needed is not 'improbable' or 'impossible', but 'absurd'.   46 Moore solemnly admits that 'our beautiful world would be better still, if there were human beings in it to contemplate and enjoy its beauty' (p. 85). Nowell-Smith, in criticism of this argument of Moore's, distinguishes 'A-words' ('Aptness-words'), or 'words that indicate that an object has certain properties which are apt to arouse a certain emotion or range of emotions'; and 'D-words' ('Descriptive words') which simply describe emotionally-neutral properties. He goes on to note that Moore's passage about the 'two worlds' is full of words ('beautiful', 'beauty', versus 'ugly', 'ugliest', 'filth', 'disgusting') which he treats as 'D-words' (neutral-descriptive), whereas they are 'A-words'. These 'cannot be understood to mean anything at all if the presence of human beings and their tastes and interests are excluded, as they must be to make Moore's point. If, for example, instead of using the word "filth" we specified what the second world was to contain in the neutral language of chemistry, it is not so obvious that, if there were no one to see or smell either world, the one would be better than the other. To imagine something as beautiful or ugly, admirable or disgusting, is already to "react" to it' (*Ethics*, Penguin Books, 1954, pp. 70–74; cf. 171).   47 p. 84.

'foreign to',[48] but something 'outside' or 'foreign to' our human existence can be no part of our ultimate end. As Aristotle pointed out, what we are looking for in ethics is a 'good for man', a good which can be the object of human action and is attainable by man. It is *beyond* man but is not outside him; because *in* man there is the 'divine principle' which aspires to the Transcendent Good.[49]

It is by the same method of abstractive intuition that Moore tries to counter Sidgwick's central thesis, that we have an 'intuitive judgment' that no object is valuable apart from 'its conduciveness in one way or another, to the happiness of sentient beings'.[50] This entails that pleasure alone is valuable in itself. Moore maintains that hedonists are thereby committed to holding that pleasure would be valuable 'whether we are conscious of it or not'; happiness must, for hedonists, be good in itself 'even on condition that we never know and never can know that we are happy'.[51] For intuitions of what is good in itself must be tested by 'considering what value we should attach to [an object], if it existed in absolute isolation, stripped of all its usual accompaniments'.[52]

By this test, we find that consciousness of pleasure is more valuable than pleasure without consciousness; and further, that many other things are more valuable than either of these. It does not seem to occur to Moore that 'pleasure' of which we are not conscious, 'happiness' of which we know nothing, are words without sense. Again, we have a classic instance of what Wittgenstein called *the* philosophical malady, that of sending language 'on holiday', leaving the language 'engine idling'[53]—which is precisely to use words or consider objects 'stripped of all their usual accompaniments'.

Moore returns to firmer ground in the pages which he devotes to ethical egoism. He shows that the doctrine is strictly irrational because its terms are simply self-contradictory. An egoistic good is private to one person. An ethical good is by definition an absolute good, a universal good, claiming the allegiance of everyone. Egoism could be ethical only if it allowed each single man to maintain that his individual interest or happiness is '*the sole good*, the Universal Good, and the only thing that anybody ought to aim at'; in other words, 'that a number of different things are *each* of them the only good thing there is—an absolute contradiction'.[54] This section contains an important affirmation of the claim to absoluteness and universality which is inherent in ethical judgments, and which

---

48 By force of long association, the phrase 'beyond human existence' conveys the suggestion of 'being above' or 'transcending human existence'. Moore seems himself to have been tricked by the general sense of 'uplift' in the phrase. But his 'beyond' is more correctly 'beneath'; it is not 'super-human' but 'infra-human' or 'non-human'. The 'end' in question is the 'beauty' of a material world—'mountains, rivers, the sea; trees and sunsets, stars and moon', all this, but no human occupant. 49 See Aristotle, *Eth. Nic.*, 1096 b. 1177 b. 50 pp. 85–7. 51 pp. 88–91. 52 p. 91; cf. p. 93–6. 53 *Philosophical Investigations*, 38, 132, 136. 54 pp. 98–102; cf. 131–3; cf. *Ethics*, pp. 228ff. Cf. K. Baier, *The Moral Point of View* (Cornell University Press, (1958) 1960), pp. 188–204; C.D. Broad, *Five Types of Ethical Theory*, pp. 54–5, 63–6.

is forgotten by those who speak of 'ethical solipsism'[55] or try to make ethics a matter of personal 'stands'.

Moore concludes that 'no form of hedonism can be true'; which means that 'half, or more than half of the ethical theories which have ever been held' are false.[56]

But of the critique of hedonism in the *Principia Ethica* we must conclude that what is valid in it becomes lost in the web of Moore's own eccentricities. The valid and cardinal point, that hedonism is wrong because it gives a naturalistic definition of 'good', is almost erased by the proposition that it is wrong because it gives a definition of 'good', and that *any* definition of good would be equally wrong and equally naturalistic. But though 'good' cannot be defined, it is not for Moore's reasons and not in his sense. 'Good' cannot be defined, in the sense of being put in a wider class of things, of which it would be a special instance; and this, for the Aristotelian and scholastic reason that 'good' is transcategorial or 'transcendent-to-the-categories'. There is no more ultimate term to which it can be reduced, no wider class in which it can be situated. In this sense, it is like 'existence' or 'being' or 'true'.[57] But we are not thereby restricted to the formula that 'good is good . . . and that is all I have to say about it'.

It has come to be generally recognised that it is part of the meaning of morals that we must have reasons for what we call good.[58] We are, to this extent, obliged to 'define' good, that we must be able to state and defend what we mean by it; we must be able to indicate the features of a situation which justify us in calling it good. Hedonism did try to do this. It is not for thus trying to 'define' good that hedonism must be judged false. It is because the reasons it gives are incommensurable with the judgment: 'This is morally good.' Hedonism gives non-moral reasons to justify a moral conclusion. That is the real 'naturalistic fallacy'.

This reduction of the moral to the non-moral, found in all forms of naturalism, is part of a monistic philosophy of man, which denies all dualism of spirit and matter, and reduces the spiritual in man to terms of the physical. All the philosophers who commit the naturalistic fallacy in ethics, commit a corresponding fallacy in their philosophy of man. They use, as if they were univocal in meaning, words which are not univocal. Hedonists are not wrong in saying that happiness is the end for man; they are wrong in failing to see that 'happiness' is polyvalent, as man is polyvalent. Happiness is not pleasure, nor is pleasure only sensory; desire is not just one impulse, nor is satisfaction just one state; because

---

55 See e.g. Alasdair MacIntyre, in *What Moral Philosophy is Not*, 1957, pp. 325–36. 56 pp. 108, 146. 57 See Aquinas, *S. Theol.* 1. 5. 1–3; *De Veritate*, 1.1, 21. 1–3, 22.1. Cf. H.W.B. Joseph, *Some Problems in Ethics* (Oxford University Press, (1931) 1933, pp. 77–80; J. H. Muirhead, *Rule and End in Morals* (Oxford University Press, 1932), pp. 75–7. Moore notes the parallelism of 'good' and 'true' (pp. 132–3, 136), and of 'good' and 'beautiful' (pp. 200–2). Any definition of 'true' or 'beautiful' would be, he holds, a form of 'naturalistic fallacy' in epistemology and aesthetics respectively. 58 See e.g. S. Toulmin, *The Place of Reason in Ethics* (Cambridge University Press, 1950). We examine this book in a later chapter.

man is not just one thing. The great error of the hedonists is, as Bradley saw, a faulty monistic metaphysics of the human person; a failure to realise the plurality-in-unity of the moral self.[59] The existentialists speak of man as ambiguous and of morality as the expression of his ambiguous situation.[60] Naturalism is the refusal of 'ambiguity', which is better called the refusal of duality or the refusal of transcendence or the spiritual. The most telling refutations of hedonism are perhaps Sartre's analyses of desire as the demand for the impossible. Sartre's testimony is all the more telling in that he agrees with the hedonist that there is only one kind of satisfaction; but he does not agree that there is only one kind of desire. Man is such that the satisfactions of this world (which is for Sartre, as for the hedonists, the only world) will never assuage his desire. He desires what, for Sartre, is not. He desires God; and therefore is a 'useless passion'.[61]

Failure to realise this deeper level of the naturalistic fallacy leads Moore himself, as we shall see, to commit the very fallacy whose 'refutation' made his book famous. Also his peculiar concomitant ideas detract greatly from the value of his naturalistic fallacy argument and from his refutation of naturalism.

3 ANTI-NATURALISM IN THE 'ETHICS'

Moore's later little book, *Ethics*, does not use the term 'naturalistic fallacy' at all; but it gives a better refutation of naturalism, based essentially on the irreducibility of moral to non-moral predicates. He considers mainly, in this book, the notions of 'right' and 'wrong' rather than the notion of 'good'. He shows that judgments of right and wrong cannot be assertions about somebody's *feelings* towards the action in question. Such judgments cannot be assertions about the speaker's feelings: because then no two persons could really contradict one another's moral judgments or really dispute about moral questions. If, when one speaker says 'x' is wrong', he means only 'I dislike x' or 'I disapprove of x'; he is not contradicted by another who says 'No, x is right', but means only 'No, I like x', or 'But I approve of x'. 'They are no more contradicting one another than if, when one had said, 'I like sugar', the other had answered, 'I don't like sugar'.[62] If it were proposed that moral judgments are assertions about the feelings of one's community, it must be replied that this would make moral disagreement or discussion between people from different societies impossible; and also that I can think an action to be right despite of the disapproval of my society or vice-versa.[63]

Moore prolongs his defence of 'the objectivity of moral judgments' by refuting the suggestion that 'x is right or wrong' merely assents 'somebody or other *thinks*

---

59 See *Ethical Studies*, pp. 85–7, 116, 124–6.   60 Note the title of Simone de Beauvoir's book, *Pour une morale de l'ambiguité.*   61 See *Being* and *Nothingness*, E. trans., pp. 86–90, 101–2, 127–9, 566ff., 575, 591–9, 615, 623.   62 op. pit., pp. 87–106.   63 pp. 107–19.

it to be right or wrong.' As in the case of the *feelings* translation of moral judgments this would mean that the same act could be both right and wrong at once, and that one speaker could not contradict another's moral judgment.[64] In a more general epistemological argument which both recalls Bradley's anti-psychologism and anticipates certain aspects of Wittgenstein's, Moore argues that 'I believe that so-and-so' can never mean 'I believe that I (or anybody else) have the belief that so-and-so.'[65] This would land us in infinite regress and would deprive the belief of any content or of any object.[66] When a man makes a moral judgment, he may be in fact merely *expressing* an opinion which he has, and which may be a false opinion; but he is not merely *meaning to* asssert that he has an opinion or that he thinks so-and-so. He is *meaning to assert* that 'x is in fact right or wrong'. I can always know my own opinions; but I can and do hesitate and doubt as to what is the moral truth.[67] All doctrines which translate moral judgments into statements about men's feelings or opinions are proposing to abolish ethics and replace it by psychological enquiries into how men feel or anthropological enquiries into what opinions men have.[68]

But ethics cannot be thus abolished; the ethical question always returns. 'This is right' can never be translated into, 'Most men feel or think it is right'; because, about what most men like or approve of, feel or think to be right we can always ask, 'But is this morally 'right'?[69] Hence,

To predicate of an action that it is right or wrong is to predicate of it something quite different from the mere fact that any man or set of men have any particular feeling towards, or opinion about it.[70]

64 pp. 119–22. 65 The whole section repeats an argument of *Principia Ethica*, directed against idealism, (pp. 131–5), which he accuses of committing a sort of 'naturalistic fallacy' about truth. He there says: 'Whether you have a certain thought or not is one question; and whether what you think is true is quite a different one, upon which the answer to the first has not the least bearing' (p. 132). He concludes: 'That "to be true" means to be thought in a certain way is, therefore, certainly false. Yet this assertion plays the most essential part in Kant's "Copernican revolution" of philosophy, and renders worthless the whole mass of modern literature, to which that revolution has given rise, and which is called Epistemology' (p. 133). This is a large claim; and we can at least say that Moore's point, valid and important as it is, has not the bearing upon this claim that he thinks it has. He did not recall that Bradley, *chef de file* of idealistic epistemologists, made an almost exactly similar point against the empiricists. He could not foresee that Wittgenstein, by appealing to a very similar point, would condemn as psychologism or epistemologism and pronounce worthless a great mass of Moore's own philosophy of knowledge. Cf. pp. 143–4. 66 pp. 122–4. 67 pp. 124–8. 68 pp. 130–1. 69 pp. 139–43. 70 p. 144. This whole line of argument is parallelled in 'The Nature of Moral Philosophy', in *Philosophical Studies*, pp. 330–39. It is common-place in British moral philosophy. For example C.D. Broad argues against Hume that on his theory, every dispute about right and wrong turns on the question whether more men 'feel an emotion of approval (or of disapproval) on contemplating' the object in dispute; and this 'is capable of being settled completely by the simple method of collecting statistics.' But this, Broad points out, 'seems utterly irrelevant to this kind of question' (*Five Types of Ethical Theory*, Kegan Paul, London, 1944, pp. 114–5). Broad is almost certainly wrong about Hume; but his argument is decisive against psychologistic and sociologistic types of ethical theory. Compare A. N. Prior, *Logic and the Basis of Ethics* (Oxford University Press, (1949) 1956), pp. 9–10, where he holds that naturalism can make itself invulnerable to Moore's argument—by denying that there is any such study as ethics, and calling the 'enquiry into the sources of pleasure, not Ethics, but some such name as "Hedonics" . . . or "Biological Strategy" '.

The same applies to translations of moral judgments into terms of the feelings or thoughts of any 'non-human being', or any mental attitudes (such as *willing* or *commanding* or *forbidding*) of any 'non-human being', be it God, or Practical Reason or Pure Will, or Universal Still, or the True Self.[71]

A prevalent theory of this type is that of religious moralists who translate 'This is right' into 'God wills or commands this'; and 'This is wrong' into 'God forbids this.' Moore finds it a 'serious objection' to such views that 'it is, to say the least, extremely doubtful whether there is any such being . . .'. In fact, his own opinion is 'that in all probability there is no such being—neither a God nor any being such as philosophers have called by the names I have mentioned'.[72]

But Moore does not know anything of the chief philosophers who held that the moral law is ultimately God's law, namely the medieval scholastics. If he did, he would not have argued, as though in refutation of this doctrine, that even people who do not believe in God know the difference between right and wrong. Nor would he have argued that the religious view prevents us from saying that 'God forbids what is wrong, *because* it is wrong', obliging us, on the contrary, to say 'that the wrongness of what is wrong consists simply and solely in the fact that God does forbid it'.[73]

Aquinas affirms that people know the difference between right and wrong by reason, and that the fundamental principles of morality are ineffaceable from the human mind. But he did not find that knowing something to be true by reason is opposed to knowing it to be true by God's disposition; for reason is the God-given means for the discovery of God-ordained reality and truth.[74] Aquinas maintains that the differences between right and wrong is written into the nature of man and the nature of things. But he does not find this incompatible with or alternative to holding that the difference between right and wrong is determined ultimately by God's Mind and Will; because the nature of man and of things is determined by God.[75] Aquinas repeats again and again that acts are right or wrong in themselves, and not by an arbitrary fiat of God; and he rejects categorically the thesis that wrong acts are wrong because they are forbidden by God; contending instead that acts are forbidden by God because they are wrong.[76] But he would have held it senseless to maintain that acts are right or wrong *independently* of God. One understands nothing of the meaning and the logic of theism unless one realises that, for theism, there is no disjunction between a thing's being true or false, right or wrong *in itself*, and being true or false, right or wrong, *by God's*

---

71 pp. 145–51. We need not comment on the grotesque misunderstanding of Kant and of the idealists which is revealed by speaking of the Practical Reason, the True Self etc. as 'non-human beings'. 72 p. 151. 73 pp. 152–4. Paradoxically, Moore objects to such views that they are incompatible with the objectivity of moral judgments (pp. 224–5). 74 *S. Theol.* 1–2. 93. 2–3; 1–2. 94. 6; *SCG* III 111–15. Aquinas says (1–2. 93. 3 and 2): 'Human law realises the definition of law insofar as it accords with right reason; and it is this which shows whether it is derived from the eternal law of God or not.' 75 *S. Theol.* 1–2. 93. 6; 1–2. 94. 2; 1–2. 94. 4–6. 76 *S. Theol.* 1–2. 18; 1–2. 54. 3; 1–2. 94. 2; *SCG* III 129.

determination. For the theist, everything exists, and has its nature, its moral quality and its truth, *both* in itself *and* from God; for it is what it is, it is *itself*, by God's creation. Yet British moralists have been monotonously repeating, since Moore, that it is a 'matter of logic' that God's Mind or Will or Command cannot 'entail' an ought-judgment.

4 MOORE'S CRITIQUE OF METAPHYSICAL ETHICS

Moore is confident that he can show metaphysical ethics to be guilty of the same sort of fallacy as the naturalistic fallacy of evolutionism and hedonism. We are now familiar with the fact that, according to Moore, the naturalistic fallacy is committed both when 'good' is claimed to be defined or explained in terms of, or to be derived from, non-moral predicates; and when 'good' is claimed to be defined or explained in terms of, or to be derived from, any predicates whatever other then 'good'. One of the oddest results of this, which becomes more explicit in the chapter on metaphysical ethics, is that 'good' or 'goodness' is said not to exist. Things or qualities which are good do exist. But goodness does not exist at all.[77] This is surprising; but part of the surprise comes from wonder at (to use Moorean language) 'what, that is true, can possibly be meant by this'. By 'exists' Moore means 'exists in time'. Only natural objects, objects of perception, exist in time. 'Good' or 'goodness' is not a natural object. Therefore it does not exist.[78] Moore announces this with the innocence of a child; and it never occurs to him to give reasons to justify this use of language.

At first sight, it would seem that metaphysics and ethics were made for one another; for metaphysics is just the study of things that are not natural objects, things that do not exist in time. The Good would seem, then, to be the proper study of metaphysics. But, alas, metaphysicians have made the fatal error of thinking that the 'objects' they study exist.

> They have in general supposed that whatever does not exist in time must at least exist elsewhere, if it is to *be* at all—that whatever does not exist in Nature, must exist in some supersensible reality, whether timeless or not.

Metaphysics has been the search for 'knowledge of non-natural existence'. Moore, with his quaint ideas about what religion is, says metaphysicians

> have held that their science consists in giving us such knowledge as can be supported by reasons, of that supersensible reality of which religion professes to give us a fuller knowledge, without any reasons.

77 p. 110; cf. p. 125. 78 pp. 110–1; cf. pp. 40–1, 124–5.

But Moore cannot give them many marks.

I think that the only non-natural objects about which it has succeeded in obtaining truth, are objects which do not exist at all.

Such objects are, chiefly, numbers and universal truths.[79]

In the sphere of ethics, metaphysicians have persisted in the belief that 'good' must be a non-natural, supersensible reality.

A 'Metaphysical Ethics' is marked by the fact that it makes the assertion: That which would be perfectly good is something which exists, but is not natural; that which has some characteristic possessed by a supersensible reality.

The Stoics, Spinoza, Kant and modern Idealists are named by Moore as typical metaphysical moralists. He concedes that they have

a merit, not possessed by Naturalism, in recognising that for perfect goodness much more is required than any quantity of what exists here and now or can be inferred as likely to exist in the future.[80]

They recognise, in other words, that good is not a natural property. But here their merit ends. For they go on to claim

that this ethical proposition *follows* from some proposition which is metaphysical: that the question 'What is real? has some logical bearing upon the question 'What is good?' . . . (But) to hold that from any proposition asserting 'Reality is of this nature' we can infer, or obtain confirmation for, any proposition asserting 'This is good in itself' is to commit the naturalistic fallacy . . . Such an assertion . . . rests upon the failure to perceive that any truth which asserts 'This is good in itself' is quite unique in kind—that it cannot be reduced to any assertion about reality, and therefore must remain unaffected by any conclusion we may reach about the nature of reality.[81]

In a curious section, which does not seem easy to correlate with the rest of his ethical thought, Moore argues that, when ethics enquires, 'What is good?' it is asking two questions, which must be clearly distinguished. The first question is: 'Which among existing things are good?' The second one is: 'What *sort of* things are good, what are the things which, whether they *are* real or not, ought to be real?' The answer to the first question depends on the answer to the second. Hence the business of ethics 'is finished when it has completed the list of things that ought to exist, whether they do exist or not'. For this purpose, fiction is as

---

79 pp. 110–2. 80 p. 113. 81 pp. 113–4. Cf. p. 118: 'What ought to be? What is good in itself? That no truth about what is real can have any logical bearing upon the answer to this question has been proved in Chapter I . . . If we ask: What bearing can Metaphysics have upon the question, What is good?, the only possible answer is: Obviously and absolutely none.'

good as truth; metaphysical Utopias as relevant as alleged metaphysical construc-
tions of Reality. In fact, in this sense 'Ethics should, far more emphatically, be
based on fiction'.[82]

But metaphysics has been trying to base ethics, not on the fictional supposed
real but on the impossible or the self-contradictory supposed real. This is the case
with their concept of Eternal Reality; for the eternal reality is by definition one
which 'no actions of ours can have power to alter'; and if it alone is the only true
reality, then 'nothing good can possibly exist in time'.[83] Moore thinks that the
same accusation of self-contradiction can be brought against Kant's notion of the
good as being what the Free or Pure Will necessarily does. This implies that
whatever the Pure Will wills is good, not because that Will is good, but simply
because it is what that Will wills. In other words, whatever the Pure Will wills is
good. This, according to Moore, makes Kant's ethics hopelessly 'heteronomous',
and is a species of 'naturalistic fallacy', 'supposing moral law to be analogous to
natural law'.[84]

It is, however, most unplausible to suggest that Kant, who built nearly all of
his philosophy on the distinction of moral law from natural law, of 'ought' from
'is', of freedom from necessity, should commit any such fallacy. In fact, Moore
has blundered badly about Kant. Despite all Kant's pains to distinguish them,
he has confused Kant's moral necessity with his physical necessity, the necessity
of duty with the necessity of physical law, the causality of freedom with the
causality of nature. He has forgotten that Kant's Pure Will or Good Will is
defined, in the most carefully non-naturalist way, as the will which does what is
morally right because it is morally right.[85] Moore finds a naturalistic fallacy too
in Kant's doctrine of the categorical imperative, which identifies what is good
with what is commanded. But, he says,

> however an authority be defined, its commands will be *morally* binding only
> if they are—morally binding; only if they tell us what ought to be or what is
> a means to what ought to be.[86]

It is preposterous to accuse Kant of reducing 'ought' to 'is', or of confusing what
ought to be done with what is commanded. Kant actually agrees with Moore that

---

82 pp. 118–23. 'Wild and extravagant', says Moore', 'as are the assertions which metaphysicians have
made about reality, it is not to be supposed but that they have been partially deterred from making them
wilder still, by the idea that it was their business to tell nothing but the truth. But the wilder they are, and
the less useful for Metaphysics, the more useful will they be for Ethics . . .' (p. 121). 83 pp. 115–7,
119–20, 140. Moore does not advert to the fact that his own concept of a perfectly beautiful world without
human occupant or observer is equally a world that 'no actions of ours have power to alter'. 84 pp.
126–7; cf. p. 174. 85 See the section on 'Solution of the Cosmological Idea of the Totality of the
Deduction of Cosmical Events from their Causes' in the second book of the Transcendental Dialectic of
the *Critique of Pure Reason* (Everyman edition, pp. 316–29); *The Fundamental Principles of the Metaphysic
of Morals*, tr. T.K. Abbott (Longmans, London, 1909, 1948), pp. 9, 55–9, 65ff.; *Critique of Practical
Reason*, op. cit., pp. 164–82. 86 pp. 127–9.

even God's commands are incapable of determining what ought to be done.[87] Kant is not proposing to translate 'this is right' into 'this is commanded'. He is translating 'this is right' into 'this is morally obligatory' or 'this is morally commanded'; he is, in other words, trying to analyse what it means to say 'this is right' or 'morally obligatory' or 'morally commanded'.

Moore is equally wrong about Green, whom he accuses of equating 'good' with what *is* willed or desired by a moral being. This identifies 'being good' with 'being desired in a particular way'. But 'being desired in a particular way' has nothing to do with ethics. Therefore, 'the *Prolegomena to Ethics* is quite as far as Mr Spencer's *Data of Ethics* from making the smallest contribution to the solution of ethical problems'.[88] Moore is very perverse here; for, in Green's context, 'being desired in a particular way' means 'being desired in an ethical way'; and it is paradoxical to suggest that this has nothing to do with ethics.

But it is by now plain that Moore has pushed his 'naturalistic fallacy' argument to the point where he refuses to allow any analysis of what it means to say 'this is good'. Ethics as an investigation of the meaning of 'good', is reduced to one sentence which is not even a sentence but only the repetition of one word: 'Good is good and nothing else whatever'—and anything said about 'good' is naturalism.[89] It is not only that to define moral good non-morally is a fallacy; but to define moral good morally is a fallacy too—or, at least, Moore is unwilling to distinguish moral from non-moral definitions of 'good'.[90]

One of Moore's arguments against idealism is particularly interesting in the light of the subsequent history of British ethics. It is that metaphysicians assimilate all propositions to 'the type of those which assert either that something exists or that something which exists has a certain attribute'. They thus force ethical propositions to conform to material-object statements. They imagine that ethical properties must somehow exist, as natural properties do; and since ethical properties do not exist in nature and time, they suppose that they must exist non-naturally or not in time. They 'confuse the necessity with which goodness inheres in good things with the necessity with which natural properties, studied by science, attach to physical things'.[91] This false logical assimilation leads them

---

87 See *Critique of Practical Reason* (Abbott), pp. 224–9; cfr. *Metaphysic of Morals* (do.) p. 25. Cf. the chapter on Kant's Prize Essay in A.E. Teale's *Kantian Ethics* (Oxford University Press, 1951), pp. 17–32. 88 137–9. 89 cf. p. 144. Cf. A.N. Prior, *Logic and the Basis of Ethics*, pp. 3–4. 90 On p. 129 he writes that the assertion, 'This is good' 'is not identical . . . with any other proposition'. 91 An odd passage occurs here, in which Moore says: 'It is immediately obvious that when we see a thing to be good, its goodness is not a property which we can take up in our hands, or separate from it even by the most delicate scientific instruments, and transfer to something else. It is not, in fact, like most of the predicates which we ascribe to things, a *part* of the thing to which we ascribe it. But philosophers suppose that the reason why we cannot take goodness up and move it about, is not that it is a different *kind* of object from any which can be moved about, but only that it *necessarily* exists together with anything with which it does exist' (p. 124). But it is not peculiar to 'goodness' that we cannot take it in our hands etc.; this applies to all 'natural properties' equally, indeed to all properties whatever. *No* predicate is 'part' of a thing in this sense.

to suppose either that 'to be good' means to be related to some other particular thing which can exist and does exist 'in reality'; or else that it means merely 'to belong to the real world'—that goodness is transcended or absorbed in reality. But all such definitions of good in terms of reality are disqualified by the fact that

> whatever we may have proved to exist, and whatever two existents we may have proved to be necessarily connected with one another, it still remains a distinct and different question whether what thus exists is good; whether either or both of the two existents is so; and whether it is good that they should exist together. To assert the one is plainly and obviously not to assert the other. We understand what we mean by asking: Is this, which exists, or necessarily exists, after all good? and we perceive that we are asking a question that has not been answered.[92]

There is nothing that Moore repeats more often, in this chapter and in his book, than this, that of everything that may be pronounced to be anything other than 'good' (e.g. 'desired' or 'desirable', 'pleasant'or 'approved', 'satisfying' or 'satisfactory', 'true' or 'real', 'existing' or 'necessary'), we may always ask, But is this thing which is so-and-so, also good?;[93] and this, for him, proves conclusively that good does not mean anything else whatever than 'good', and that nothing else whatever can be said about it than that it is 'good'.

But, we must again object, in this 'good' does not differ from any other property. 'Yellow' means 'yellow' and nothing else whatever. But we are not therefore confined to saying that 'yellow is yellow', and we are not committing a 'chromatic fallacy' when we talk about it in terms of light waves etc. Moore has pushed a perfectly valid proposition about the irreducibility of ethics to science to such an absurd extreme that it involves the reduction of ethics to silence. As we noted already, the logic of his motto, 'Everything is what it is, and not another thing', is the end of all rational discourse about anything.

5 MOORE'S OWN 'NATURALISTIC FALLACY': THE RIGHT

Moore's ethics ought to have stopped, therefore, with the critical or negative portion. But a substantial part of his book is a positive doctrine of what actions are right, and what things are good. We should, however, be prepared to find that Moore cannot make any positive assertions whatever about right and good

---

The error Moore finds in the idealists was repeated by his own immediate successors in British ethics 'the Oxford Intuitionists', of whom we treat in the next chapter. The later Oxford school of neo-Wittgensteinians have often made of them the same criticism as Moore here makes of the idealists. The point Moore makes here was independently and powerfully developed in the philosophy of Wittgenstein's second period.   92 pp. 123–26; cf. pp. 15–17.   93 pp. 113–4., 118, 122, 129–39; cf. pp. 15–17.

without violating his own canons, and committing a 'naturalistic fallacy' in his own sense of the term. Of *anything* he may put forward as an explicitation or analysis of 'good', we may ask, 'But is this good?' Moore does speak of good as 'that which has intrinsic value or intrinsic worth', or as 'that which ought to exist'.[94] On his own terms, we could retort: 'But is that which has intrinsic value, or that which ought to exist, good?'[95]

Since, however, Moore's canon is fallacious, he is rather to be congratulated on violating it. Much more important is the fact that he repeatedly commits the 'naturalistic fallacy' in its genuine sense by confusing moral with non-moral terms. This is glaringly the case in his chapter on 'Ethics in Relation to Conduct'. This chapter introduces for him the first of the two questions of practical ethics, for which the proof of the indefinability of good has laid the foundation. These questions are: What actions are right? and, What states of affairs are good? Moore insists that 'right' does and can mean nothing but 'cause of a good result'. 'What is right?' is therefore a double question: it is first an empirical, causal question, which is like any other causal question in the natural sciences. It asks, 'What effects will this action have?'; or 'What are the efficacious means to secure such and such effects?' It is or implies, secondly, an ethical question: 'What effects are good in themselves?'[96] About 'right' in its first aspect, as *cause* of a good result, Moore is frankly and avowedly naturalistic, through and through utilitarian. He does not think that this makes his ethics naturalistic; because he thinks he has a non-naturalistic way of conceiving the *goodness* of the good result in relation to which right actions are defined. We shall see, however, that his doctrine of good is itself crypto-naturalistic; and that therefore his whole ethics collapses into naturalism. First let us take note of the naturalistic fallacies in his doctrine of 'right'.

He begins by affirming categorically that

'right' does and can mean nothing but 'cause of a good result', and is thus identical with 'useful'; whence it follows that the end always does justify the means and that no action which is not justified by its results can be right.[97]

---

94 pp. 17, 25–9, 187ff.; *Ethics*, pp. 223ff.; 'The Conception of Intrinsic value', in *Philosophical Studies*, pp. 253–75. **95** In 'A Reply to My Critics' in *The Philosophy of G.E. Moore*, ed., P.A. Schilpp, Moore acknowledged that it was a 'sheer error' on his part to speak of "good" as being identical with that which ought to exist. He says that what he really meant was that 'good' is 'logically equivalent' with 'that which ought to exist' (pp. 555–608). But criticised in *Principia Ethica*, claimed to be explaining 'good' in all the theories of good, naturalistic and idealistic, which are terms 'logically equivalent' to it; yet Moore maintained they were refuted simply by pointing out that one could ask of each proposed equivalent: 'But is this good?' Cf. M.J. Charlesworth, *Philosophy and Linguistic Analysis*, pp. 31–3. **96** pp. 146–8; cf. pp. 21–7. On p. 146, he says: 'Every judgment is practical. Ethics may be reduced to the form: This is a cause of that good thing.' **97** p. 147. He recognises a sense in which it is true that 'the end never justifies the means' and that 'we never should do evil that good may come'. It is when 'means' and 'evil' mean 'moral rules generally recognised and practised' and which must therefore, be presumed to be 'generally useful' and to prevail over the opposing opinions or interests of an individual (p. 163).

He holds it to be 'demonstrably certain' that 'the assertion "I am morally bound to perform this action" is identical with the assertion "this action will produce the greatest possible amount of good in the Universe".' The 'demonstration' is that to assert that a certain action is our absolute duty is to assert that that action is 'unique in respect of value', which is to say that 'the whole world will be better if it be performed, than if any possible alternative were taken'. If any other action would conceivably make 'the sum of good in the Universe' greater, then it, and not the first, is the action which is our duty.

> Our 'duty', therefore, can only be defined as that action which will cause more good to exist in the Universe than any possible alternative. And what is 'right' or 'morally permissible' only differs from this as that which will *not* cause *less* good than any possible alternative. . . . If we are told that 'to do no murder' is a duty, we are told that the action, whatever it may be, which is called murder, will under no circumstances cause so much good to exist in the Universe as its avoidance.[98]

The 'right' is, then, the same as the 'useful'. There is no real distinction between 'right' or 'duty' on the one hand, and the 'useful' or 'the expedient' on the other. These terms have not precisely the same meaning, but they designate one and the same act, the act, namely, which is 'a means to the best possible', or which 'will produce the best possible results on the whole'.[99] The difference in meaning between 'duty' and 'expediency', consists solely in this, that the ethical term has a hortatory force which the other lacks, and is applied to 'actions which it is more useful to praise and to enforce by sanctions, since they are actions which there is a temptation to omit'.[100] The same applies to the terms 'virtue' and 'vice'. These also

> are ethical terms: that is to say, when we use them seriously, we mean to convey praise by the one and dispraise by the other. . . . As duties from expedient actions, so virtues are distinguished from other useful dispositions, not by any superior utility, but by the fact that they are dispositions, which it is particularly useful to praise and to sanction, because there are strong and common temptations to neglect the actions to which they lead.

But 'so far as the definition goes, to call a thing a virtue is merely to declare that it is a means to good'.[101] The suggestion that ethical terms are characterised by their hortatory force was to enjoy a brilliant career in subsequent British moral philosophy: the 'emotive' and the persuasive' theories of ethics developed it extensively.[102]

. 98 pp. 147–8. 99 pp. 167–9; cf. p. 147; *Ethics*, pp. 171–3. 100 pp. 169–71. 101 pp. 171–3. Cf. *Ethics*, pp. 188–9, 216. 102 Moore's thought here is closely followed also by Nowell-Smith, *Ethics*, pp. 303–6.

There can be no question, therefore, but that the end always justifies the means, and the only justification of morality is by its results. People have grandiloquently said, 'Let justice be done should the heavens fall' but such people will be found generally

> disposed to believe that justice never will, in fact, cause the heavens to fall, but will rather be always the best means of upholding them.[103] . . . 'Fiat iustitia, ruat coelum' can only be justified on the ground that by the doing of justice the Universe gains more than it loses by the falling of the heavens. It is, of course, possible, that this is the case: but, at all events, to assert that justice *is* a duty, in spite of such consequences, is to assert that it is the case.[104]

Russell has spoken of a certain 'moralistic fierceness' that marks certain passages of *Principia Ethica* and has not usually been noticed.[105] It is here that this is most in evidence. Seldom has the criterion of utility, of efficacity, in morals been asserted and defended with such cool, obstinate logic. But this whole doctrine of 'right', 'duty' and 'virtue' is a tissue of naturalistic fallacies. Moore goes on talking about 'good result', 'better result', 'better total results', 'greater balance of good', 'best possible result on the whole'; 'the sum of good in the Universe', 'the whole world (being) better', 'the greatest total value'; about what is 'useful', 'expedient', 'generally useful', 'advantageous'.[106] He does not see that *each single one* of these terms and phrases has a two-fold use, a moral and a non-moral use; and that his whole argument, like Mill's, rests on a failure to distinguish the two.[107]

But to fail to distinguish moral from non-moral predicates is, as Moore saw in his critique of Mill, to miss the point of morality completely. To say that 'by the doing of justice the universe gains more than it loses by the falling of the heavens', and that therefore justice is justified by its results, is to slur over the moral issue by what is no better than a pun. The moral issue is that people feel that *material* gain does not excuse or justify *moral* corruption; that an action may have the best possible material results on the whole and yet lead to a worse state of the world. People can quite soberly judge it better that their nation and civilisation should perish rather than that they should adopt immoral principles. Liberals in many countries, who once accepted the theory of justification of morality by results, are now sincerely contending that it is better that their countries should be

---

103 *Ethics*, p. 177.   104 *Principia Ethica*, p. 148.   105 See *The Listener*, 30 April 1959.   106 See pp. 146–8 150, 153, 158, 160–7, 169, 172, 180. Cf. *Ethics* pp. 176–7, 180–1.   107 Because of this confusion, Moore actually thinks that the idealists' doctrine of 'self-realization' or of duty as the obligation 'to do what will conduce to [a man's] own 'perfection' or his own'salvation', is the same as saying 'that it must always be an agent's positive duty to do what is best for *himself*'; and is indistinguishable from egoistic hedonism (*Ethics*, p. 228–9). It would be interesting to have Bradley's comment on this. The Christian doctrine of heaven is also, according to Moore, a form of egoistic hedonism (see op. cit., p. 230; *Principia Ethica*, pp. 174, 195–6).

obliterated than that they should use nuclear weapons of defence. That is not an appeal to results. It is a protestation that moral results are not comparable to non-moral results. These people could be wrong in their particular judgment; but they have seen what morality is. Morality is the conviction that moral and non-moral considerations belong to different orders; that good non-moral consequences will never balance bad moral consequences, and that physically good but immoral ends will never justify morally bad means. The naturalistic fallacy eliminates ethics because it abolishes this distinction. The question which goes to the root of the naturalistic fallacy is the question: 'What doth it profit a man if he gain the whole world and suffer the loss of his own soul?'

In this part of his ethics, because it is sheerly utilitarian, Moore inevitably falls into the familiar difficulties and dilemmas of the utilitarians. Since it is never possible for us to know what the total effects of any action will be or which action will produce 'the greatest possible amount of good in the Universe', Moore is forced to concede, and he imperturbably admits, 'that we never have any reason to suppose that any action is our duty'.[108] At best, all we can 'hope to discover is which, among a few alternatives possible under certain circumstances will, on the whole, produce the best result'.[109] It should be noted that this is to abandon the definition of duty from which the whole argument proceeds, which was that duty means that *unique action* which will produce *absolutely* 'the greatest possible amount of good'.[110] But even the changed definition of duty presents 'immense difficulty'.

> It is difficult to see how we can establish even a probability that by doing one thing we shall obtain a better total result than by doing another. . . . No sufficient reason has ever yet been found for considering one action more right or more wrong than another.[111]

We cannot see far ahead. In the long run, all acts would seem to come to pretty much the same thing. Indeed (it is Moore who speaks):

> it does in fact appear to be the case that, in most cases, whatever action we now adopt 'it will be all the same a hundred years hence', so far as the existence at that time of anything greatly good or bad is concerned.[112]

It would seem that Moore should give up the notion of duty or right altogether, as Bentham was ready to do; or, more properly, that he should give up a theory which so conflicts with plain moral facts. But he perseveres. We can make a reasonable estimate about 'which, among a few alternatives, will *generally* produce the greatest balance of good in the immediate future'. Setting aside 'theological dogmas' (he has, it will be remembered, argued in the *Ethics* that to claim religious

---

108 p. 149; cf. *Ethics*, pp. 178–9. 109 pp. 150–1. 110 p. 147. 111 p. 152. 112 p. 153.

authority for morality is to undermine the objectivity of moral judgments"[113]),— immediate effects and advantages are all that any ethics can ever hope to be based upon. We must, therefore give up all notion of absolute moral precepts.

We can secure no title to assert that obedience to such commands as 'Thou shalt not lie', or even 'Thou shalt do no murder', is *universally* better than the alternatives of lying and murder.[114]

We can only have probable and conditional generalisations in ethics as in science. But in ethics, the possibility of error is ever so much greater, and

owing to the comparative absence of accurate hypothetical knowledge on which the prediction should be based, the probability is comparatively small.[115]

Murder, for example cannot be proved absolutely wrong; because we cannot prove that human life is in itself good, nor can we be sure that people will always persist in preferring life to death. However, so long as they do, then 'it seems capable of proof that under these circumstances it is generally wrong for any single person to commit murder.'[116] The same goes for honesty, promise-keeping, respect for property, so long as men have that 'intense desire for property of some sort, which seems to be universal'.[117] These rules, however, seem to be based on tendencies 'so universal and so strong that it would be impossible to remove them', and we may say that 'under any conditions that could actually be given, the general observance of these rules would be good as a means'.[118] Indeed, we may further say that these rules are necessary for 'the preservation of civilised society', which, in turn, is 'necessary for the existence, in any great degree, of anything that may be held to be good in itself'.[119]

Not quite the same can be said about 'most of the rules comprehended under the name of chastity'. The sentiments of 'conjugal jealousy and paternal affection' seem indeed 'sufficiently strong and general to make the defence (of these rules) valid for many conditions of society'.

However, 'it is not difficult to imagine a civilised society existing without them'; and, in that case,

if chastity were still to be defended, it would be necessary to establish that its

---

113 *Ethics*, pp. 149–55, 224–5.   114 p. 154. Compare *Ethics*, pp. 178–9: 'If we do take the view that right and wrong depend upon consequences, we must, I think, be prepared to doubt whether any particular kind of action is absolutely always right or absolutely always wrong. For instance, however we define "murder" it is unlikely that absolutely *no* case will ever occur in which it would be right to commit a murder; and however we define "justice", it is unlikely that no case will ever occur in which it would be right to do an injustice. . . . In the case of most of the ordinary moral rules, it seems extremely unlikely that obedience to them will *absolutely always* produce the best possible results. And most persons who realise this would, I think, be disposed to give up the view that they ought absolutely *always* to be obeyed. They would be content to accept them as *general* rules, to which there are very few exceptions, without pretending that they are absolutely universal.'   115 p. 155; cf. pp. 22–4, *Ethics*, pp. 192–5.   116 p. 156–7.   117 p. 157.   118 Ibid.   119 p. 158; but see *Ethics*, pp. 178–9, cited in n. 189 above.

violation produced evil effects other than those due to the assumed tendency of such violation to disintegrate society.

'Such a defence, may, no doubt, be made'; but it will require a great deal of ethical research, Moore thinks.[120]

The test of utility, by which duty is determined, is therefore passed by most of the rules 'which are in general both recognised and practised'. On the other hand,

a great part of ordinary moral exhortation and discussion consists in the advocating of rules which are *not* generally practised; and with regard to these it seems very doubtful whether a case for their general utility can ever be conclusively made out.[121]

Even with regard to rules which are generally recognised and practised, we can never be sure that in some exceptional cases 'neglect of an established rule' will not be 'the best course of action possible'. Can the individual, then, ever be justified in assuming that his is one of the exceptional cases? Moore is quite firm: the answer is No! The general probability must outweigh the individual's judgment. 'The individual can be confidently recommended *always* to conform to rules which are both generally useful and generally practised.'[122] 'Proposed changes in social custom, advocated as being better rules to follow than those now actually followed' can not, apparently, claim the support of ethics, for 'it seems doubtful whether *Ethics* can establish the utility of any rules other than those generally practised'.[123] There is, however, the probable exception of chastity, mentioned above; and it is to be presumed that moral pioneers do not need the support of Ethics! More seriously, it is surely a fatal flaw in any ethical theory that it cannot, consistently with itself, allow for moral progress.

On Moore's theory, 'the general utility' (and hence the rightness) 'of an action depends on the fact that it is generally practised'. In a society where theft is the rule,

the utility of abstinence from theft on the part of a single individual becomes exceedingly doubtful, even though the common rule is a bad one. There is therefore a strong probability in favour of adherence to an existing custom, even if it be a bad one.[124]

A person may even be punished for doing an action

right in his case, but generally wrong, even if his example would not be likely to have a dangerous effect. For sanctions have, in general, much more influence upon conduct than example; so that the effect of relaxing them in an exceptional case will almost certainly be an encouragement of similar action in cases which are not exceptional.[125]

---

120 Ibid.   121 p. 160.   122 p. 164. On p. 165, he speaks of 'rules which are both generally practised and strongly sanctioned among us'.   123 p. 161.   124 p. 164.   125 Ibid.

It is the nemesis of every utilitarian theory of punishment that it can give punishment no meaning except that 'of encouraging the others' or improving the culprit; and, as in the argument of Dr Pangloss, so in that of Moore, the two are often irreconcilable.

Can it be denied that, in these passages we have been quoting, it is not ethics that Moore has been speaking about, but 'something quite different'—social success, 'lifemanship' or whatever we might call it? Ethics has been replaced by something else—and this is the essence of the naturalistic fallacy.[126] 'When 'virtue' is pronounced to be 'useful', 'good as means', but is said to have generally 'no intrinsic value whatever';[127] when conscience is described as 'one of the things which are generally useful'[128] the naturalistic fallacy is glaring. With regard to 'right' and 'duty', Moore may protest that he has granted their non-ethical character, and has given an empirical, a non-moral definition of them. But it cannot be sensibly maintained that 'right' and 'duty' are non-moral, and any non-moral definition of them must be fallacious. It is perverse to maintain, as Moore's theory compels him to maintain, that actions can be right, or can be my duty, without having any intrinsic goodness or value; or, that judgments about rightness or duty are empirical or, causal, not strictly ethical in character,[129] or that motive, while relevant to some other moral judgments, is irrelevant to the rightness or wrongness of actions.[130]

In his later volume, *Ethics*, Moore defends the irreducibility of ethics against naturalism by speaking precisely of 'right', not of 'good'. He there shows that 'right' cannot be replaced by assertions about what 'is generally approved in the society to which I belong', or generally approved by all mankind, etc. 'Right' is 'something quite different' from all such assertions.[131] All such translations of 'right' abolish ethics.[132]

Paradoxically, in the same book in which he is categorically non-naturalist about the *meaning* of 'right', he persists in being naturalistic about the criterion and content of 'right'.[133] We must conclude that, to make Moore consistent with himself, we should have to pronounce his whole doctrine of 'right', by his own prosecution, guilty of the naturalistic fallacy.

6 MOORE'S OWN 'NATURALISTIC FALLACY': THE GOOD

The same fallacy infects Moore's theory of the Good, in a more subtle form, but in a form destined to have even greater influence in subsequent British philosophy. This theory is expounded in the last chapter of *Principia Ethica*, on 'The

---

126 See pp. 11–12, 39–40. 127 pp. 171–8, 181–2. 128 p. 180. 129 See e.g. pp. 21–7, 146–8. 130 *Ethics*, pp. 182–90; cf. *Principia Ethica*, pp. 177–80. This tenet of Moore's, as taken up by Ross, is criticised by Joseph, *Some Problems in Ethics*, pp. 37–4, 94–5. 131 op. cit., pp. 108ff., 139–44. 132 op. cit., pp. 130–1. 133 See the whole of chapter V, 'Results the Test of Right and Wrong', pp. 170–95.

Ideal'. We have noted already that the question of what things are intrinsically good must, and can only be decided, according to Moore, by intuition; answers to it are incapable of proof.[134] We have seen also that Moore has a technique for submitting objects and situations to the judgment of intuition: namely, the technique of 'absolute isolation'. In the present case,

> it is necessary to consider what things are such that if they existed *by themselves*, in absolute isolation we should yet judge their existence to be good.[135]

We have seen already that this technique is an error, exposed and refuted decisively by Wittgenstein. For the moment, we are interested only in the results Moore thinks he has established by it.

When we apply this method to the question, 'What things are good?', the answer, Moore holds,

> appears to be so obvious that it runs the risk of seeming to be a platitude. By far the most valuable things, which we can know or imagine, are certain states of consciousness, which may be roughly described as the pleasures of human intercourse and the enjoyment of beautiful objects. No one, probably, who has asked himself the question, has ever doubted that personal affection and the appreciation of what is beautiful in Art or Nature, are good in themselves: nor, if we consider strictly what things are worth having *purely for their own sakes*, does it appear probable that anyone will think that anything else has *nearly* so much value as the things that are included under these two heads.[136]

It is to be noted that Moore's 'intrinsic goods' are a plurality; they form 'immense variety' having nothing in common except that they *are* 'intrinsic goods'. They depend each upon a separate and unique intuition; and these intuitions have no reasons founding them or connecting them.[137]

Moore becomes warmly eloquent in advocacy of this doctrine:

> What has not been recognised is that it is the ultimate and fundamental truth of Moral Philosophy. That it is only for the sake of these things—in order that

---

134 See Preface, pp. viii, x. 135 pp. 187–8; cf. 208, 223; *Ethics*, 243–50. 136 pp. 188–9. He sums up: '. . . personal affections and aesthetic enjoyments include *all* the greatest, and *by far* the greatest, goods we can imagine' (p. 189). 137 *Ethics*, pp. 247–9. 'So far as I can see, there is no characteristic whatever which belongs to all things that are intrinsically good and only to them—except simply the one that they all *are* intrinsically good and *ought* always to be preferred to *nothing* at all, if we had to choose between an action whose sole effect would be one of them and one which would have no effects whatever. . . . There are an *immense variety* of different things, *all* of which are intrinsically good; and . . . their variety is so great that they have [no characteristic] which, besides being common to them all is also *peculiar* to them. . . . All that can, I think, be done by way of making plain what kinds of things are intrinsically good or bad . . . is to classify some of the chief kinds of each pointing out what the factors are upon which their goodness or badness depends.' Moore has a section on the comparison of intrinsic values with one another, in reading which we might sometimes forget that he is comparing *values*, rather than, e.g., grading apples (ibid., pp. 243–7).

as much of them as possible may at some time exist,—that any one can be justified in performing any public or private duty; that they are the *raison d'être* of virtue; that it is they . . . that form the rational ultimate end of human action and the sole criterion of social progress: these appear to be truths which have been generally overlooked.[138]

The things in question are wholes, 'organic unities', which must include consciousness, knowledge or true belief, pleasant emotions or feelings.[139] In so far as personal affections are concerned 'the mental qualities of the person towards whom the affection is felt' are obviously important. But appreciation of these cannot be isolated from appreciation of the other's 'corporeal beauty'.[140] Matter without mind is indeed valueless; but so is mind without matter. When idealistic metaphysicians pronounce matter as 'essentially imperfect, if not positively evil' and propose a purely spiritual Supreme Good from which all material properties are absent, they are proposing to exclude 'many, if not all, of those things which we know most certainly to be great goods'. 'To deny and exclude matter, is to deny and exclude the best we know.'[141] It is fairly clear, however, that there is much more to be said than Moore recognises, about metaphysicians who are not idealists; about philosophers of the spiritual who do not deny or exclude matter; as also about what we, in our material condition, *know* about our transcendence of the material; and about the impossibility of accounting for all the dimensions and the complexities and the paradoxes of human love by reference to beautiful bodies or congenial minds or both together.

The same method of absolute isolation enables Moore to determine what things are evil. These he finds also to be organic unities, including an object, consciousness of that object, and some emotion. Among them are cruelty, lasciviousness or lust, hatred, envy or contempt. The first two are intrinsic evils, including in them 'an enjoyment or admiring contemplation of things which are themselves evil or ugly'.[142]

To return to the theory of intrinsic good, we wish to show in what sense and why we hold it to be a crypto-naturalistic theory. The 'pleasures of human intercourse and the enjoyment of beautiful objects' cannot be held to be unconditionally good except by the surreptitious addition to them of moral epithets. It is only the *morally lawful* pleasures of human intercourse and the *morally right* enjoyment of beautiful objects which can be unconditionally or intrinsically good. Obviously there can be 'pleasures of human intercourse' and 'personal affections' accompanying lasciviousness; and Moore would hold these to be intrinsically evil. There can be enjoyment of beautiful objects which have been acquired by theft, or through wealth unjustly amassed; and such enjoyment is evil. Moore has

---

138 p. 189. 139 pp. 27–36, 189–202; cf. *Ethics*, pp. 242–3. 140 p. 203–4. 141 pp. 205–7. 142 pp. 208–14.

confused the moral and the non-moral uses of the word 'good'. This is the naturalistic fallacy, truly so called.

The content of his 'intrinsic good' is an empirical, a non-moral content. The whole object and the sole justification for the intuitive judgment, 'This is intrinsically good', are the empirical features of the situation. The judgment predicating goodness of it is an unprovable, unarguable, unreasoning intuition, expressing a moral appraisal of an object already fully constituted and solely constituted in its objective nature by its empirical properties.

No relevant evidence whatever can be adduced: from no other truth, except themselves alone, can it be inferred that they are true or false . . . When I call such propositions 'Intuitions', I mean *merely* to assert that they are incapable of proof; I imply nothing whatever as to the manner of our cognition of them.[143]

We can put [the question] clearly by the method of isolation; and the sole decision must rest with our reflective judgment upon it, as thus clearly put.[144]

Our only means of deciding upon . . . intrinsic value and its degree, is by carefully distinguishing exactly what the thing is, about which we ask the question, and then looking to see whether it has or has not the unique predicate 'good' in any of its various degrees.[145]

In his lecture on 'The Conception of Intrinsic Value', Moore maintains that 'intrinsic value' is not an 'intrinsic property' or part of the 'intrinsic nature' of a thing; but it 'depends solely and necessarily' on the intrinsic nature of the thing. 'Intrinsic properties', by which Moore means the empirical properties of a thing, also depend solely and necessarily on the intrinsic nature of the thing. There is an irreducible difference between the type of 'necessity' or 'unconditionality' with which ethical values and empirical properties respectively accompany their objects, and this makes ethical predicates unique; but Moore does not know what the difference is.[146]

I can only vaguely express the kind of difference I feel there to be [between intrinsic or empirical properties and ethical predicates] by saying that intrinsic properties seem to *describe* the intrinsic nature of what possesses them in a sense in which predicates of value never do. If you could enumerate *all* the intrinsic properties a given thing possessed, you would have given a *complete* description of it, and would not need to mention any predicates of value it possessed; whereas no description of a given thing could be *complete* which omitted any intrinsic property.[147]

Strictly, in Moorean terminology, no reason can be given, no argument or

---

143 Preface, pp. viii, X. 144 p. 197. 145 p. 223. 146 *Philosophical Studies*, pp. 260–75. 147 Ibid., p. 274.

proof or evidence supplied, to justify the value judgment. But in fact, considerations are presented (the 'question is clearly put by the method of isolation')—and these considerations are, as we have seen, solely of the empirical order. Moore is therefore grounding a moral intuition on non-moral facts. This is surely not essentially different from deducing a moral conclusion from non-moral premisses; or from 'defining' 'good' in non-moral or naturalistic terms. It has the same vice as the naturalistic fallacy. The vice is repeated by philosopher after philosopher in subsequent British ethics. Many of them, especially after Toulmin's *The Place of Reason in Ethics*, accept it as a definition of moral judgments that they are evaluations backed by reasons; Moore's intuitionism of 'good' and later intuitionisms of 'ought', would, in this sense, have to be pronounced non-ethical. But these philosophers commit the same mistake as Moore: the reasons they advance as backing for moral evaluations are empirical or non-moral reasons. They too commit a naturalistic fallacy.

But an even more plausible development of Moore's doctrine is in the direction of emotivism. It seems paradoxical to assimilate Moore, who talked so much about the objectivity of moral judgments, to the subjectivists; but the connection is undeniable. If the judgment 'This is good' (or 'This is evil') is not provable, not analysable, not expressible in any other words but itself, how can it be a 'genuine proposition' at all? Is 'good' (or 'evil') any more than an interjection, evincing the speaker's feelings of approval (or disapproval)? Are moral sentences any more than 'expressions and excitants of feelings which do not necessarily involve any assertions'. In other words, is the youthful Ayer a, or the, legitimate heir of G.E. Moore?

7 LORD KEYNES ON MOORE'S INFLUENCE

An irreplaceable commentary on the contemporary impact of Moore's ethical teaching is provided in a memoir by John Maynard Keynes, entitled 'My Early Beliefs'.[148] Keynes came up to Cambridge in 1902. Cambridge's confident rationalism was then at its height and there seemed no limit to what reason could dare and do through its dedicated spirits. As we have seen, some of England's most brilliant intellects of the first half of this century were met together at Cambridge in the dozen years before 1914. In the philosophical field, Moore, with astonishing rapidity, ousted McTaggart and eclipsed Russell in the eyes of this generation of young genius.

---

148 See *Two Memoirs*, ed. David Garnett (Rupert Hart-Davis, London, 1949), pp. 75–103. The memoir in question is dated 9 September 1938.

Moore's *Principia Ethica* appeared in 1903, at the end of Keynes' first year. Keynes writes about it:

> We were at an age when our beliefs influenced our behaviour, a characteristic of the young which it is easy for the middle-aged to forget; and the habits of feeling formed then still persist in a recognisable degree.[149]

Moore's influence was, he says, exciting and exhilarating; it gave a sense of mission and emancipation and fearlessness; it gave the disciples 'supreme self-confidence, superiority and contempt towards the rest of the unconverted world'.

From Moore, they took only what Keynes calls his 'religion', discarding his Benthamite, utilitarian doctrine about the 'general rules of correct behaviour'. They contrasted Moore's 'religion', by which they meant 'one's attitude towards oneself and the ultimate', with his morals, by which they meant 'one's attitude towards the outside world and the intermediate'; and they felt attracted to the 'religion' precisely because 'it made morals unnecessary'.[150] On Moore's 'religion', Keynes has this to say:

> Nothing mattered except states of mind, our own and other peoples, of course, but chiefly our own. These states of mind were not associated with action or achievement or with consequences. They consisted in timeless, passionate states of contemplation and communion, largely unattached to 'before' and 'after'. . . . The appropriate subjects of passionate contemplation and communion were a beloved person, beauty and truth; and one's prime objects in life were love, the creation and enjoyment of aesthetic experience and the pursuit of knowledge. Of these, love came by a long way first. . . . Our religion closely followed the English puritan tradition of being chiefly concerned with the salvation of our own souls. . . . There was not a very intimate connection between 'being good' and 'doing good' . . . and the latter might interfere with the former.[151]

The question, 'What states of mind are good?' could not be settled by argument; it had to be decided by intuition.

> This was a matter of direct inspiration, direct unanalysable intuition, about which it was useless and impossible to argue.

How disputes regarding ultimate good could arise, on what precisely they bore, and how they could be settled, were difficult theoretical problems. But, Keynes drily remarks,

---

149 p. 81.   **150** p. 82.   **151** pp. 83–4.

in practice, victory was with those who could speak with greatest appearance of clear, undoubting conviction and could best use the accents of infallibility.

Of this method, he continues, Moore was himself the master.[152]

Yet, Keynes insists, they held morals to be scientific, not mystical or religious.

Like any other branch of science, it was nothing more than the application of logic and rational analysis to the material presented as sense data. Our apprehension of good was exactly the same as our apprehension of green and we purported to handle it with the same logical and analytical technique.

Russell's *Principles of Mathematics* came out in the same year as *Principia Ethica*, and the former provided the principles of a method for handling the material of the latter.

Keynes has some remarks on Moore's religious unworldliness, surpassing, he holds, that of Plato or the New Testament, which a different reading of Plato, and any reading of the New Testament, make to seem very queer. Keynes still judges the 'religion' of *Principia Ethica* 'a truer religion than any other', and sees 'no reason to depart from its fundamental intuitions'. Its great enemy they used to hold to be Christianity. But, in truth, he later came to see, 'it was the Benthamite calculus, based on an over-valuation of the economic criterion'? It was the escape from Bentham, he thinks, which served 'to protect the whole lot of us from the final *reductio ad absurdum* of Benthamism known as Marxism'.[153] It may well be felt, however, that an important role in saving Britain from Marxism was played by Keynesian economics; and this, though it had nothing whatever to do with Moore's pseudo-religion, had some connection with the Christian command to feed the hungry and clothe the naked.

But Keynes, looking back on these early beliefs, finds them sadly defective: they were 'far too narrow to fit actual experience'. Moore, he recognises, 'was oblivious of the value of the life of action and of the pattern of life as a whole'; he 'existed in a timeless ecstasy', academically isolated from the world of real people and their passions and problems.[154] In the disciples, this attitude expressed itself in an irresponsible antinomianism. 'We entirely repudiated a personal liability on us to obey general rules. We claimed the right to judge every individual case on its merits, and the wisdom and especially the self-control to do so successfully.' They were, precisely, 'immoralists' entirely opposed to 'morals, conventions and traditional wisdom'. They owned no moral obligation to obey the moral rules of society.

All this, Keynes, thirty years older, judges to have been naïve. It was 'flimsily based on an a priori view of what human nature is like, both our own and other

---

152 pp. 84–5.　153 pp. 92–7. Of the chapter on 'The Ideal', Keynes proclaims: 'I know no equal [to it] in literature since Plato.'　154 pp. 92–4.

people's, which was disastrously mistaken'. They were, he acknowledges, among the last Utopians or meliorists, who felt that people were fundamentally decent and good, and would be good without moral rules, if left alone.

> We repudiated all versions of the doctrine of original sin, of there being insane and irrational springs of wickedness in most men. We were not aware that civilisation was a thin and precarious crust, erected by the personality and will of very few and only maintained by rules and conventions skilfully put across and guilefully preserved.

Keynes' concept of how civilisation is erected is vague; his notion of how it is maintained is unprofound; but the essential criticism of Mooreanism reamins impressive. He admits the justice of the charge made by D.H. Lawrence and repeated often by Wittgenstein that he and his friends 'lacked reverence . . . for everything and everyone'. They were too individualist; too unaware of the value of community life and of society. They had a naïve and unrealistic confidence in the rationality of man and in the power of reasoning to make men good. 'Our comments on life and affairs were bright and amusing but brittle . . . because there was no solid diagnosis of human nature underlying them.'[155]

8 MOORE'S PLACE IN BRITISH ETHICS

A.N. Prior has shown[156] that Moore's sort of anti-naturalism has been a recurring feature in British ethics since the Cambridge Platonists' reaction against Hobbes. He has found parallels to Moore's reasoning in Cudworth's arguments against Hobbes; in the polemic of Clarke, Wollaston, Reid and Price against Locke and Hutcheson and Hume. He shows a particularly close correspondence between Richard Price's arguments against Locke in the mid-eighteenth century and Moore's refutation of naturalism.[157] Price already held 'right' and 'wrong' to be 'simple perceptions of the mind', intuitively apprehended and incapable of being defined or analysed. He gave essentially the same reasons for this view as Moore was to give: namely that every definition of a moral notion presupposes that moral notion, for of every proposed definition—psychological or theological—we can always ask: 'But *is* this (desire . . . divine command . . . etc.) morally right?'[158] Price and others among the authors mentioned had argued, as Moore was to argue, that any 'definition' of a moral term would reduce ethical statements to barren tautologies and would trivialise the whole subject of ethics.[159]

---

155 pp. 97–102.   **156** In *Logic and the Basis of Ethics*.   **157** Of Price he says: '. . . no other writer has anticipated Professor Moore quite so completely' (p. 98) Cf. D.D. Raphael's Introduction to his edition of *Price's Review of Morals* (Oxford, Clarendon Press, 1948), p. x.   **158** See Raphael's edition of the *Review of Morals*, pp. 13–17, 40–56, 110–9; cf. A.N. Prior, op.cit., pp. 98–101.   **159** Prior, op. cit., pp. 95–104; cf. pp. 18–25.

But Prior shows, too, that it was not only the rationalist or anti-empiricist moralists who stressed the autonomy of ethics, or the underivability of ethical conclusions from non-ethical premises.[160]

Hutcheson and Hume held this just as strongly; and argued that rationalistic 'definitions' of 'ought' were tautologous, just as stoutly as the rationalists argued that 'sentimentalist' or empiricist accounts of 'ought' were trivialising.[161] Reid was already able to turn Hume's logic against Hume's ethics. The rationalist or intuitionist moralists of inter-war Oxford (whom we shall be examining in the next chapter), were also able both to invoke Hume's argument for the autonomy of ethics and to condemn Hume by it as a naturalist.[162]

It was Sidgwick, Moore's teacher, who came closest both to Moore's 'naturalistic fallacy' argument and to Moore's intuitionist and 'non-naturalist' position in ethics.[163] Sidgwick is quoted by Moore as being the 'only one ethical writer . . . who has clearly recognised and stated' the fact 'that "good" is indefinable'.[164] Against Bentham, Sidgwick argued that utilitarian 'definitions' of 'right' reduced ethics to something very close to tautology. Prior quotes from Sidgwick's *The Ethics of Green, Spencer and Martineau* passages in the same sense which come very close to the language of Moore. Sidgwick found a common error in the evolutionary naturalism of Spencer and the metaphysical ethics of T.H. Green— the error of denying the autonomy of ethics by reducing ethics to some other sort of knowledge, whether it be natural science or metaphysics. This is, needless to say, what Moore was to call the 'naturalistic fallacy'. Sidgwick's book was published (posthumously) the year before the appearance of *Principia Ethica*. Prior is satisfied that it was Sidgwick who inspired Moore's work on the 'naturalistic fallacy'; and that Sidgwick in turn would have claimed no originality for himself here, for he traced the doctrine of the indefinability of 'right' and 'wrong' back to Price.[165]

The passage in which Hume asserts the autonomy of ethics and the irreducibility of 'ought' to 'is', is capital in the history of British ethics; and though it has been quoted with monotonous frequency, it must be quoted again.

---

160 See Prior, op.cit., pp. 18, 22, 24.　161 Prior, op. cit., pp. 30–5.　162 Prior, op.cit., pp. 35, 46–53. 163 C.D. Broad devotes a long chapter to Sidewick in his *Five Types of Ethical Theory*, pp. 143–256. It is a tedious chapter, about one who strikes us nowadays as a tedious moralist. Broad begins by the claim: 'Sidgwick's *Methods of Ethics* seems to me to be on the whole the best treatise on moral theory that has ever been written . . .'; and this may stand as an example of the self-sufficiency of English philosophers! Broad was, of course, also a Cambridge man—a successor of Sidgwick in the Knightsbridge Professorship of Moral Philosophy!　164 *Principia Ethica*, p. 17.　165 pp. 104–7. Prior concludes his book by saying: 'Nor need any more be said in order to establish the fact that Professor Moore's achievement has not been to work a revolution in Moral Philosophy, but simply to help keep alive, in our own age, the eighteenth-century tradition of sanity and logical rigour which Sidgwick . . . kept alive in his.' But Prior, in his extremely valuable book, did not consider the logical and ethical eccentricities of Moore's personal thought.

In every system of morality, which I have hitherto met with, I have always remarked, that the author proceeds for some time in the ordinary way of reasoning, and establishes the being of a God or makes observations concerning human affairs; when of a sudden I am surprised to find, that instead of the usual copulations of propositions, *is* and is *not*, I meet with no proposition that is not connected with an *ought* or an *ought not*. This change is imperceptible; but it is, however, of the last consequence. For as this *ought* or *ought not*, expresses some new relation or affirmation, 'tis necessary that it should be observed and explained; and at the same time that a reason should be given, for what seems altogether inconceivable, how this new relation can be a deduction from others, which are entirely different from it. But as authors do not commonly use this precaution, I shall presume to recommend it to the readers: and am persuaded, that this small attention would subvert all the vulgar systems of morality, and let us see, that the distinction of vice and virtue is not founded merely on the relations of objects, nor is perceived by reason.[166]

There is nothing of importance in Moore that is not anticipated in this passage.

But there is a good deal of importance in Hume that is missing in Moore. Hume does not say that 'ought' *cannot* be 'explained', but that it *needs* to be explained. He does not say that 'ought propositions' cannot be 'a deduction' from 'is propositions', but that 'a reason should be given' for the transition from the one to the other.[167] He objects to 'the vulgar systems' of rationalist morality that they do not recognise or account for the unique character of moral judgements as being not merely theoretical comparisons of abstract notions but as having 'an influence on the actions and affections' of men.[168] A great weakness of Hume's critique of rationalism, as of many modern critiques of rationalism, is that he virtually adopts the rationalist definition of reason as the faculty of 'abstract reasoning concerning quantity or number'—though allowing to reason also the separate functions of 'experimental reasoning concerning matter of fact and existence'.[169] Since morality is not reducible to either of these functions, he holds that it is not a matter of reasoning at all but of sentiment', 'feeling' or passion.

This is the background to Hume's famous but often misunderstood outburst:

We speak not strictly and philosophically when we talk of the combat of passion and of reason. Reason is, and ought only to be the slave of the passions, and can never pretend to any other office than to serve and obey them.[170]

---

166 *A Treatise of Human Nature*, Book III, Part i, Sect. i, ad fin. (ed. Selby-Bigge), (Oxford, Clarendon Press, (1888) 1949), pp. 469–70.   167 Compare Alasdair MacIntyre, in *The Philosophical Review*, October 1959.   168 Ibid. (ed. Selby-Bigge) pp. 456–68; cf. *Enquiries*, ed. Selby-Bigge (Oxford, Clarendon Press, (1902) 1951), pp. 163–5, 170–5, 287–94.   169 See *Enquiries*, ed. Selby-Bigge, p. 165; *Treatise*, ed. Selby-Bigge, pp. 265–6, 463–4.   170 *Treatise*, ed. Selby-Bigge, p. 415; cfr. pp. 468–9, 521ff.

What Hume is really looking for, as the foundation of morality, is a reason which shall 'have an original influence on the will and must be able to cause, as well as to hinder any act of volition'.[171] In other words, he is looking for the concept of Practical Reason. But he has so defined 'reason' that it *cannot* be 'practical'; he has so defined 'reason' that morality cannot be rational. The dilemma persisted among British moral philosophers for many generations, though it has increasingly been challenged by more recent writers.

Yet Hume's merit was to see that moral judgments cannot be either a collection of unreasoned intuitions or a system of deductively demonstrated axioms.[172] They must find their justification in the 'principles of human nature', in a 'science of Man', or 'science of human nature'.[173] For Hume, the 'autonomy of ethics' does not mean the isolation of ethics from the philosophy of man. Unfortunately, his philosophy or science of man, constructed on the model of Newton's experimental philosophy of nature, is conceived as a purely descriptive, observational science. It can issue only in 'copulations of propositions, *is* and is *not*'; and fails to fulfil his own requirement of explaining or justifying the transition to propositions 'connected with an *ought* or an *ought not*'. He does not see that the science of man, the knower of norms, must be partly a normative science; that man cannot be described adequately in terms of 'is-propositions'. Man *is* also what he *ought-to-be*; for he knows that he could be and ought-to-be more and other and better than he is. Hume should have seen that an 'ought' which is irreducible to any 'is', can reside only in a being who is not merely 'experimentally observable' but also metaphysical.

But Moore does not even get this near to the problem. He thinks that 'intrinsic goods' can be intuited without any reference to human nature or to any kind of knowledge or reality other than themselves. It is strange that he did not see a problem in the fact that, on his theory, man is capable of apprehending this 'non-natural' quality of goodness; and that the things which possess the 'non-existing' quality 'good' 'form the rational ultimate end of human action'. What kind of being can this be whose end and value and meaning come from that which does not exist in time or in nature, which does not indeed exist at all?

Moore seems unaware of any problem. But awareness of it has been a constant theme of ethical thought. Kant saw that the fact that man is conscious of the 'ought' makes him transcendent to the empirical or the phenomenal, makes him *also* noumenal.[174] Kant saw that:

> Supposing there were something *whose existence* has *in itself* an absolute worth, something which, being *an end in* itself, could be a source of definite laws, then in this and this alone would lie the source of a possible categorical imperative.

171 Ibid., p. 415.   172 Ibid., pp. 455–70.   173 See Hume's Introduction to the Treatise. The *Enquiry Concerning Human Understanding* opens with the words: 'Moral Philosophy or the science of human nature . . .'.   174 *Critique of Pure Reason*, Everyman ed., pp. 323–9.

He also saw that man *is* this being who '*exists* as an end in himself',[175] and that morality consists in respecting, in oneself and in others the absolute and transcendent dignity which inheres in the empirical existence and nature of men. The thought of Aquinas is not fundamentally different, when he speaks of man as ordained to God alone as ultimate end, and of everything else in creation as ordained to God through men.[176] Above all, Aquinas saw that the true foundation and explanation and justification of the moral 'ought' is the nature of man who *is* oriented to God, who *is*—obliged towards good, whose nature is *also* value. But even Sartre is more profound than Moore when he at least gives the 'non-existing good' its name—the 'missing God'; and concludes that man, whose meaning comes from the 'missing God', is meaningless and absurd.[177]

Moore transmits to his successors an insolvent estate; an ethics that negates naturalism but affirms nothing that can be supported either by reason or by nature. From this point of view he is in regression as compared both with idealism and with utilitarianism. His immediate successors take his debts for riches and push the autonomy of ethics still farther towards arbitrariness. It will be nearly fifty years before people begin to realise that non-naturalism is not enough;[178] and that ethics can be saved from vacuousness only by asking again the question which Bradley asked but did not answer: 'What is the moral self?' 'What is the nature of man and what is man's place in the Universe?'[179] As Nowell-Smith has written:

> Men choose to do what they do because they are what they are; and moral theories which attempt to exclude *all* consideration of human nature as it is do not even begin to be moral theories.[180]

---

175 *Fundamental Principles of the Metaphysic of Morals*, tr. T. K. Abbott, p. 46.   176 *SCG*, III, 115.
177 *Being and Nothingness*, E. trans., pp. 623–8.   178 Mary Warnock (see *The Listener*, 8 January 1959) has said: 'English moral philosophers in the last sixty years sometimes seem to have spent most of their energy and ingenuity on one single project, the refutation of utilitarianism. The utilitarians were attacked by Moore because they committed what he called the naturalistic fallacy, and a hostility to ethical naturalism has been the most obvious common element in the vast majority of English writings since Moore's *Principia Ethics*'. She criticises this onesidedness here and in *Ethics since 1900*. (See e.g. pp. 31, 136–7, 204.) Cf. Iris Murdoch, 'Metaphysics and Ethics', in *The Nature of Metaphysics*, ed. D.F. Pears (Macmillan, London, 1957), p. 106; P.H. Nowell-Smith, *Ethics* (Penguin Books, 1954), pp. 180–2. A.N. Prior writes: 'A siginificant non-naturalism must comprise more than mere freedom from the naturalistic fallacy' (op. cit., p. 12).   179 Bernard Mayo, *Ethics and the Moral Life* (Macmillan, London, 1958), p. 184.   180 *Ethics*, p. 182.

CHAPTER THREE

The Oxford Intuitionists

We have seen, with A.N. Prior, that intuitionism has had a long history in British ethics. It has been the doctrine usually espoused by defenders of traditional moral principles, and of ethical objectivism generally, against the subjectivist and relativist tendencies associated with empiricist moral theories. Thus the naturalism of Hobbes, the 'sentimentalism' of Shaftesbury, Hutcheson, Hume and Smith, provoked each in their time a reaction of an intuitionist variety. The intuitionists of inter-war Oxford and Cambridge saw themselves, in turn, as defenders of the objectivity of ethical judgments against hedonism and more modern versions of naturalism, just as Moore had claimed to be earlier. But paradoxically, they fell, as Moore had fallen, into a subjectivism of their own, indeed into a crypto-naturalism of their own. They were not all directly or consciously influenced by Moore; but in fact they continue along Moore's lines and they commit similar errors. We feel it is not unjust to say that they make ethical judgments ultimately arbitrary.

In this chapter, we shall be concerned with the pre-war school of Oxford intuitionists, of whom the outstanding were Prichard, Carritt and Ross.

1 PRICHARD AND CARRITT

Prichard and Carritt can be taken together. E.A. Prichard did not publish much or leave such behind in a publishable form. W.D. Ross collected and published some of his papers and manuscripts in 1949. These included the draft of a considerable part of a projected book on 'Moral Obligation'. Along with this, Ross republished the well-known *Mind* article of 1912, 'Does Moral Philosophy Rest on a Mistake?', and the British Academy Lecture of 1932 on 'Duty and Ignorance of Fact'; and published for the first time a critique of T.H. Green's theory of obligation together with other shorter papers, the whole in a volume to which he gave the title, *Moral Obligation*.[1] Prichard had great influence as a teacher and tutor. Even though his 1912 article contained nothing that had not already been said by Moore and indeed, earlier by Sidgwick, it had an air of confident novelty

---

1 Oxford, At the Clarendon Press, 1949. Ross, in a prefatory note, says: 'I believe no one can read [these essays] without feeling that in [Prichard] we had one of the very finest philosophical minds of the whole generation to which he belonged.' This recalls C.D. Broad's encomium of Sidgwick and shows that neither of the great British universities is outdone by the other in superb insular self-sufficiency.

64

and the tone of a manifesto; and it did for a time mark a date in British moral philosophy. E.F. Carritt had Prichard for tutor and friend, and his ethical thought remained very close to that of the older man.[2] These two together give us the most unsophisticated version of intuitionism one could desire.

1.1 *Does moral philosophy rest on a mistake?*

The mistake on which Prichard suggested in his *Mind* article of 1912 that moral philosophy rested, was the mistake of attempting to answer an improper question, namely *why* 'we ought to act in the ways usually called moral'. This question cannot be answered because the demand for proof that I ought to do my duty is illegitimate.[4] It is illegitimate in the same way as that in which a demand for a test or proof of knowledge is illegitimate. The mistake of moral philosophy in parallel to the mistake of theory of knowledge: that of trying to *prove* what can only be '*directly apprehended*'.[5] We know that we know many things, and that is all there is to it. We know that we have duties and that they oblige us, and that is all there is to it.

The mistake of supposing that we must find reasons to *prove* that we ought to do our duty has led moral philosophers into two types of false theory. One group of theories seeks the reason why we ought to do our duty in the fact that doing so will 'be for our good', which Prichard says is the same as to say, will be 'for our advantage or for our happiness'.[6] Another type of theory proposes to prove that we ought to do the act which is our duty because it is intrinsically good in itself.[7] But both are mistaken. In his later writing, Prichard gives more detailed analysis of the type of fallacy which he supposes them to involve—the fallacy of substituting 'good', which in the context means happiness, pleasure or advantage, for 'ought' which means 'ought' and nothing else. In the paper we are summarising, he repeats that these theories fail because they 'suppose the possibility of proving what can only be apprehended directly by an act of moral thinking'. When we are in a moral situation, we *know* our obligation; we *know* it as self-evident and we

---

2 See his *The Theory of Morals. An Introduction to Ethical Philosophy* (Oxford University Press, (1928) 1945); and *Ethical and Political Thinking* (Oxford, Clarendon Press, 1947). In a prefatory note to the former volume, Carritt reports that Prichard found it differed from his thought 'in almost every particular'; but, seen from this distance in time, the differences seem quite academic. There is a splendid Oxonian note in the Preface to the second volume: 'For nearly fifty years, most of the time as an Oxford tutor, I have spent some twelve hours weekly each term in discussing moral, political and aesthetic philosophy with pupils and with colleagues, either singly or in very small groups. This gives in round numbers nearly 15,000 hours of opportunity for mass observation of Ethical and Political Thinking.' An important paper by Carritt, 'Moral Positivism and Moral Aestheticism', first published in *Philosophy*, 1938 is reprinted in *Readings in Ethical Theory*, eds. Sellars and Hospers, pp. 405–14. 3 *Moral Obligation*, p. 2. 4 Ibid. p. 14. 5 pp. 1–2, 14–17. 6 Ibid. pp. 2–5. 7 pp. 6–7. We shall point out below that Prichard distinguishes two uses of the term good; the adjectival use in which (as here) it denotes an ethical character; and the substantival in which it coincides with 'the pleasant', and is non-ethical. (See pp. 59–102.)

know that we know it to be self-evident; and no reasons can be given because no reasons are needed.[8] Prichard's conclusion is:

> Hence, if as is almost universally the case, by Moral Philosophy is meant the knowledge which would satisfy the demand [for proof that we ought to do our duty], there in no such knowledge, and all attempts to attain it are doomed to failure because they rest on a mistake. . . . Nevertheless the demand, though illegitimate, is inevitable until we have carried the process of reflection far enough to realise the self-evidence of our obligations i.e. the immediacy of our apprehension of them. This realisation of their self-evidence is positive knowledge and so far, and so far only, as the term Moral Philosophy is confined to this knowledge and to the knowledge of the parallel immediacy of the apprehension of the goodness of the various virtues and of good dispositions generally, is there such a thing as Moral Philosophy.[9]

It is surprising that Prichard gives no sign of awareness that Bradley had, many years before, pronounced the question, 'Why should I be moral?', to be a question that 'has no sense at all [and] is simply unmeaning'.[10] Nor does he seem conscious that Moore, nine years before, had traced the 'difficulties and disagreements' of which the history of ethics is full, to one simple cause, the failure to distinguish different questions clearly from one another, and, in particular, to distinguish questions where proof is possible from questions where no proof can be given and only intuition or immediate inspection or 'looking to see' can be invoked.[11]

1.2 *The indefinability of ethical terms*

The affinity between Prichard's thought and that of Moore, in this early article and throughout his work, is close. Just as Moore held that 'good' is a simple, unanalysable, indefinible notion; and as, in the *Ethics*, he held 'right' and 'wrong' to be ultimate, untranslatable notions; so Prichard declares that 'the sense of obligation to do, or the rightness of, an action . . . is absolutely underivative or immediate'.[12] Similarly he elsewhere argues that 'being under a moral obligation to do an action', is 'a kind of attribute [which is] *sui generis*, i.e. unique, and therefore incapable of having its nature expressed in terms of the nature of anything else.'[13]

Prichard also maintains that the term 'good' when used ethically, is indefinable. He distinguishes two different uses of the term 'good'. 'Good' used adjectivally is an ethical term, though not a moral one; it is predicated of virtuous acts, virtuous motives, good dispositions; but it cannot be defined.

---

8 pp. 16–17. On p. 9 he says 'our sense of the rightness of an act is not a conclusion from our appreciation of the goodness either of it or of anything else'.   9 p 16.   10 *Ethical Studies*, p. 64.   11 *Principia Ethica*, Preface, pp. 21–7, 77, 144, 188, 223–4. Prichard's implied epistemology is of course also akin to Moore's; see e.g. *Principia Ethica*, pp. 131–5.   12 p. 7.   13 p. 94. He speaks on the next page of 'the unique and therefore indefinable character of the thing meant by our being morally bound to do some action'.

When we use the term 'good' as an adjective, as when we make the statement 'Courage is good' . . . we can be said . . . to be attributing to what we state to be good a certain character or quality which it possesses in itself, i.e. independently of its relatedness to other things. . . . The quality, however, to which we refer by 'good' plainly cannot be defined . . . we can no more state the nature of this character in other terms than we can in the case of 'red' . . .[14]

'Good' used substantively (where it means 'someone's good' or 'the Good for man') is indistinguishable from 'something which *pleases*, i.e. excites pleasure in us'; and it therefore is a non-ethical term and differs totally in meaning from 'good' used adjectivally.

If, as seems clear, we mean by 'a good to us' something which indirectly or indirectly excites pleasure in us, the difference in meaning between it and the term 'good' must be radical in spite of the occurrence of the word 'good' in both. Indeed, we have to allow that statements of the form 'X is good' and 'X is a good to us' are *totally* different in meaning, so that the meaning of neither is capable of being stated in terms of, or even derivable from, the meaning of the other.[15]

Of the two uses of the term 'good', therefore, one is ethical but not moral and the other is neither moral nor ethical. A paradoxical result of this is that Prichard has to distinguish morality from virtue. Morality is exclusively a matter of *duty*: it consists in doing the act which we 'directly apprehend' to be our duty, irrespective of any consideration of desire, disposition, purpose or motive other than that involved in the doing of the act in question. Virtue, on the other hand, is a matter of good motives and dispositions.

It is a fundamental principle with Prichard, as we shall see more fully later, that motives and desires are not under the control of our will and cannot be required of us as our duty.

[This] view implies that an obligation can no more be based on or derived from a virtue than a virtue can be derived from an obligation. . . . Take the case of courage. It is untrue to urge that, since courage is a virtue, we ought to act courageously. It is and must be untrue, because . . . to feel an obligation to act courageously would involve a contradiction. For . . . we can only feel an obligation to *act*; we cannot feel an obligation to *act from a certain desire* . . . Moreover, if the sense of obligation to act in a particular way leads to an action, the action will be an action done from a sense of obligation, and therefore not an act of courage.[16]

14 p. 99; he gives another example of a simple indefinable thing on p. 189, namely, 'willing': 'While we know the general character of that to which we refer when we use the word 'willing', this character is *sui generis* and so incapable of being defined i.e. of having its nature expressed in terms of the nature of other things.' 15 p. 101. 16 pp. 12–13; see the whole section, pp. 9–13.

The conclusion is:

> We must sharply distinguish morality and virtue as independent, though related, species of goodness, neither being an aspect of something of which the other is an aspect, nor again a form or species of the other, nor again something deducible from the other; and we must at the same time allow that it is possible to do the same act either virtuously or morally or in both ways at once.[17]

It is curious that Prichard continually appeals to our ordinary moral consciousness, our ordinary knowledge and unsophisticated language; but seems unaware that the views just expressed mark a complete departure from common-sense convictions and common usage.

Whereas Moore claimed that 'good' was the primary ethical notion and indeed 'the only simple object of thought which is peculiar to ethics',[18] Prichard makes this claim for 'obligation' or 'duty' or 'right'. In this, he was preceded by all the British intuitionists of earlier centuries and followed by all the modern Oxford and Cambridge intuitionists.

In support of his view that 'moral obligation' is indefinable, Prichard uses the same sort of arguments as those which Moore used against naturalism under the name of the naturalistic fallacy. Any 'definition' of 'obligation' would resolve it into 'something else'; it would turn the moral 'ought' into a non-moral 'ought' and substitute for morality some non-moral consideration or enquiry.[19]

All theories which define obligation in terms of good or final end or happiness —and that, in effect includes all theories in the history of ethics other than intuitionist ones of Prichard's own variety—are lumped together. They are labelled teleological or quasi-teleological. Teleological theories are those which define 'duty' or 'right' in terms of what is alleged to be the Good for man, however this may be conceived. The hedonists have interpreted this as pleasure; Plato and Aristotle conceived it in terms of the life which gives satisfaction or happiness; Green and the idealists think of it as the realisation of the self. But there is no essential difference between these philosophers. All of them are equivalently saying that we ought to do our duty because 'we shall gain by doing our duty'. And this is to replace (to use Kant's terms) the categorical imperative by the hypothetical imperative; it is to say, not 'It is your *duty* to do so-and-so', but, '*If you wish* for such-and-such advantages, you ought to do so-and-so'. This is to reduce the moral to the non-moral 'ought'; it is simply to abolish ethics.[20]

---

17 p. 11. It is characteristic of Prichard to go on: 'And surely this is true.' Moore would have underlined 'surely'. Compare Carritt, *The Theory of Morals*, pp. 47–8, 73, 137; *Ethical and Political Thinking*, pp. 83–6.   18 *Principia Ethica*, p. 5. As in the *Ethics*, the emphasis is on 'right' and 'wrong' as the primary or irreducible ethical notions; but no attempt is made to reconcile this with the position of the earlier book, or indeed with the definition of 'right' in terms of 'results' in the same volume.   19 pp. 95, 117, 119, 163. Moore had equally insisted that 'good' does not mean any of the things proposed as definitions of it, but 'something' else'.   20 pp. 95–101, 110–11, 114–28, 158–63.

It is an extraordinary historical and philosophical blindness which causes Prichard to persist in making Plato and Aristotle into hedonists, and even egoistic hedonists. In spite of all Plato's polemic against the naturalism of Glaucon and Thrasymachus and the relativism of the sophists; in spite of all Aristotle's precise discussion of the pleasure principle, all his careful critique of Eudoxus, Prichard insouciantly includes them in the same list with Hobbes, Bentham and Mill, as philosophers who all of them ignored the difference between the moral and the non-moral.[21] Green and the idealists are placed by Prichard in the same incongruous class.[22] How quickly had Bradley been forgotten and the crushing refutation he made of the view that to aim at the realisation of the better self is only a form of selfishness.[23]

It is surely clear that there is a sort of naturalistic fallacy involved in Prichard's reasoning. As we saw above, he allows only one meaning to 'good', used as a substantive, namely 'pleasant' or 'advantageous'—and this is precisely the error of all naturalists, from Glaucon and Thrasymachus to Hobbes and Mill. Muirhead protested that, to say there is no difference of principle between Plato and the Sophists, is almost the same as to say that 'there is no difference of principle involved in a famous question as to the exchange value of the world as against one's 'soul'.[24] But Prichard imperturbably replied that 'though, of course, there can be different views as to what is profitable, there are not two "senses" of "profitable", and even to differ from another as to what is profitable is to imply that there is only one sense.'[25] There could hardly be a clearer case of the naturalistic fallacy than to say that 'profitable' has only one sense, and that a self-interested one; and that in the Gospel context it enjoins a form of selfishness.

'Quasi-teleological' is the name Prichard gives to theories which hold 'that there is a single something at which we *ought* to aim' and that duty is to be defined in terms of conduciveness to this. Sidgwick is cited as the chief exponent of this type of theory. Against it Prichard urges that there is no one thing at which we ought to aim;[26] and that, if there were, the 'ought' in question would be a

---

21 'The idea that we always seek, i.e. act for the sake of, our own good is one which has not infrequently been held. Aristotle shared this idea with Plato, and it was in effect held by Hobbes, Bentham, Mill and T.H. Green' (p. 111). '[Between the ideas of Mill, on the one hand, and those of Plato, Aristotle and Green, on the other] there is no distinction of importance. . . . Given the necessary correction, the one view will be that our final aim is our being constantly in the state of feeling enjoyment, and the other will be that it is our being constantly in the state of feeling gratified. And since it must be allowed that enjoyment and gratification are species of pleasure, the views only differ in that the one implies the idea that enjoyment is the only form of pleasure and the other the idea that gratification is the only form of pleasure. Further, as there seems to be no denying that by being happy we mean being pleased . . . both views seem only different forms of the view that our final end or purpose is always our happiness' (p. 117). Cf. pp. 2, 97–108, 110–14 (on Plato). Prichard has a paper on 'The Meaning of *Agathon* in the Ethics of Aristotle', whose purpose is to defend the 'heresy' that Aristotle was a 'psychological hedonist' (—and Prichard remarks that the same can be proved of Plato). (Op. cit. pp. 40–53; cf. pp. 108–9.) 22 pp. 54–86, 111, 120–8. Cf. Carritt, *The Theory of Morals*, pp. 49–56. 23 *Ethical Studies*, pp. 250–62; cf. pp. 109, 124–5. 24 *Rule and End in Morals* (Oxford University Press, 1932), p. 25. 25 p. 118. 26 p. 136.

non-moral 'ought', not the 'ought' of duty. 'Aim' implies 'desire' and 'desire' is a psychological datum, not a moral activity. It is not within our power, and cannot therefore be our duty, to call up a desire at will. 'Aim' also implies 'motive'; and motive can be no part of our duty either. We cannot produce motives at will any more than desires. To suppose that we are obliged to have motives would imply that we were obliged to have motives for having motives . . . and so on; it would involve an infinite regress. But duty prescribes the doing of certain actions, not the doing of them from certain motives. The goodness of the motive comes from the rightness of the act, and not vice versa. 'The rightness or wrongness of an act has nothing to do with any question of motives at all.'[27] All this Prichard holds to be self-evident. We know that to have an obligation is to be bound to perform a certain action, not to have a certain motive.[28]

Prichard rejects Moore's view of obligation on the ground that, making the obligatory act a means to a good result it supposes that motive is a part of obligation; which is false.[29] Kant's theory is rejected for the novel reason, not hitherto or since encountered in Kantian studies, that according to Kant, 'there are no acts which we ought to do, and our duty is only to have a certain idea as our motive'.[30] Philosophers like Rashdal, Joseph Laird and Muirhead are criticised for trying to relate 'ought-to-do' with 'good' through defining 'good' as what 'ought-to-be'.[31] But this, according to Prichard, is to forget that obligatoriness characterises persons not actions. Typically, Prichard claims, as Moore was fond of claiming for his assertions, that one has only to reflect in order to see that this is true.

> As we recognize when we reflect, there are no such characteristics of an action as ought-to-be-doneness and ought-not-to-be-doneness. This is obvious; for since the existence of an obligation to do some action cannot possibly depend on actual performance of the action, the obligation cannot itself be a property which the action would have if it were done. What does exist is the fact that you or that I ought or ought not, to do a certain action . . . and when we make an assertion containing the term 'ought' or 'ought not', that to which we are attributing a certain character is not a certain activity but a certain man.[32]

The moral 'ought' is, therefore, always of the form 'I ought-to-do' or 'someone ought-to-do'. The theories Prichard is examining translate 'ought' into something-ought-to-be-done. Their heads, therefore, fall under the same guillotine as that which slaughters all teleology: they, too, replace the moral 'ought' by a

---

27 pp. 5–7, 12–13, 129–31. Cf. Carritt, *Ethical and Political Thinking*, pp. 26, 83–4. We shall meet with this notion again in Ross. 28 pp. 129–31. 'It is really self-evident that an obligation is necessarily an obligation to perform a certain action, and not to have a certain motive'. (p. 131) 29 pp. 152–4. 30 pp. 155–6. Carritt's critique of Kant even more caricatural, partly because it is a good deal longer. See *The Theory of Morals*, pp. 76–86. 31 pp. 117–8, 131–6, 158–63. Moore is included under this rubric also. 32 p. 37; cf. p. 159.

non-moral ought, and thus abolish ethics.[33] The familiar doctrine that an 'ought' can only be derived from another 'ought'[34] has been narrowed and hardened into the doctrine that 'someone ought-to-do' can be derived only from another 'someone ought-to-do'.

A step has been taken beyond Moore towards the more complete separation of 'ought' from any justification or explanation other than the agent's direct apprehension of 'oughtness'. Prichard writes

> The negative side of all this is, of course, that we do not come to appreciate an obligation by an *argument*, i.e. by a process of non-moral thinking, and that, in particular, we do not do so by an argument of which a premiss is the ethical but not moral activity of appreciating the goodness either of the act or of a consequence of the act; i.e. that our sense of the rightness of an act is not a conclusion from our appreciation of the goodness either of it or of anything else.[35]

E.F. Carritt strongly supports Prichard in all these opinions. His point of departure is that ethical conceptions cannot be derived from, or defined in terms of, non-ethical conceptions.[36] It is on this principle that his excellent criticisms of hedonism, evolutionary ethics, utilitarianism, subjectivism, emotivism turn.[37] But, like Prichard, he holds that all doctrines of 'good' or 'end' in morals are hedonistic or naturalistic and result in the abolition of ethics. Logically, though *grandly*, he concluded that 'owing to [its] ambiguities it is usually better to avoid the term good in ethics'.[38] Another bold saying is that 'the *Summum Bonum* has . . . been the *ignis fatuus* of moral philosophy'.[39]

1.3 *The ambiguities of self-evidence*

Prichard's ethics is doubly an ethics of self-evidence. He holds that 'moral obligation' is a self-evident intuition, independent of any other concept; and he holds that it is a self-evident intuition that 'moral obligation' is a self-evident intuition. The 'realisation of the self-evidence [of our obligations] is positive knowledge'.[40] His supreme argument in every discussion is 'we are *certain* i.e. *know*';[41] 'it is really self-evident'.[41]

Prichard, and Carritt with him, intended their doctrine of the self-evidence of obligation to be a defence of the objectivity of moral truths against all forms of subjectivism and naturalism. As the intuitionist of earlier centuries had done, Carritt assimilates moral judgments to mathematical and logical ones.

33 pp. 157–63. 34 pp. 4, 163. 35 p. 9. The element of argument by definition, or of 'persuasive definition', in the text is marked. 'Argument' is defined as non-moral thinking, whence it follows that moral thinking must be intuitive; and 'appreciating the goodness of an act' is defined as being not a moral activity. See also pp. 110ff., 128, 142. 36 *The Theory of Morals*, pp. 28–9, 33; *Ethical and Political Thinking*, pp. 12–13. 37 Op. cit. See in addition, the paper 'Moral Positivism and Moral Aestheticism', referred to n. 2 above. 38 *The Theory of Morals*, p. 48. 39 Ibid., p. 74. 40 p. 16. 41 p. 38; cf. p. 146.

I know the reality of obligations and goodness with as much self-evidence as I know logical, geometrical or causal necessitation. It is less self-evident to me that there are other human beings I can affect than that, if there are, I have obligations to them.[43]

Moral rules have for Prichard and Carritt a self-evidence akin to that of the principle of contradiction. One cannot, for example, deny the obligatoriness of promises without self-contradiction. 'I promise' means 'I hereby place myself under an obligation'; therefore I cannot say I promise but am not obliged by my promise'.[44] In general, the obligatoriness of duty as such is self-evident. To be aware of a duty is to know that one is obliged; and one cannot without self-contradiction deny that one is obliged by a duty.[45] All this seems highly acceptable to one who is convinced that moral judgments are propositions which can be true or false and are objectively true or false. But the difficulties of the intuitionist doctrine soon appear. Intuitions may contradict one another. Prichard's study of 'moral obligation' provides a beautiful example. He is discussing Sidgwick's view that, in a conflict between the desire of our whole good and the desire of some particular good,

> it is self-evident that we ought to aim at, i.e. be moved to act by the desire of our whole good, rather than aim at, i.e. be moved to act by our desire of, the particular good.

To which Prichard replies:

> On this part of the argument, the only comment needed is that it is self-evident that there is no such duty.[46]

When 'self-evident' statements contradict one another, which shall prevail? Is there any settlement possible except the one humorously proposed by Keynes in speaking of Moore—that, in practice, victory shall lie 'with those who [can] speak with greatest appearance of clear, undoubting conviction and [can] best use the accents of infallibility'.[47] Prichard was as good a master of this technique as Moore.

1.4 *The arbitrariness of intuition*

Since no reasons can be given for moral judgments, since there is in fact no such thing as moral reasoning, there can be no criterion of moral truth except the

---

42 p. 131. 43 *Ethical and Political Thinking*, p. 43; cf. p. 3. Cf. Price, in *Price's Review of Morals*, ed. D.D. Raphael, pp. 41–2, 50–2. 44 Carritt, *Ethical and Political Thinking*, p. 102; cfr. pp. 4, 37; cf. Prichard, op. cit., pp. 169–79. 45 Prichard, op. cit. pp. 1–2, 7–9. He quotes Cudworth and Clarke on pp. 77–9. Cf. Carritt, *Ethical and Political Thinking*, pp. 2–3, 37. Cf. Price, op. cit., p. 110. See A.N. Prior., op. cit., pp. 47ff., for other quotations from seventeenth- and eighteenth-century rationalists in the same sense. 46 p. 139. 47 *Two Memoirs*, p. 85.

individual conscience; and there is no appeal beyond each person's 'moral reason'. In his 1912 article. Prichard wrote:

> Suppose we come genuinely to doubt whether we ought, for example, to pay our debts, owing to a genuine doubt whether our previous conviction that we ought to do so is true. . . . The only remedy lies in actually getting into a situation which occasions the obligation or . . . imagining ourselves in that situation, and then letting our moral capacities of thinking do their work. Or to put the matter generally, if we do doubt whether there really is an obligation to originate A in the situation B, the remedy lies not in any process of general thinking, but in getting face to face with a particular instance of the situation B, and then directly appreciating the obligation to originate A in that situation.[48]

Similarly Carritt writes:

> You cannot prove to a man that he has duties or should do his duty, or that justice is a duty, or that this act is just. All you can do is to give his fuller information of the consequences and antecedents of what he is doing and then ask him to agree with you that it is right or wrong, If he knows the situation and consequences as well as you do and still differ, one of you must be wrong, yet there is no proof. All you can do is to get him to imagine the situation again and repeat the act of moral thinking with greater attention.[49]
>
> Moral philosophy . . . should not try to play the part of that conscience or moral reason which acts primarily upon particular situations and whose immediate judgments neither need nor can be demonstrated.[50]

There is surprisingly little difference between this language of the 'objectivist' Carritt and the language of the 'emotivist' Ayer. Ayer wrote:

> When someone disagrees with us about the moral value of a certain action or type of action, we do admittedly resort to argument in order to win him over to our way of thinking. But we do not attempt to show by our arguments that he has the 'wrong' ethical feeling towards a situation whose nature he has correctly apprehended. What we attempt to show is that he is mistaken about the facts of the case. . . . We do this in the hope that we have only to get our opponent to agree with us about the nature of the empirical facts for him to adopt the same moral attitude towards them as we do.[51]

Prichard and Carritt call the moral judgment an act of thinking; Ayer calls it an expression of feeling. But for all three it is unreasoned, irreducible to any terms

48 pp. 16–17. 49 *The Theory of Morals*, p. 72; cf. *Ethical and Political Thinking*, pp. 4, 8. 50 *The Theory of Morals*. p. 84; cf. pp. 114–6. 51 *Language, Truth and Logic*, 2nd. edit. (Gollancz, London, (1946) 1950), pp. 110–1. The text of the second edition is, of course, unchanged from that of the first edition of 1936.

other than itself, unprovable. Prichard and Carritt in effect accept Ayer's statement 'that the fundamental ethical concepts are unanalysable, inasmuch as there is no criterion by which one can test the validity of the judgments in which they occur'.[52] It is hard to resist the conclusion that Ayer was more logical than they in naming them 'pseudo-concepts' and holding that the judgments in which they occur 'do not express genuine propositions'.[53]

Intuitionist and emotivist in fact commit a common error. We have met it in Moore and called it in him a quasi-naturalistic fallacy. It is the fallacy of denying that there is such a thing as *moral* reasoning; of affirming that moral judgments are an intuitive leap of the mind from *empirical* facts, descriptions and reasons to moral, that is to say, *non-empirical* evaluations. Prichard repeatedly denies that there is any such thing as argument or proof in morals: we have seen him define 'argument' as 'non-moral thinking', and the 'appreciation of the goodness' of an act or of its consequences as an 'ethical but not moral activity'.[55] What precedes and justifies the moral judgment is 'a process of general and not of moral thinking', that is to say, an empirical description of the facts of the case and of the effects of my proposed act.[56] Carritt, too, as we have just seen, supposes the moral judgment to spring parthenogetically out of empirical descriptions of the 'consequences and antecedents' of an act or the factual circumstances of a situation.[57] But this is surely little different from 'deducing' a moral conclusion from non-moral premises, which the intuitionists, before and after Moore, are so quick to condemn.

It can hardly be denied that intuitionism tends to make moral judgments arbitrary and irrational. On Prichard's theory, moral judgements are unrelated to one another, in the sense that they have no common character or ground. He anticipates the objection that his theory makes 'our various obligations . . . an unrelated chaos', and he accepts it as valid.[58] Carritt holds that moral rules or principles are only generalisations from particular intuitions; the rules must be tested by the intuitions and not vice versa. At best moral rules are 'a very good practical dodge'; at worst they turn into an 'idolatry of rules', which can work *on the side of passion* against genuine moral insight'.[59] Carritt is convinced that people who believe in absolute, immutable and universal moral principles are really seeking to escape from the responsibility, and the worry, of deciding for themselves where their duty lies, in each new situation as it arises.[60] We shall meet with

---

52 Op. cit., p. 107. 53 Op. cit., pp. 107, 109. 54 See 'G.E. Moore and Non-naturalism in Ethics', in *Philosophical Studies*, Maynooth, V–XII, 1963, pp. 25–65. 55 *Moral Obligation*, p. 9. 56 Op. cit., p. 8, 21–2, 37. 57 *The Theory of Morals*, pp. 72, 84; cf. *Ethical and Political Thinking*, pp. 4, 8, 10, 11. 58 p. 9. He pleads only, as an *argumentum ad hominem*, that 'the various qualities which we recognise as good are equally unrelated; e.g. courage, humility, and interest in knowledge". Cf. p. 114. 59 *The Theory of Morals*, pp. 114–9. 60 See *Ethical and Political Thinking*, p. 1: 'Men hope to save themselves the worry of deciding on their duties if they can discover some foolproof earmark of right and wrong, of good and evil. Cf. p. 11: 'A chief reason for the obstinate effort to find a common non-ethical character in all obligations or in all good things is the desire to escape the trouble of using our moral judgments.' Cf. pp. 5–6.

the same attitude in virtually every contemporary British moralist. They are almost unanimous in fearing that belief in fixed moral standards will lead to fanaticism, or at least to what Iris Murdoch has called 'moral degeneration through lack of reflection'.[61] This belief has become virtually part of the culture of the western world in this last decade of the century.

1.5 *Relapse into subjectivism?*

The mistrust of general moral rules is so great that it leads the intuitionists, who began by boldly affirming the self-evidence and the objectivity of moral truths, to end by weakly agreeing that objective moral truth is unattainable and that obligation is subjective. Prichard argues that since duties can always conflict with one another, no duty can be absolutely and always binding. Therefore

> no kind of action whatever can strictly speaking be a duty, if only for the reason that if it were, there might be occasions on which we were bound to do two actions, although we could only do one or other of them. This reflection forces us to allow that what we at first think of as a duty must really be something else, for which, in my opinion, the least unsatisfactory phrase is 'a claim'.

In cases of conflicting duties, the question becomes, 'Which of these duties has the stronger claim?'[62] As Carritt makes plain, it is only the individual who can, in the concrete situation, 'decide which is the stronger obligation that will constitute [his] duty in the situation'.[63]

But the doctrine of 'self-evident duty' has not finished its surprises. In his British Academy Lecture on 'Duty and Ignorance of Fact', Prichard examined two views of what we may call the ground of the 'ought' judgment: the 'objective view', which holds that obligation 'depends on certain characteristics of the situation'; the 'subjective view', which holds that it 'depends on our being in a certain attitude of mind towards the situation in respect of knowledge, thought or opinion'.[64] Prichard defends the subjective view. He argues that I can never know the objective facts of the situation with sufficient accuracy, or know the effects my efforts will produce with sufficient certainty, to be sure what duty the situation imposes. Among the examples that Prichard chooses are the problems whether I ought to shout to revive a man who has fainted, or whether I ought to tell someone the truth. But whether I objectively have these duties or not depends on many things. I can never know . . . whether the man *is* fainting, for example, or whether my shouting will revive him. It is not even certain that I *can* shout or make a loud noise when I want to; or that making the noises I call speaking will, in fact, produce knowledge of the truth in the secret recesses of another's mind.

---

61 "Metaphysics and Ethics", in *The Nature of Metaphysics*, ed. D.F. Pears, p. 109.   62 op.cit., p. 86.
63 *Ethical and Political Thinking*, pp. 3–4; cf. p. 84.   64 Prichard, op. cit., pp. 21–5.

I *may* have duties, depending on these various unverifiable conditions; but I can never and shall never know that I have them. 'There is absolutely no occasion on which a moral rule applies to me on which I can know that I have the duty in question.'[65]

The subjective view, therefore, is the only one that can be defended. Having a duty depends, not on what the situation is, but on the 'state of our mind' towards it. As we have seen in an earlier section, Prichard holds, and here repeats, that obligatoriness characterises not actions but persons.

> Since, in fact, it is a characteristic of ourselves, there is nothing to prevent its existence depending on our having certain thoughts about the situation. . . . Indeed, for this reason, its existence must depend on some fact about ourselves.[66]

Prichard holds that this explanation corresponds 'with the thought of ordinary life'.[67]

But even when we know our subjective duty, there remain conditions, most difficult to fulfill, for its successful performance. Since my present duty is necessarily absolute, it must bear on some act which I know for certain that I am free and able to do. Prichard asks us to consider well some weighty tasks and reflect on what we could be sure of being free and able to do in respect of them. Could we be *sure and certain* that we could thread a needle, draw a line through a point on a piece of paper, move our arms or make a loud noise? Presumptuous indeed would he be who would so claim in face of the always possible contingency that he might become suddenly paralysed, or who knows what?[68] The fear of paralysis seems to have been endemic among inter-war Oxford moralists. Carritt

---

65 Op. cit., p. 23.   66 p. 37, pp. 25–8.   67 p. 28 and ff. Carritt has the same doctrine: see *The Theory of Morals*, pp. 93–4. Much of what he says deserves to be reproduced; seeing is believing: 'There appear, in any situation, to be three acts, possibly all different or by chance coinciding. . . . First there is the absolutely right act, the right act for an omniscient being; second, there is the right act for me, the one which is really the duty of a being with my knowledge of the facts; and last, the act I think right, which is moral if done for that reason (if I know it to be right, the last two coincide). To which of these three is properly applicable the phrase 'the act I ought to do' or 'my duty'? Not, apparently, to either of the two first; for when I cannot know them I cannot do them except by accident. Yet to apply these phrases to the third and say that the act I think right is my duty . . . seems equivalent to saying that what I think right for me to do always is right for me to do and that what I think to be my duty is my duty: which seems to be plain nonsense. If it were true, any opinion as to my duty would be as good as 'any other . . . I suppose we may conclude that I ought to try to do what is absolutely right since I might by luck succeed and the harder I try the better the chances. . . . My duty is to be moral, and that is to try to do what is right.' Cf. *Ethical and Political Thinking*, pp. 23–6, where Carritt concludes: 'we always know our putative duty, sometimes a subjective obligation, but our objective duties never'.   68 p. 34. The passage must be quoted. 'Two conclusions are at once obvious. (1) The first is that the true answer to any question of the form "Can I do so and so?" must be "I don't know". . . . Plainly we never *know* that if we were to set ourselves to thread a needle we should thread it; or . . . draw a line through a point. . . . But in the last resort, this is the only answer ever possible, since we never know that we have not become paralysed.' (This seems odd . . .) 'Even in the case of moving our arms or making a noise we do not *know* that, if we were to set ourselves to do it, we should do anything, though, of course, we may think it very likely both

had it.[69] We shall meet it again in Ross. It must have made the writing of books on ethics very difficult! Hence, Prichard concludes,

> an obligation must be an obligation, not to *do* something but to perform an activity of a totally different kind, that of setting or exerting ourselves to do something i.e. to bring something about.

We must note that this time Prichard finds himself opposed to 'the implication of ordinary language and of moral rules in particular'; yet what he says is held no whit less 'obvious' for that.[70] So, finally, the doctrine that duty is objective and absolute and self-evident has turned into the doctrine that I have a subjective duty to set myself to do something which may possiblyv result in something which may probably be my putative duty.

Such were the problems gravely discussed by Oxford moral philosophers in the nineteen-thirties. It is largely a myth that there was a post-war 'revolution' in British ethics. The later Oxford moralists largely continued in the methods and, to a large extent, also in the doctrines of the preceding generation. Carritt already defined 'the main purpose of moral philosophy' as being

> to analyse and clarify our moral thinking . . . [which is thinking] about the meaning of such words as 'right', 'obligation', 'good', 'merit' and their opposites. . . . [The method of moral philosophy] is to define or discriminate the meanings of various terms and phrases commonly used in the commendations

that we should do something, and also that we *should* move our arms, or make a noise, in particular. (2) The second conclusion is that whatever we are setting ourselves to do, we never in so setting ourselves *know* that we shall be doing what we are setting ourselves to do, bringing about what we are setting ourselves to do., or indeed that we are doing anything at all.'   69 *Ethical and Political Thinking*, p. 23: 'Our subjective duty can only be to try to effect or prevent a certain change when we think either possible, since we can never be sure of our success; even the limb we try to move may have gone to sleep or become paralysed. An objective duty would never be to try but always to effect or to prevent; an omniscient being would know whether he was able or not, and it would not be his duty to try the impossible. So objective and subjective duties never strictly coincide. In one sense we cannot try to do our objective duty since we do not know what it is. . . .' See the whole chapter on 'The Ground of Obligation', p. 14–27.   70 pp. 34–5; cfr. pp. 86, 196. On p. 33 we read ' "choosing to make a loud noise" becomes "setting or exerting myself to make a loud noise" '. On pp. 192–3, the worry of how we shall ever be able to do anything at all has become almost paralysing. 'Where we think we have done some action, e.g., have raised our arm or written a word, what we willed was some change, e.g., some movement of our arm or some movement of ink to a certain place on a piece of paper in front of us. But we have to bear in mind that the change which we willed may not have been the same as the change we think we effected. Thus, where I willed some movement of my second finger, I may at least afterwards think that the change I effected was a movement of my first finger, and, only too often, where I willed the existence of a certain word on a piece of paper, I afterwards find that what I caused was a different word. Again, in two cases of the act which we call trying to thread a needle, that I willed may have been the same, though the changes I afterwards think I effected were very different, being in the one case the thread's going through the needle and in the other its passing well outside it.' There is, once more, the worry about our hands becoming 'either paralysed or numb with cold, whether we knew this or not'. We do not seem far removed from the world of Samuel Beckett's *Malone Dies* or *End Game* or *Comment c'est*.

or censure of characters and actions, and to check these distinctions by instances.[71]

Linguistic philosophers will not define ethics differently. Nothing so resembles the style and content of the more dreary linguistic analysts as that of Prichard's later papers.[72]

It is hardly necessary to point out the total absence of any awareness of the unity of the moral life, any sense of the existence of a moral self or moral person, any consciousness of morality as the effort to give unity, consistency and value to one's life. It is typical of Prichard that he should record his 'extreme sense of dissatisfaction' with Aristotle's *Ethics*; and that he should, in the same place, declare that

> a systematic account of the virtuous character . . . at best can only make clear to us the details of one of our obligations, viz. the obligation to make ourselves better men; but the achievement of this does not help us to discover what we ought to do in life as a whole, and why; to think that it did would be to think that our only business in life was self-improvement.[73]

Wittgenstein was, about the same time, beginning to discover for himself and to convince a few students that to isolate words from their place 'in the stream of life' was to deprive them of meaning.[74] That is what the intuitionists did. They isolated duty from its context in the moral life, and from all context whatever; they left it without content and ultimately without meaning.

2 SIR DAVID ROSS

We have examined the theories of Prichard and Carritt in some detail, because they give the most categorical statement of intuitionism, and thereby incidentally most clearly display its weaknesses; and also because they seem seldom to receive extensive treatment. Ross wrote more voluminously; but he depends, for most of his central ideas, on Prichard and on Moore. He enjoyed however, much prestige and had considerable influence; he may be said to typify a whole period of Oxford and British ethics.

71 *Ethical and Political Thinking*, pp. 8–10. On p. 97, he writes: 'Any definitive classification of obligations is neither to be expected nor desired; it is mainly a linguistic question, dependent upon usage which fluctuates with time and company in its treatment of border-line or mixed cases . . .'. 72 On 'The Object of a Desire', 'The Obligation to keep a Promise', 'Exchanging', 'The Time of an Obligation', 'The Psychology of Willing', 'Acting, Willing, Desiring', 'Ought'. See op.cit., pp. 164–98. 73 p. 13. 74 *Philosophical Investigations*, 241; cf. 544. See also N. Malcolm, *Ludwig Wittgenstein. A Memoir* (Oxford University Press, 1958), p. 93, where Wittgenstein is recorded as saying: 'An expression has meaning only in the stream of life.' Some interesting remarks about 'Ethical Intuitionism' . . . from the standpoint of a 'neo-Wittgensteinian', are made by P.F. Strawson in a paper published in *Philosophy* in 1949, which is reprinted in *Readings in Ethical Theory*, eds. Wilfrid Sellars and John Hospers, pp. 250–9.

His first book on moral philosophy, *The Right and the Good*, was published in 1930.[75] He availed of the occasion of being asked to give Gifford Lectures in 1935–6 in order to pursue 'further reflections on moral theory'; and these were published as *Foundations of Ethics* in 1939.[76] The second book follows meticulously, point by point, the questions discussed in the first, taking account of later writing and replying laboriously to various criticisms. It is a dull book and a monument to a dull philosophical period. Ross also published a commentary on Kant's 'Grundlegung zur Metaphysik der Sitten', with the title, *Kant's Ethical Theory*.[77] Some of his criticisms of Kant seem unfounded; but, in contrast to the criticisms made by the British moralists we have so far examined, it is recognisably of Kant that they are criticisms.

In the Preface to *The Right and the Good* Ross acknowledges his debt to Prichard and to Moore.

> My main obligation is to Professor H.A. Prichard. I believe I owe the main lines of the view expressed in my first two chapters[78] to his article 'Does Moral Philosophy rest on a Mistake?' . . . In addition to this, I have repeatedly discussed many of the main ethical problems with him, and have learned something from every discussion; I have also had the advantage of reading a good deal that he has written but not published. And finally, he has read in manuscript most of what I have written, and has helped me greatly by exhaustive comments and criticisms. These have been very profitable to me both where (as in the treatment of rightness) he is (I believe) in general agreement with my point of view, and where (as in the treatment of the question what things are good) he to a large extent disagrees.
>
> I wish also to say how much I owe to Professor G.E. Moore's writings. . . . Where I venture to disagree, no less than where I agree, I have always profited immensely from his discussions of ethical problems.

2.1 The indefinability of 'right'

Ross has told us that his theory of the meaning and ground of 'right' or of obligation is mainly derived from Prichard; we can therefore deal with it briefly. Ross naturally rejects Utilitarian definitions of right as 'conducive to greatest happiness', for the reasons now familiar to us from Moore and Prichard. But he also rejects Moore's definition of 'right', as 'productive of the greatest possible good'. Moore had said ' "right" does and can mean nothing else' but this.[79] Ross

---

75 Oxford, At the Clarendon Press. Our edition is a reprinting of 1946.   76 Oxford, At the Clarendon Press. Our edition is a reprinting of 1949.   77 Oxford. At the Clarendon Press, 1954.   78 i.e., the chapters on 'The Meaning of "Right" ', and 'What makes Right acts Right?'   79 *Principia Ethica*, p. 147.

says it is 'plain on reflection that this is not what we *mean* by right . . .'.[80] What is plain, at least, is that two opposite things can both be said with the same 'accent of infallibility'.[81] Ross is correct, however, in his point that Moore's view 'differs from hedonism not in logical form but just by the substitution of "good" for "pleasure" '.[82] His argument virtually is that Moore's definition of 'right' conflicts with Moore's own principle of the indefinability of ethical terms. It may be replied that Moore did not regard 'right' as a strictly ethical term. This, however, as we have seen, is true only of *Principia Ethica*. In *Ethics* he does treat 'right' as though it were the primary ethical notion and were irreducible.

For Ross there is no question but that 'right' is the fundamental and distinctive concept of ethics. It is indefinable. Ross does not go back on this position when, in *Foundations of Ethics*, he accepts Broad's view that 'rightness' means ' "appropriately" or "fittingly" related to the rest of the situation'. This is not a 'naturalistic' definition, for he is using 'fittingly related' in a moral sense, where it means 'morally suitable' to the situation. This kind of suitability which is moral suitability cannot be further explained; especially it cannot be 'explained in terms of any non-moral reaction'; he agrees with Broad that it is 'specific and analysable'. This 'definition' of right, he claims, 'has the great merit of connecting the ethical sense of right and wrong with other uses of the words'.[83] It may be doubted, however, whether it does much to elucidate the meaning of right; and it would surely be more illuminating, as well as more consistent with his theory, for Ross to have tried to connect 'right' with other ethical words rather than with non-ethical ones; whereas, as we shall see, he determinedly cuts all the attachments of 'right' with 'good', 'morally good', 'virtue', 'value'.

To say that 'right' is 'an irreducible notion', ultimate and self-evident,[84] is, for Ross, just a way of asserting the objective validity of moral truth. Sociological 'explanations' of moral convictions fail: 'right' does not mean, even for primitive men, just 'what my race and age ordain'.

> Moral progress has been possible just because there have been men in all ages who have seen the difference and have practised, or at least preached, a morality in some respects higher than that of their race and age. And even the supporters of the lower morality held, we may suspect, that their laws and customs were in accordance with a 'right' other than themselves. 'It is the

---

80 *The Right and the Good*, pp. 8–9; cf. *Foundations of Ethics*, pp. 42ff. In the latter book, p. 69, Ross says: 'Professor Moore definitely says that for him the principle is self-evident. For my part, I can find no self-evidence about it.'   81 In the same place in 'My Early Beliefs' from which we have already quoted this phrase, Keynes recalled how Moore would say. : '*Do* you *really* think *that*? . . .', and answer was impossible (*Two Memoirs*, p. 85).   82 *The Right and the Good*, p. 10; cf. pp. 16–17. He calls Moore's view 'Ideal utilitarianism' or 'Agathistic utilitarianism' (op. cit., p. 9), or simply 'non-hedonistic utilitarianism' (*Foundations of Ethics*, p. 67).   83 op. cit., pp. 51–5, 79–82, 146, 315.   84 *The Right and the Good*, p. 12; cf. *Foundations of Ethics*, pp. 315–6.

custom' has been accompanied by 'the custom is right', or 'the custom has been ordained by someone who has the right to command'.[85]

It is false to say that

no one moral code is any truer, any nearer to the apprehension of an objective moral truth than any other; that each is simply the code that is necessitated by the conditions of its time and place, and is that which most completely conduces to the preservation of the society that accepts it. But the human mind . . . is competent to see that the moral code of one race or age is in certain respects inferior to that of another. . . . It has in fact an *a priori* insight into certain broad principles of morality and it can distinguish between a more and a less adequate recognition of these principles. There are not merely so many moral codes which can be described and whose vagaries can be traced to historical causes; there is a system of moral truth, as objective as all truth must be, which, and whose implications, we are interested in discovering; and from the point of view of this, the genuinely ethical problem, the sociological enquiry is simply beside the mark. It does not touch the questions to which we most desire answers.[86]

This (apart from a query one would wish to enter about the phrase '*a priori* insight') seems as good a statement of ethical objectivism as one could desire. We shall see what becomes of it as Ross's enquiry proceeds.

2.2 *The indefinability of 'good'*

Ross's doctrine of 'good' owes as much to Moore as his doctrine of 'right' does to Prichard. He begins his discussion of 'good' in both his books by referring to the Oxford English Dictionary definition, according to which 'good' is 'the most general adjective of commendation'.[87] As far as we know, Ross was the first moral philosopher to quote this definition. But no definition of the OED was to have so many articles, chapters, books written around it by philosophers as this one was to have within the next thirty years.[88]

---

85 *The Right and the Good*, p. 12.   86 Op.cit., pp. 14–15. In chapters III and IV of *The Foundations of Ethics*, Ross advances criticisms, close to those made by Moore, of evolutionistic, psychological and hedonistic theories of right, all of which, he finds, simply eliminate ethics. He also rejects Moore's own view of 'right' as productive of most good. He seems, therefore to be rejecting all 'consequentialism', and declares that right is right in itself regardless of its consequences. The example of an objective moral truth for Ross is always the obligation of keeping a promise; and this, for him, 'arises solely from the fact that a promise has been made, and not from the consequences of its fulfilment'. He goes on: 'I would go so far as to say that the existence of an obligation arising from the making of a promise is so axiomatic that no moral universe can be imaged in which it did not exist' (op. cit., pp. 76–7). Ross quotes Samuel Clarke and Butler in support.   87 *The Right and the Good*, p. 66; *Foundations of Ethics*, p. 254.   88 R.M. Hare, for example, puts the definition at the head of Part II, 'Good', of his book *The Language of Morals*. See also P.H. Nowell-Smith, *Ethics* (Penguin Books), p. 95.

What Ross is concerned to establish is the nature of 'intrinsic goodness', that is the nature of 'that which is good apart from any of the results it produces', or of 'what would be good even if it existed quite alone'.[89] This is obviously Moore's criterion of isolation, and is understood with all of Moore's literalism. What would be good even if nobody existed to have any knowledge of it or take any interest in it? This can be settled only by inspection. Among the situations we may be called on to inspect is the following:

> a state of affairs in which A is good and happy and B bad and unhappy, [compared with] one in which A is good and unhappy and B bad and happy, even if A is equally good in both cases, B equally bad in both cases, A precisely as happy in the first case as B is in the second and B precisely as unhappy in the first case as A is in the second.

Ross, for his part, is satisfied that the former state of affairs is the better and feels that most people will agree.[90]

What the adjudicator has to determine, in this somewhat dizzy-making contest, is the presence or absence of, and the degree of, what Ross decides is a *quality* of 'goodness', 'a quality resident in the object itself, independently of any subject's reaction to the object'. It is odd that Ross never noticed the incongruity of asking a subject to decide by 'attending to' an object whether that object would be good even if nobody ever attended or could attend to it.[91] This is, however, only an infelicitous way of saying something that is true and important. What he really wants to stress, is that 'goodness' is an objective character of things and not a subjective attitude of persons. It is in this context that he pronounces 'good' indefinable. Even though it is the case that, when we use the term 'good', we are expressing a feeling of approval or interest towards the thing; yet 'the existence of that interest is not what we assert when we so describe things'.[92]

> In my attitude towards the things I call good, my opinion that they are good seems to be the primary thing, and my feeling to be consequent upon this. . . .
> If we ask ourselves what 'approval' is we find that the basic element in it is not feeling at all but the judgment that an object is good.

---

89 *The Right and the Good*, pp. 68–9, 74, 75.   90 Op. cit., p. 72.   91 p. 89; cf. pp. 81–2. He wants to exclude all forms of the doctrine that good is relational, because for him to be 'related-to' is the same thing as to be 'relative'; and all relational theories of 'good' destroy its objective character. There is clearly a confusion here. Truth obviously requires some kind of relation between things and the mind; but this does not make truth relative to individual minds. Similarly 'goodness' requires some relatedness of things to the will; but this does not make goodness relative to individual wills. See Aquinas, *De Veritate*, 1.1. 92 pp. 90–1; cf. *Foundations of Ethics*, pp. 254–5. In the latter place, Ross invokes Meinong's distinction between *expressing* and *meaning*, and goes on: 'In the same way, what we *express* when we call an object good is our attitude towards it, but what we *mean* is something about the object itself and not about our attitude towards it. When we call an object good we are commending it, but to commend it is not to say that we are commending it, but to say that it has a certain character, which we think it would have whether we were commending it or not.'

Ross concludes that 'goodness is entirely objective and intrinsic to the "good" things that are good'.[93] This truth about the use of the term 'good' was often forgotten by the later protagonists of 'good-as-commending'.

Ross is strongly influenced by Moore's language and ideas when he is trying to determine what we mean by saying that goodness is an intrinsic quality of things. It is a quality which *results* from the other qualities or from the whole nature of the thing, apart from its goodness. Goodness is a 'consequential attribute', a 'toti-resultant property, based on the whole nature of its possessor'.[94] This way of speaking is unhappy. In Moore, we pointed out, it amounts to a quasi-naturalistic fallacy. Ross seems to be, most of the time, immune from naturalism in his use of this language; for many of the examples he gives of the 'other qualities' or 'whole nature' in question, are ethical and not natural qualities. But, then, it seems anomalous to speak of 'conscientiousness'. . . 'benevolence', etc., as qualities of a thing 'apart from its goodness', or as 'something in its nature other than goodness'.[95] If we empty 'goodness' of the content provided by 'conscientiousness' etc., there seems nothing left for 'goodness' to be except an exclamation of approval or a piece of rhetorical commendation, as Ayer and Stevenson were to urge.

But when Ross sets himself to identify the sorts of thing that are intrinsically good, he does seem to fall into the same fallacy as Moore. The list he draws up is a curious one, corresponding to the curious method of isolation and direct inspection by which it is established. It comprises 'virtue, pleasure, the allocation of pleasure to the virtuous and knowledge (and in a less degree right opinion)'.[96] Since these are found to be 'intrinsically good' precisely by 'inspecting' them in isolation from one another, we are being asked to say that pleasure in itself and knowledge in itself are intrinsically good.[97] But, as we maintained against Moore,

---

93 *The Right and the Good*, pp. 131–2; cf. *Foundations of Ethics*, pp. 257–62. 94 *The Right and the Good*, pp. 79, 88, 104–5, 109–10, 114, 121–3, 155. 95 Op. cit., pp. 79, 88. 96 p. 140. See the whole section, pp. 134–41. On p. 122, he says: 'Good is a characteristic belonging primarily only to states of mind and belonging to them in virtue of three characteristics—the moral virtue included in them, the intelligence included in them, and the pleasure included in them'. On p. 130 we have the typically Moorean question 'whether there could be beauty in a world in which there were no minds at all'. Ross decides there could not, except such as might be appreciated by 'such minds as might later come into being'. On p. 140, we are invited to 'contemplate' [with our minds . . . ?] 'any imaginary universe from which [we] suppose mind entirely absent'; and we are asked do we not agree that we 'fail to find anything in it that [we] can call good in itself'. 97 The following passages are typical: 'Two states of mind alike in respect of virtue and intelligence are not equally good if they differ in their degree of pleasantness; nor two states alike in virtue and pleasantness equally good if they differ in their degree of intelligence; nor two states alike in intelligence and pleasantness equally good if they differ in their degree of virtuousness' (pp. 122–3.) 'It seems at first equally clear that pleasure is good in itself. Some will perhaps be helped to realise this . . . if they suppose two states of the universe including equal amounts of virtue but the one including also widespread and intense pleasure, and the other widespread and intense pain' (p. 135). Cf. *Foundations of Ethics*, pp. 270–9. On p. 271 of the latter book he writes: 'When we turn to consider whether, and if so in what sense, pleasure is good, we come to what is for me one of the most puzzling problems in the whole of ethics'. And in the *Right and the Good*, p. 24, he says: 'The case of pleasure is difficult'. It is perhaps sentences like this which gave rise to the story that Ross once said in a lecture: 'I am not too happy about pleasure.'

this cannot be sustained except by surreptitiously qualifying the pleasure as 'good pleasure' and the knowledge as 'good knowledge'; and this reduces the claim to a non-significant tautology. Or else, as Ayer concluded, when we say 'pleasure is good', the word 'good' is only an exclamation expressing our approval of pleasure.

The absurd consequences of isolating 'pleasure', 'knowledge', 'virtue' from one another and from 'the stream of life', are made plain in the chapter on 'Degrees of Goodness'. Here Ross solemnly assures us that he has devoted 'a good deal of reflection' to, and has discussed with 'many others who have reflected' on them, such questions as whether any amount of pleasure is equal to any amount of virtue or whether moral goodness is infinitely better than knowledge.[98] When thrown out of connexion with one another and with the rest of moral life, these words, as Wittgenstein showed, simply spin around idly and convey no meaning. As Ross himself points out against the hedonists in this same chapter, the goodness of pleasure depends on the goodness of what we are taking pleasure in.[99] It is impossible to draw up a scale of degrees of goodness except by appealing to the 'quality of the function' of man which is involved, the relative 'qualities of a specifically human life' in which these 'goodnesses' are embodied.[100]

2.3 *Moral goodness*

The dismantling of moral language, the dissection of the moral life, is carried further by Ross when he distinguishes 'moral goodness from the 'goodness' he has hitherto been discussing. Surely what he has been discussing in the passages considered in our last section was moral goodness in any ordinary sense of this term. But Ross gives a special definition to 'moral goodness' which we now proceed to note. It means 'good either by being a certain sort of character or by being related in one of certain definite ways to a certain sort of character'.[101]

Moral goodness is determined chiefly by motives and desires. It attaches to conscientious acts, or acts done from a sense of 'devotion to duty' to acts done from the desire to produce something good; and to acts done from the desire to cause pleasure or prevent pain to some other person.[102]

Of these, by far the highest degree of moral goodness belongs to conscientiousness. To this extent Kant was right; but he was wrong to say that dutiful action is action done without desire. Ross says that duty itself creates a desire, provides a motive.[103] Discussing Kant's antithesis of duty and inclination, he makes the sensible and valuable point that a dutiful action which, through the formation of a moral habit, has become less difficult to perform, does not thereby

---

98 *The Right and the Good*, pp. 142–54. 99 pp. 145, 151. 100 The former phrase is from Bradley, *Ethical Studies*, p. 125, the latter from Muirhead, *Rule and End* in Morals, p. 107. Muirhead makes the point in criticism precisely of this section of Ross. 101 *The Right and the Good*, p. 155. 102 Op. cit., pp. 155–6; cf. p. 82; *Foundations of Ethics*, pp. 292–309. 103 *The Right and the Good*, pp. 156–8; *Foundations of Ethics*, pp. 206–7, 226–7.

become less morally good. 'Goodness is measured not by the intensity of the conflict but by the strength of the devotion to duty.'[104] Ross has, however, the notion that the better a man is, the less he will be subject to evil desires. 'A perfect character would, *ex hypothesis*, have no bad desires.'[105] This is another example of the mistake of reasoning from abstract ideas and not from facts and experience. This notion has no foundation in the history of sanctity. It completely misses the complexity, the 'ambiguity' of human 'desire'. But it is a notion which was given authority by Kant and which, in various forms, has become a common-place in modern moral philosophy.

But Ross's Moorean method of isolation leads him again into false abstractions and unreal antitheses.

> Suppose that some one is drawn towards doing an act A by a sense of duty, and towards doing another, incompatible, act B by love for a particular person. *Ex hypothesi* he thinks he will not be doing his duty in doing B. Can we possibly say that he will be acting better if he does what he thinks not his duty than if he does what he thinks is his duty. . . ? We may like better the man who acts more instinctively from love but we are bound to think the man who acts from sense of duty the better man.[106] In a purely conscientious act . . . there is no wish to promote the relief of another man's suffering, independent of the thought that it is one's duty to do so.[107]

In order to attenuate the stoicality and the paradox of this doctrine, Ross contrives an incredible couple of pages of moral arithmetic out of which he draws the conclusion that, provided there is unused sense of duty left over from an act done 'from sense of duty and love', this act may be morally better than an act 'done from duty alone'. This enables Ross to end his book, *The Right and the Good*, with the words:

> Thus we can, while agreeing with Kant that the sense of duty is the best motive, justify the generally entertained preference for actions in which some more instinctive generous impulse is present as well. And it is possible . . . to value highly the presence and operation of warm personal feeling, without disparaging, as it is often being thought necessary to do, the supreme moral value of the sense of duty.[108]

---

104 *The Right and the Good*, pp. 158–9, 164–5, 172; *Foundations of Ethics*, p. 206, Kant would not, however, have denied this. Ross seems to have come to see this later. In *Kant's Ethical Theory*, p. 17, he writes: 'In fact Kant is far from insisting, as he has often been charged with insisting, that there is a natural opposition between duty and inclination; what he does insist on is that there is a complete difference between the two.' 105 *The Right and the Good*, pp. 160. 106 Op. cit. p. 164. 107 *Foundations of Ethics*, p. 207. 108 *The Right and the Good*, pp. 170–2. The 'moral arithmetic' begins thus: 'Let us suppose that in the scale of values, sense of duty is represented by 10, love by 8, desire of an innocent sensuous pleasure by 0, malice by -8: and let us suppose an act in which two of these motives co-operate, with equal strength in producing an act.' The Kant-weight and the Ross-weight of different acts thus can be (and are) computed. Ross continued 'We are suggesting that there may be some [motivation] to spare,

But this is all wrong. There is no such thing as a 'purely conscientious act'—as if you could separate the conscientiousness from the act and call the former morally good whatever the moral quality of the latter. Conscientiousness is *not* morally good by itself: what can be morally good is the doing of something with conscientiousness. Whether this is morally good or not depends on the moral nature of that something. To use Ross's favourite example, in the posting back to the owner of a borrowed book, it is not the conscientiousness which is morally good but the *posting*-with-conscientiousness. And conscientious posting, in turn, is not necessarily morally good; it depends on what is posted. Bombs too can be posted conscientiously. It is true that one's concientious judgment may be at variance with the objective moral truth; and in that case conscientiousness (which is here only another name for inculpable ignorance) may excuse the agent from guilt. But we have a duty not to be ignorant of moral truth; and if we neglect this duty our conscientiousness is evil and can increase the evil of our works.[109]

2.4 *The right is not good*

Moral goodness depends mainly on motives. But it is a basic principle with Ross that one can never have a moral obligation to act from a good motive. This follows from the fact that 'I ought' implies 'I can'. For

> it is not the case that I can by choice produce a certain motive . . . in myself at a moment's notice, still less that I can at a moment's notice make it effective in stimulating me to act. I can act from a certain motive only if I have the motive; if not, the most I can do is to cultivate it . . . so that on some future occasion it *will* be present in me, and I shall be able to act from it. My *present* duty, therefore cannot be to act here and now from it.[110]

---

so that in a man who does an act, e.g., from sense of duty + love, the sense of duty may yet be strong enough to have secured the doing of the act from it alone. . . . And while we hold that there are actions in which sense of duty + an inferior good motive are just enough to secure the doing of the act, and that in that case the value of the action is reduced, we suggest that there are other cases in which, though an inferior good motive is present, the sense of duty is strong enough to have secured by itself the doing of the act, and that in such a case the value of the action is greater than if it had been done from duty alone.' **109** Peter Geach writes: 'A man may be got by training into a state of mind in which "you *must* not" is a sufficient answer to "why shouldn't I". . . . Moral philosophers of the Objectivist School, like Sir David Ross, would call this "apprehension of one's obligations"; it does not worry them that, but for God's grace, this sort of training can make a man "apprehend" practically anything, as his "obligations". (Indeed they admire a man who does what he thinks he *must* do regardless of what he actually does; is he not acting from the Sense of Duty which is the highest motive?) But even if *ad hominem* "You mustn't" is a final answer to "Why shouldn't I?", it is no rational answer at all' ('Good and Evil', in *Analysis*, 17.2, December, 1956, p. 40). **110** *The Right and the Good*, p. 5; cf. pp. 133, 156–8. On p. 43 he says: 'Motive never forms part of the content of our duty; if anything is certain about morals, that, I think, is certain.' *Foundations of Ethics*, pp. 115–6, repeats the same argument, adding that having a motive means having a certain opinion about the nature and consequences of an act, and desiring to do the act thus envisaged. 'But it is surely clear that neither opinion nor desire is under our immediate control.'

Secondly, Ross argues, to suppose that I have a duty to act from a motive involves an infinite regress; for it requires that I must have a motive for doing my duty, which is to have a motive for doing my duty . . . and so on.[111]

'The only conclusion which can be drawn,' Ross says, 'is that our duty is to do certain things, not to do them from the sense of duty.'[112] Ross has established, he thinks,

> that nothing that ought to be done is ever morally good . . . that what is morally good is never right . . . [113]

If we contemplate a right act alone, it is seen to have no intrinsic value.[114]

When we read passages like these, we must surely have sympathy with Wittgenstein's demand for attention to the ordinary usage of words, with his slogan, 'The meaning of a word is its use in the language'. This was not a plea for philology but a protest against arbitrariness.

This arbitrariness has, as Wittgenstein was to see, one main cause, the abstracting of concepts out of their living context. In real life, the inter-relationship of act and motive, intention, purpose, desire, love, sense of duty, is infinitely more complex than Ross's method of isolation has permitted him to see. He has not seen the complexity, the 'ambiguity' of 'I' and of 'desire' and 'will',[115] for he has been studying ethics as if it were all about words and their definitions, not about people. Ross refers to the story adduced in this connection by G.C. Field about Plato saying to his slave, 'I should punish you if I were not angry.' On which Ross comments: 'If Plato actually reasoned on Professor Field's lines, he can only be judged to have dealt very perfunctorily with a case of conscience';—and he proceeds to lecture Plato on how to solve 'his problem' properly.[116] It is enough to say that one feels that Plato was living and Ross lecturing.

2.5 *Prima facie duties*

We have seen what duty is not; it remains to see what duty is and what our duties are. Ross leads into this from his doctrine that right is indefinable, which is mainly a weapon of attack against 'definitions' of right in terms of results. In fact, if we look at 'what we really think', we shall see that we justify our duties to ourselves, not by looking ahead to their results, but by looking back to our relationships with other persons, our promises, contracts and other responsibilities. This, we feel,

---

111 *The Right and the Good*, p. 4; cf. pp. 45–7; *Foundations of Ethics*, pp. 165–7. 112 *The Right and the Good*, p. 6; *Foundations of Ethics*, pp. 122–4. 113 *The Right and the Good*, p. 41; cf. pp. 45–7; *Foundations of Ethics*, pp. 165–7. 114 Op. cit., pp. 132–3. 115 St.Thérèse of the Child Jesus, for example, said, speaking of the difficulty of religious life and of how it runs counter to natural inclination: 'I assure you that I would not remain in the convent a single instant by force. If anyone were compelling me to live this life I could not live it. But it is I who will it. I will everything that goes against my grain. Yes, it is I who will everything that goes against my will . . .'. (See *Conseils et Souvenirs de Ste. Thérèse de l'Enfant Jesus*, Carmel de Lisieux, 1952, p. 128, cf. p. 141), 116 *Foundations of Ethics*, pp. 135–6.

is surely true. Ross is undoubtedly right in accusing the utilitarians and Moore of reducing all my morally significant relations with my neighbours to that in which they are 'possible beneficiaries by my action'.

But they may also stand to me in the relation of promisee to promiser, of creditor to debtor, of wife to husband, of child to parent, of friend to friend, of fellow-countryman to fellow-countryman and the like . . .[117]

This brings Ross to the concept by which he is best known, that of *prima facie* duty. Ross is bothered about how to name this. He suggests 'conditional duty' as an alternative to '*prima facie* duty'.

He is not altogether happy about Prichard's term 'claim'. In his second book, he gladly accepted Carritt's suggestion of 'responsibility'.[118] But Carritt later withdrew this and substituted 'obligation'.[119] Whatever about the name, the concept is that of a presumptive duty; of what tends to be a duty, of what will be a duty unless over-ruled by some more imperious duty. This characteristic of being a *prima facie* duty belongs to acts objectively in themselves in virtue of their character as being acts of promise-keeping, etc. Ross draws up a list of six categories of *prima facie* duties.[120] These have been derisively referred to as just 'the code of the English gentleman'. But surely Ewing is right in protesting that they are 'statements of principles which would be accepted as grounds of obligation within any civilised community'.[121]

In fact, Ross has simply taken some of the moral beliefs of civilised communities and called them prima facie duties. He says: 'the moral convictions of thoughtful and well-educated peoples are the data of ethics'. He speaks of 'the existing body of moral convictions of the best people . . . ; the verdicts of the moral consciousness of the best people.'[122] These are indeed part of the data of ethics. But the business of ethics is to examine their foundations, their presuppositions, their justification. So far from finding any philosophical foundation for these duties, Ross actually deprives them of the foundations they do have in unreflective 'ordinary moral consciousness'.

Our quarrel is not with the notion or with the list of *prima facie* duties, but with the fact that they are *only prima facie*, and that they have no authentication or justification in Ross's system except personal intuition. In talking of duties as inter-personal, he seemed to be promising some study of the moral person as a

---

117 *The Right and the Good*, pp. 17–19, 22.   118 *The Right and the Good*, pp. 19–20; *Foundations of Ethics*, p. 85.   119 *Ethical and Political Thinking*, p. 3 n. 2.   120 *The Right and the Good*, p. 21. They are: 1. Duties resting on previous acts of my own, including; (a) duties of fidelity—those resting on an actual or implied promise; (b) duties of reparation, resting on a previous wrongful act. 2. Duties resting on previous acts of other men, or duties of gratitude. 3. Duties of justice, concerned in preventing the distribution of pleasure or happiness or the means thereto otherwise than in accordance with merit. 4. Duties of beneficence. 5. Duties of self-improvement. 6. Duties of non-injury to others. It will be noted that Ross is here immune from naturalism, since he makes duties rest on ethical situations.   121 *Second Thoughts in Moral Philosophy* (Routledge and Kegan Paul, London, 1959), p. 40.   122 *The Right and the Good*, pp. 40–1.

foundation of ethics; but the promise is not fulfilled. *Prima facie* duties are self-authenticating. They are just self-evident. They are *facts* that *we know*. They are

just as much part of the fundamental nature of the universe (and, we may add, of any possible universe in which there were moral agents at all) as is the spatial or numerical structure expressed in the axioms of geometry or arithmetic.[123]

This seems an excellent statement of the rationality and objectivity of ethics. But it is not well begun until it has started to wobble. First we note that there is no common 'ground of the rightness of all right acts'; *prima facie* duties are a plurality, having no common foundation and no principle of unity. They are like Prichard's obligations, an 'unrelated chaos' of separate intuitions, 'self-evidently necessary' facts, but nonetheless 'brute facts'.[124] But this is not all. It is only the general principles of duty which are self-evident. But these are only hypothetical duties. To discover what is my actual duty in the particular case, I have neither self-evidence to appeal to nor reasoning, but only perception. Ross compares moral perception to aesthetic perception;[125]—and the comparison is not encouraging from the point of view of its objectivity. It is a matter of assessing the relative 'claims' of conflicting '*prima facie*' duties in order to

form the considered opinion (it is never more) that in the circumstances one of them is more incumbent than any other; then I am bound to think that to do this *prima facie* duty is my duty *sans phrase* in the situation.[126]

In this, we can have, at most, only 'more or less probable opinions'; 'we are taking a moral risk'; the right act is 'a fortunate act . . . ; it is our good fortune if the act we do is the right act'.[127] The fear of subjectivism which this language arouses is not allayed by statements such as that it is our duty to keep promises irrespective of consequences—even when Ross brings moral weighing-machines into the lecture hall to persuade us that this is so.[128]

---

123 Op. cit., pp. 29–30; cf. pp. 20, n.1 , 32–3; *Foundations of Ethics*, pp. 1–3, 76–7, 144–5. The comparison of ethical with mathematical truths is, we have seen, common among intuitionists. 124 *Foundations of Ethics*, pp. 319–20; cf. pp. 82–4. 125 *The Right and the Good*, p. 31; cf. p. 40. 126 Op. cit., p. 19. He speaks of *prima facie* duty as a 'parti-resultant attribute' of an act: it is a 'tendency to be' a duty, 'Being actually a duty is a 'toti-resultant attribute', belonging to an act 'in virtue of its whole nature and of nothing less than this' (pp. 28, 33). 127 Op. cit., pp. 30–1, 33, 40, 42. 128 Op. cit., pp. 34–5. 'Suppose . . . that the fulfilment of a promise to A would produce 1,000 units of good for him, but that by doing some other act I could produce 1,001 units of good for B, to whom I have made no promise, the other consequences of the two acts being of equal value; should we really think it self-evident that it was our duty to do the second act and not the first? I think not.' Supposing the two acts were to be done for the same man duty + 1,000 units of good being in one pan of the balance, 1,001 units of good being in the other . . . what then? Ross still thinks the promise side has it; 'though a much greater disparity of good' might turn the scales the other way. There is more moral arithmetic of this sort in *Foundation of Ethics*, pp. 180–4.

2.6 *No absolute right and wrong*

The self-evidence of *prima facie* duties guarantees only that certain types of act tend to be right or wrong; it can never guarantee that they *are* in fact right or wrong. It all depends on the particular case, which has to be judged by individual perception.

> Rules such as 'tell the truth', 'injure no man', cannot survive if they are taken to be absolute rules of such a kind that any and every act which is an instance of telling the truth is thereby rendered right, and any act which is an instance of injuring another man is thereby rendered wrong. The rules cannot *both* be true, when thus understood, if there is a single case in which one cannot tell the truth without inflicting pain. And we find, further, that we cannot believe that there is any *one* of them which is universally true, as thus understood. At any rate, we feel sure that it is sometimes right to say what is not true, that it is sometimes right to break a promise, and so on with any one of such rules. The only way to save the authority of such rules is to recognise them not as rules guaranteeing the rightness of any act that falls under them, but as rules guaranteeing that any act which falls under them tends, so far as that aspect of its nature goes, to be right, and can be rendered wrong only if in virtue of another aspect of its nature it comes under another rule by reason of which it tends more decidedly to be wrong.
>
> Kant overshot the mark when he tried to vindicate for such rules absolute authority admitting of no exception; but he would have been right if he had confined himself to insisting that any act which violates such a rule must be viewed with suspicion until it can justify itself by appeal to some other rule of the same type.[129]

Ross was, of course, not thinking about what his words would mean in real life; he was only giving lectures. Nor was he thinking of what he was saying when, in another place, he wrote:

> The interests of the society may sometimes be so deeply involved as to make it right to punish an innocent man 'that the whole nation perish not'. But then the *prima facie* duty of consulting the general interest has proved more

---

129 *Foundations of Ethics*, pp. 312–3; cf. pp. 86, 137; *The Right and the Good*, p. 31. In *Kant's Ethical Theory*, pp. 33–4, Ross argues that absolute moral rules sin by abstraction. 'The whole method of abstraction, if relied upon . . . to answer for us the question, 'What ought I to do?', is a mistake. For the acts we have to choose between, say the telling of the truth or the saying of what is untrue, in some particular circumstance, or the keeping or the breaking of a promise, are completely individual acts, and their rightness or wrongness will spring from their whole nature, and no element in their nature can safely be abstracted from. To abstract is to shut our eyes to the detail of the moral situation, and to deprive ourselves of the data for a true judgment about it.'

obligatory than the perfectly distinct *prima facie* duty of respecting the rights of those who have respected the rights of others.[130]

A theory which leads to these conclusions is obviously false. The reason for its falsity in this particular domain is, once more, the error of abstractness. The definitions Ross gives or implies in the above passages, of telling the truth, avoiding injury, consulting the general interest, respecting the rights of others, are unreal, abstract definitions. The moral obligation of telling the truth does not mean telling all that we know to be true to everyone; and the moral obligation of avoiding injury does not mean that we may never cause pain. Otherwise we could never keep a secret or extract a tooth. The kindest as well as the most obligatory truth may be the truth that hurts. Similarly, the general interest, morally conceived, cannot be served by judicial murder of the innocent, cannot conflict with our moral duty towards individuals. Ross's *prima facie* duties clash because he defines them out of relation to human reality, that is to say, out of their context of moral reality. As he defines them, they are not moral duties at all.

2.7 Can duty ever be done?

The actual doing of dutiful acts encounters in Ross the same paralysing difficulties as it did in Prichard. Ross agrees that we cannot have a duty to do acts, but only to 'set ourselves to produce certain results' like loud noises etc. There is the ever-present possibility of being struck dumb or paralysed. All we can be obliged to do is to exert ourselves in a way morally suitable to the circumstances.[131]

> The only thing to which a man can be morally obliged is what I will call a self-exertion; a setting oneself to effect this or that change or set of changes. He cannot be obliged to perform an 'act' in the ordinary sense. For the noun 'act', as we ordinarily use it, stands for a complex thing; viz. the causing of a certain change by setting oneself to cause it; and this includes as an element in it the occurrence of the change. . . . Now the occurrence of the bodily change involved in the use of such words or phrases as 'kill', 'hit', 'tell the truth', cannot even be part of what is right or what is wrong. This follows directly from the fact that if a man had, without knowing it, become paralysed, since the last time he had tried to effect the given type of change, his self-exertion, though it would not produce the effect, would obviously be of exactly the same character as it would have been if he had remained unparalyzed and it had therefore produced the effect. The exertion is all that is his, and therefore all that he can be morally obliged to; whether the result follows

---

130 *The Right and the Good*, p. 61. Peter Geach comments: 'We must charitably hope that for him the words of Caiaphas that he quotes had just the vaguely hallowed associations of a Bible text, and that did not remember whose judicial murder was being counselled.' (See his article, "Good and Evil", in *Analysis*, vol. 17, 17.2, December 1956, p. 42.) 131 *Foundations of Ethics*, pp. 155–63, 233–4.

is due to certain causal laws which he can perhaps know but certainly cannot control, and to a circumstance, viz. his being or not paralysed, which he cannot control, and cannot know until he performs the exertion.[132]

There is, lost in all this verbal maze, a real problem, that of the distinction, relation and possible divergence between the morality of the act and the morality of the intention;[133] but distinctions are not separations. The occurrence of active, transitive verbs is sufficient proof that our wills act on the world and in the world of facts, and are responsible for the changes they effect there.

2.8   *From anti-subjectivism back to subjectivism*

Ross lets himself be led by Prichard also into the subjective view of the ground of duty, namely that a duty

> is made a duty by the subjective facts of the situation, viz. by my state of knowledge or opinion about the facts of the case.[134]

These philosophers suffered from crises of agnosia, as well as fears of aphasia and motor ataxia.

> I can never *know* nor can come to *know* that some state which I can bring about will produce an effect of the kind x, though I may have reason to *think* it.

Hence, if duty were made to depend on the objective facts of the case, I could

> never know that I have any particular duty, or even that any one has ever had or will ever have a duty.[135]

It follows that the correct view of duty in the concrete is that it obliges a man to

> the self-exertion which he *thinks* to be morally most suitable in the circumstances as he takes them to be.[136]

Ross agrees that this is 'a subjective account' of duty, but holds it is not 'subjective in any objectionable sense'.[137] The trouble again is that it is an unnecessary difficulty created by false abstractions. Ross, after Prichard, so defines 'knowledge' that nothing in ordinary life can ever be *known*. He, in this context, also pulls at a distinction between objective and subjective morality until it becomes a total separation of one from the other. The garment of morality becomes in the hands of the intuitionists a thing of shreds and tatters.

---

132 Op. cit., p. 160.   133 See Aquinas, *S. Theol*, 1–2, qq. 18–20.   134 *Foundations of Ethics*, p. 150.
135 Ibid.   136 Op. cit., pp. 161–5; cf. p. 207.   137 Op.cit., p. 164.

2.9 *The trivialising of ethics*

The younger Oxford moral philosophers of the 1950s, most of them linguistic analysts, were sometimes accused of having trivialised ethics by discussing absurd or unimportant problems, or giving banal examples. The assumption frequently is that they were innovators in this respect, betraying a nobler Oxford tradition of moral seriousness. The accusation is unfair, the assumption untrue. We shall here enumerate some of the examples we have found in the works of Prichard, Carritt, Ross and some others of their time.

(1) 'When I see someone who shows symptoms of having fainted and it occurs to me that if I shouted, I might revive him', am I morally bound to shout? And if I am, is it to shout or to set myself to do so, that I am bound?

(2) Can I *know* that I can thread a needle, or only that I can set or exert myself to thread a needle? Am I bound to tell the truth, or only to set or exert myself to tell the truth?

(3) When I tried to jump a ditch, did I will a movement which I was sure would get me well across or did I only will 'that movement the willing of which, if I were to will it, I thought the most likely of all the willings of movements in my power to result in my landing on the farther bank?'

(4) 'Suppose I have a spare banana and X has a spare apple, and we meet. I realise that I should gain if it happened that I lost the banana and also gained control of the apple. But I want not to lose control of the banana unless somehow I do it by an act which will give me control of the apple. I may, for example, resolve to hand over the banana, if I can be assured that if I do I shall in consequence receive the apple. But I shall not hand over the banana unless I have some confidence that if I do I shall in consequence get the apple. How am I to acquire this confidence?'

(5) A and B are two sick musicians. A has promised B that before 5 p.m. to-day he will put a new E-string on B's violin. If at 4.45 p.m. B is evidently dying, is A still bound by his promise?

(6) The vicar of my parish asks me to send my piano to the parish hall next Thursday afternoon. I promise categorically. I later hear that the concert he had been arranging is off. Am I still bound to send the piano?

(7) Is a promise to attend an At Home much less binding than one to attend a dinner-party?

(8) Is there a moral difference between the state of a man who is habitually selfish and that of a man who is habitually unselfish during times when both men are asleep or otherwise engaged?

(9) When I have borrowed a book, is my obligation to return it discharged (a) when I have packed it and posted it; or (b) when he has actually received it? Again, is my duty done (a) if I pack the book carelessly and yet it does reach my friend; (b) if I pack the book carefully and yet it does not reach him? And do I deserve more praise in the one than in the other case?

(10) What is the moral position if, after I have handed the parcel in at the Post Office, the Post Office goes on fire?

(11) A man habitually locks his roll-top desk. One day there happen to be confidential papers on his desk which he has the moral obligation to keep from view. He locks the desk from force of habit, without adverting to his duty? Is the act of locking the desk a moral act? Is it a right act?

(12) 'A man who was fond of oysters might eat a plateful put before him for the sake of their flavour; a man who loathed them might do so to avoid hurting his host's feelings; a man who loathed or was indifferent to them might do so to prevent his neighbour, whom he knew to be fond of them and whom he disliked, from having two portions.' Are these three instances of one act, or three different acts?

(13) 'Suppose that I have promised to take Paul to see a race, though I am not fond of Paul or his company, and that the day before the race a friend of mine, Peter, whom I have not seen for many years, writes to ask me to meet him at the hour of the race elsewhere . . . I decide to break my promise [to Paul]; and then, at the last moment, Peter wires to me to meet him at the race instead. If now, after deciding to break my promise to Paul for the sake of meeting Peter, I take him because I am going anyhow, and not because I had promised to'— is my act a right act?; is it a moral act?

Such were among the subjects solemnly discussed by the solemn generation of morally serious Oxford philosophers who preceded the Angry Young Men of British philosophy. This may help us to understand a little why the young men were angry.[138]

---

138 Nos. 1–4 come from Prichard; these or similar examples are found also in Carritt; Nos. 5–7 were creations of Pickard-Cambridge in criticism of Ross, and are discussed by Ross, in reply, throughout a whole chapter of *Foundations of Ethics*, on 'The Obligation to Fulfil Promises', Nos. 8–9 are Ross's original work; No. 10 is L.A. Reid's contribution to the borrowed book saga; Nos. 11–13 come from H.W.B. Joseph, No. 12 being carefully discussed, in reply to Joseph, by Ross.

CHAPTER FOUR

Inter-War British Ethics

Intuitionism dominated British moral philosophy during the whole period from Moore and Prichard until the Second World War. Its premisses, methods and main conclusions were rarely called in question. Critics were usually content to accept intuitionism as a true account of a part of moral experience, but set themselves to complete it by reconciling its partial truth with the truths of more comprehensive moral theories. Some form of philosophical idealism was professed by most of these critics. Others tended to accept intuitionism as being on the whole a valid account of ordinary morality; but went on to say, 'So much the worse for ordinary morality'; and to seek the morality of perfection and holiness beyond 'right' and duty, in 'creative living' or in religion. We confine ourselves, in the main, to Oxford philosophers, or to philosophers whose contribution was inspired more immediately by the Oxford discussions.

1 PRIORITY OF GOOD

Examples of the former category of critics are H.W.B. Joseph and J.H. Muirhead. Joseph's book, *Some Problems in Ethics*, was published in 1931,[1] Muirhead's book, *Rule and End in Morals*, in 1932.[2] Both find intuitionism incomplete. It fails to do justice to the wholeness and unity of the moral life, and especially to the place of Good and End in Morals. Both plead for a return to the neglected truths of older traditions—Joseph looking to Aristotelianism and idealism, and Muirhead mainly to idealism, to complete the inadequacies of the moralists of intuitive duty.

1.1 *Joseph*

Joseph begins by a summary outline of the scientific account of the world and of man, and he shows that this is inconsistent with the existence of moral experience. The scientific account, therefore, cannot be absolutely true. 'This result,' he concludes, 'illustrates the necessity to Ethics of a metaphysical foundation.'[3] He does not, however, do much to show what form his metaphysical foundation would take; or to reassure anti-idealists that metaphysics is not wild fiction substituted for human experience and for common sense. Joseph does not make

---

1 Oxford University Press. Our edition is a second impression, of 1933. 2 Oxford University Press.
3 *Some Problems in Ethics*, p. 15.

95

sufficiently clear what for us is the basic issue, namely that the sciences of man, separately and collectively, do not constitute an adequate description of human reality; and that an adequate account of man must be also at once moral and metaphysical. The foundation of ethics is a metaphysics of integral human experience.

Among Joseph's best pages are those in which he criticises the Prichard-Ross notion that motives cannot be obligatory, that duty binds only to do acts, not to do them for good motives; and that therefore right acts and morally good or valuable acts are distinct and separate from one another. This for Joseph is false abstraction. An action without its motive is not a human or moral action. The same physical performance done with, say, three different motives is not one but three different human acts. You cannot 'abstract from an act something essential to its being', e.g, the element of common purpose from a conspiracy.

> For a conspiracy is a common purpose working itself out through diverse persons into a change in a state of things; and an action is one man's purpose working itself out through him into a change in the state of things. Take away the common purpose, and there is no conspiracy. . . ; take away the single man's purpose, and there is no act, and nothing right or wrong.[4]

It is another false abstraction, Joseph urges, to separate 'right' from 'good'. Why should I or how could I feel obliged to do an act which is, by definition, without value?[5] Action in the ethical sense is not an isolable physical occurrence, like action in physical science; it is a 'piece of living'. A morally right action is 'something which a man judges that he ought to include in his life'.[6] To judge of the rightness or wrongness of actions and rules of conduct, we must look at the 'whole form of life' which these actions and rules 'embody and promote'.[7] It is fallacious to separate 'rightness' from 'goodness' and to suppose a plurality of unrelated grounds of 'rightness'. Rightness presupposes goodness; it 'is a sort of goodness'. Right acting is both determined by and determines right living which is also good living; and right living requires a growth towards unity and harmony both within the individual personality and between persons in society as well as between nations in the world community.[8]

Joseph rejects the Prichard-Ross thesis that 'rightness' is an obligation on us and not an obligatoriness in things. Rightness is for him a character in things.[9] But, we should say to Joseph, surely the truth is that obligation is both in us and in things. The parallelism of 'good' or 'right' and 'true' or 'knowable' is here close. 'Truth' resides both in the mind and in things. 'Goodness' resides both in the will and in things. A proposition is true when the judgment the mind has formed about a thing corresponds to or is adequate to the reality of the thing. An action

4 p. 44; cf. pp. 41–3, 45, 55–6.   5 p. 33.   6 pp. 94–5.   7 pp. 98–9.   8 pp. 87, 92, 102–3, 107, 118–9, 133–5.   9 p. 92.

is good or right when my appreciation of its goodness corresponds to the goodness it has in itself; when my recognition of its worthiness-to-be-valued is proportionate to its value. I am truly obliged in respect of an action when the action is genuinely obligatory-on-me.

Absolute objectivism and absolute subjectivism of value are both false: 'value' is what 'ought-to-be-valued by me', 'good' is what 'ought-to-be-pursued by me'. Modern phenomenological analyses have shown the same thing to hold of knowledge and truth. Here too, both extreme objectivism and extreme subjectivism are false. The 'thing-in-itself' is a myth. Everything that I know and everything I believe to be true is something known-by-me, is part of my experience. But it is not *only* known by me, not merely part of my experience. It is known by me as existing independently of me. My experience is of things that *are there*. As the phenomenologists put it, knowledge and truth are not creative construction, as rationalism thought, but the 'unveiling of being'. Being is known as 'being-always-already-there' before being known. It is the same with value. It is I who discover value; its reality is related to me; I discover it in its relation to me. But I discover it as having an objective claim upon me, as being transcendent-to-me. Its relation to me is the tie it holds over me. Its relatedness is its obligatoriness, which is the source of my obligation.

Joseph comes close to this analysis of 'goodness' when, following Plato and Aristotle, he connects 'good' with 'real', and argues that Moore, Prichard and Ross are wrong to regard 'goodness' as a quality. Goodness is the whole substance of the thing, it is one and the same with the complete reality of the thing. Joseph does not however provide any means for distinguishing between the goodness and the reality of a thing. He refers to scholastic discussions of goodness in God.[10] It is a pity that he did not also consult scholastic discussions of goodness in man and in morals.

1.2 *Muirhead*

Muirhead is more strongly under the influence of the British idealists than Joseph; but on the whole the things that Muirhead admired in Bradley, Green and Bosanquet were sound things and he was right to plead for their restoration to ethics. His view-point is, indeed, in the main, the Socratic one.

> Socrates made no mistake in the answer he gave to what he saw to be the central question of an ethics that would penetrate beneath the apparently isolated moral judgments of right and wrong, good and bad, to the assumption which underlies them of the reality of something—whatever we may call it, chief

10 pp. 76–80. He points out in the same place that Moore seems to have thought of 'analysis' exclusively in physical or chemical terms, ignoring 'intelligible' distinctions such as those which the scholastics called 'metaphysical division'.

end, ideal good, perhaps best what he himself called it, 'justice' or the spirit of integrity—that makes life worth living.[11]

He too finds guilty of false abstraction the intuitionist doctrine of right. Their rejection of teleology was due to a false separation of end and means, which caused them to fear that teleological ethics made all means indifferent and valueless, when it did not justify evil means in service of a good end. But, Muirhead replies, the proper sense of end, the Greek *telos*, is not that of an objective eventually attained by a series of means, but that of an ideal, an essence, *immanent in* a series of means—'the fulfilment or realisation in a thing of the principle inherent in its nature'.

From this point of view the philosophical life [according to Aristotle] would appear, not as a highest good to which everything else stands as a more or less indifferent means, but as the permeation of the ordinary duties of life with a sense of their significance as the expression of the principle implicit in *all* action which is characteristically human. The question what this principle is constituted to the Greeks as to ourselves the central problem of ethical philosopy.[12]

The intuitionist separation of 'right' from 'good' is criticised for like reasons. It is true that

we mean one thing by goodness or value and another thing by the claim it lays upon us to be realised by or in our actions and to become our rule of life. But this does not exclude the possibility that the two ideas stand in an essential relation to each other as two aspects of a real situation . . .[13]

The idea of the Good 'carries with it the meaning of something that "ought" to be realised', 'something which it is right and obligatory to pursue', and this is the explanation of its moral hold upon us.[14] Furthermore, our different moral

---

11 *Rule and End in Morals*, p. 25. In the Preface, he says the 'issue at stake' in ethical discussions is 'none other than the possibility of making any general statements as to what makes life worth living and so of having anything that can be rightly called a Moral Philosophy at all'. He presents his book as a 'Comment on the informal symposium which some of my younger Oxford contemporaries have been recently conducting among themselves on the idea of Right in Morals.' 12 p. 61; cf. pp. 62–4. 13 p. 45. 14 p. 90. This is said in support of the doctrine of the priority of 'right' over 'good'; but Muirhead seems to follow the intuitionists in giving a curiously narrow sense to 'moral' and in thinking of 'good' as if it were, by itself alone, not a fully moral notion. What we, however, mean by 'good' here is 'the-good-for-man', and we hold that this is moral good and the foundation of moral duty. What Muirhead says in the phrases quoted is true independently of his assumptions or conclusion in the context. He seems unexpectedly to fall into what we have called in Moore and the intuitionists a quasi–naturalistic fallacy when, siding in this particular with the utilitarians, he speaks of 'goodness or value as implying contributoriness'. 'Could it not still be argued that the rightness or goodness of the act . . . consists in its being the kind of action which on the whole contains more of the promise of non-moral Goods, in other words just of the Goods in which the good 'form of life' must in the end be conceived of as consisting?' (pp. 87–8).

judgments and our duties are not mere isolated intuitions but are organically related to one another, finding their ultimate justification in the claim of other persons upon our respect and in the claim upon our allegiance of a 'form of life' in which 'the vocation of man, as primarily a social, ultimately a supra-social, being' can best be realised.[15]

The idea and the ideal of man, 'the only mediator we know of between the ideal and the actual', should therefore be central in ethics, according to Muirhead.[16] The 'qualities of a specifically human life' provide the foundation and the unification of our moral obligations.[17] The 'much criticised formula of "self realisation"' may, he thinks, contain more truth than its critics allowed.[18]

Finally we note an aspect of Muirhead's ethical thought which will frequently recur later, namely the contrast he draws between the 'morality of rules' and 'creative morality', between law and love; his suggestion that sanctity lies beyond morality. We present this in his own words:

> We should insist that . . . *prima facie* rules of right and wrong and *prima facie* ends are precipitates of the creative spirit of man, his will and intelligence, seeking to express itself in ordered forms which shall unite and harmonise human interests at continually deeper levels, spreading from the material to the mental and from the mental to the spiritual. We should insist that there are rules beyond rules and ends beyond ends, both of them prescribed by a deeper sensitiveness to the values that life contains, and entailing not only for great moral leaders like Buddha or Socrates or the creative statesmen of Plato's *Symposium*, but for all who see life with any degree of fresh, imaginative insight, a break-away from the morality of checks and balances which is all that 'first-look' rules and ends can give. It is to this creative spirit in man which sees in the situations of life opportunities of good rather than calls to conform to rule that these leaders appeal when they would substitute love for law as the directing principle of life. They know that love and the sensitiveness to values which it gives take us deeper into the secrets of life and give us a more integrated view of its contents than either any moral rules or any moral reasoning can do.[19]

---

15 pp. 46–8, 79, 96, 107–9. 16 p. 100. 17 p. 107. Cf. pp. 102–4: 'Our immediate apprehensions [of duties] . . . presuppose a ground. . . . To attempt to cut off one's judgments of the Right and obligatory from their background in the objective Goods or values of human life is as impossible as to cut off our judgments of truth from their background in the objective reality of the world to which they refer. . . . The things that ought to *be* . . . are at once the inspiration and content of what we ought to *do*.' 18 pp. 101–2. 19 p. 105. On p. 112, he says that for the 'door of entry [to the Kingdom of Heaven] we have to look beyond morality'. We have, in connection with these passages, to deplore the irritating habit idealists have of annexing Christian terminology for their own philosophical uses.

A group of philosophers whom one can broadly associate with the moderate ethical idealism of C.A. Campbell, could be cited in support of views resembling those of Joseph and Muirhead;[20] but we shall not discuss their contributions here.

20 See C.A. Campbell, *On Selfhood and Godhood* (the Gifford Lectures, 1953, 4, 5, published by Allen and Unwin, London, 1957) especially the constructive part (pp. 200–8) of his Lecture X, on 'Moral Experience and its Implications for Human Selfhood'. J. Laird, in *A Study in Moral Theory* (Allen and Unwin, London, 1926), has passages which put the case for the unity of the moral life very well. We quote: 'Moral theory is concerned with the reasons that justify action; or else that condemn it. . . . The essential contrast here is between reasons that are simply explanatory and reasons that justify or condemn' (p. 12). 'It is plain that the only consideration relevant to the justification or condemnation of an action is its value or lack of value, its goodness or badness' (p. 17). 'A justifying reason, then (or a reason which shows that a given action *ought* to be performed), is a reason in terms of value; and anything that ought to be done, ought to be done for a sufficient reason. . . . The *ought* of morality may very well justify itself; but . . . it can do so only if it contains within itself the reason for its indefeasible authority. And this reason must be the supremacy of the value it enshrines, conjoins or sustains. . . . The good will is self-justifying because of its intrinsic value, and . . . nothing except unconditional goodness can justify unconditionally. . . . We are asserting a necessary and a fundamental connexion between value and obligation, excellence and authority, worth and duty' (pp. 20–1). 'In our own case the 'ought' presents itself as a command to action self-accepted and self-imposed. . . . In accepting it, however, we do not accept it as a thing without reason, but as something which has a reason. This is because we recognise that the knowledge of good and evil imposes an obligation to act in accordance with such knowledge' (p. 23). 'The ultimate analysis of moral experience in this matter is that the best does command' (p. 24). In a later book, *An Enquiry into Moral Notions* (Allen and Unwin, London, 1935) Laird departs somewhat from this position and takes some steps towards a more pluralistic ethical theory. In this volume he also commits the fallacy of making moral rightness depend, at least in part, on the pursuit of 'non-moral goods'—and this largely because he, like the intuitionists, defines moral good as conscientiousness. (See especially pp. 168–82, 265–300, 309–10.) Professor A. Macbeath, formerly of Queen's University, Belfast, in *Experiments in Living* (Gifford Lectures, 1948–9, publ. by Macmillan, London, 1952) defends a position similar to that of Laird's earlier book. For Macbeath, ethics deals with, (1) the pursuit of ends; (2) under the guidance of rules or principles; (3) in a certain spirit or attitude of mind. The notion of 'right' has to do with the rules; 'good' with the ends; 'moral good' with the spirit (conscientiousness, devotion to duty); 'merit' with the effort of will and struggle against natural inclination which the doing of duty involves. He rejects intuitionism, on the ground mainly that actions, ends and rules do not occur in isolation but are parts of a whole of living from which they take their meaning and their value (pp. 9–10; 356–63, 367–9, 395, 406–7). 'We find the grounds of the rightness of moral rules in a form of life which is the realisation of a system of ends; and we find the grounds of the goodness of good ends in the same form of life. . . . That form of life is both unconditionally good and the source of moral obligation' (p. 33). 'The moral good or ideal makes a demand upon the moral agent that he do or refrain from doing those acts and realise or repress those ends which are here and now required for its realisation. It is this demand which is experienced as the sense of duty or obligation. The acts thus demanded are morally right' (p. 60). 'The way of life stands for the good which is the source of moral obligations; and we accept its demands as binding because, our nature being constituted as it is, we cannot do otherwise. 'When we carefully contemplate the form of life which we take to be the good for man, we cannot help recognising its requirements as obligatory on us' (p. 102). He criticises the ends-means terminology for reasons similar to those of Muirhead (pp. 43–4, 400). He describes his theory as 'a reformulation or modification of a self-realisation type of theory in the light of an anthropological analysis of primitive ways of life' (pp. 413–4). He is mistaken in assigning non-moral ends to morally right and morally good acts: 'The ends which are pursued in such acts are . . . the ends of desires which are rooted in human nature and required to satisfy its needs—ends such as food, shelter, health and freedom, knowledge, beauty and friendship. . . . Strictly speaking, all these ends are non-moral ends. . . . The moral ideal has in fact no contents but these non-moral goods. . . .' (pp. 59–60). But food and shelter etc. for human beings are not non-moral: they are either moral or else wicked (as when supplied by cannibals or white slave-traffickers to their victims). These things are contents of the moral ideal only when they are morally good: otherwise we have a form of naturalistic fallacy.

2 FROM OBLIGATION TO INSPIRATION : DE BURGH, REID, LINDSAY.

Intuitionism provoked an interesting contemporary reaction from a group of religious moral philosophers. Broadly speaking, they took the intuitionism of their time to be the most developed and complete expression of ethics; and went on to judge ethics, thus expressed, to be either afflicted with inner contradictions or inadequate to man's aspirations after perfection. They argued that ethics must look beyond itself to metaphysics and religion for the solution of its antinomies; and that man must transcend ethics, or at least the ethics of duty, in order to achieve sanctity.

2.1 *Duty versus good: de Burgh*

Among these, it was W.G. de Burgh who laid most emphasis on the 'inner contradictions' of ethics. The phrase is reminiscent of Bradley and de Burgh's thought in fact resembles Bradley's. In two papers on 'Right and Good', published in 1930,[21] he presented the ideas which he was later to develop more thoroughly in his Gifford Lectures of 1938, *From Morality to Religion.*[22] In the third paper, he accepts the contention of Prichard and Ross that I can never know what my real objective duty is. I am however obliged to do what is my real duty. Duty, therefore, obliges me to do the impossible. If, therefore, 'I ought' implies 'I can', how can duty be my duty at all? Yet it is impossible to escape from the certainty that I must do my duty. Here is a fundamental antinomy within ethics, the solution of which cannot be found in ethics, but must be sought 'beyond the confines of ethics [in] the field of religion'.[23]

Unfortunately for this argument, however, the alleged antinomy in ethics is only an error in de Burgh, which he inherited from Prichard. It is an error which contemporary studies of the problem of knowledge have exposed again and again —the error of so defining knowledge that large areas, if not the whole, of what we ordinarily mean by knowledge would not fulfil the conditions laid down. Prichard, Carritt and Ross so define 'knowing my duty', that only an omniscient

---

21 "On Right and Good: Preliminary Survey", *Journal of Philosophical Studies* (later *Philosophy*), V.V, 1930, pp. 246–56; "On Right and Good: the Problem of Objective Right", ibid., pp. 422–34; "Right and Good: the Contradiction of Morality", ibid., pp. 582–93; "Right and Good: Action sub ratione Boni", V.VI, 1931, pp. 72–84; "Right and Good: Conclusion—the Limits of Ethics", ibid., pp. 201–11. 22 Macdonald Evans, London, 1938. 23 *Journal of Philosophical Studies* (*Philosophy*), vol. V, October 1930, pp. 582–8. 'We can never know, in any particular situation, what it is really right to do. We know indeed that it is always right . . . to do what we believe to be right. . . . But this knowledge is purely formal and gives us no clue to the matter of moral obligation. . . . Our beliefs and judgements as to material rightness . . . are notoriously liable to error. . . . We never get beyond what we, or other persons, judge to be right. . . Once again, to put the paradox in its most glaring form, if we are never able to know our duty, how can we perform it? And if we are never able to perform it what meaning is there in calling it our duty? . . .' Morality is therefore the command to will 'what can neither be willed or known . . . the endeavour to achieve the impossible.'

being could ever know what objectively was his duty. It is the old sceptics' error of so defining knowledge that in fact only God's knowledge could be held to be true, and all human knowledge must be condemned. It is the rationalist's error of so defining knowledge or proof that, say, mathematical knowledge or deductive demonstration alone would be true or proven. Against this error, philosophers following Wittgenstein have been right to advance the paradigm case argument. It is ordinary knowledge that gives meaning to the word 'knowledge', and that provides us with a standard of rationality and of truth and falsehood.[24] As inductive reasons are what we mean by 'good reasons' in science, so ordinary moral certainty is what we mean by 'knowing our real duty' in morals. Moral knowledge is no more disqualified because we are not omniscient or infallible, than physics is disqualified because it is not geometry or logic. We must not invoke religion under false pretences.

In his Gifford Lectures, de Burgh discovers other 'antinomies' in ethics. In each case, his starting point is some conclusion of the intuitionists. First of all, he finds the distinction between 'duty' and 'good' to be irreducible. It is the difference between compulsion and love, between struggle and vision, between action and contemplation. Duty and duty alone founds moral value; but 'good' inspires intrinsic value, which goes beyond moral value.[25] He rejects all attempts to derive 'ought' from 'good'. I can never know what will turn out to be good, or what actions of mine will lead to good. But I do know duty by direct intuition as an indubitable, self-evident datum of experience; and I know duty to have its characater of dutifulness or rightness in itself, independently of all consideration of good. It is just a fact of experience that duty is duty and good is good and neither can be reduced to the other.[26]

In itself, he argues, the experience of duty implies and reveals a fundamental dualism in human nature. It imposes a struggle against desires that are alien and recalcitrant to the moral law. We know that these desires ought not to exist, yet if they did not exist, there would be no 'ought'. We feel obliged to fulfil our duty perfectly, to bring all our nature under the absolute control of duty. Yet we know that duty cannot be perfectly fulfilled and that nature can never be brought

---

24 See A.J. Ayer's chapter, 'Scepticism and Certainty', in *The Problem of Knowledge* (Penguin Books, 1956). He writes: 'The upshot of our argument is that the philosopher's ideal of certainty has no application. . . . [The sceptic's] victory is empty. He robs us of certainty only by so defining it as to make it certain that it cannot be obtained.' (p. 68; cf. pp. 75, 127–9, 222). See Wittgenstein, *Philosophical Investigations*, 472–86 (on induction). In fact, the 'paradigm case argument' is not essentially different from Aristotle's injunction that 'the man of education will seek exactness so far in each subject as the nature of the thing admits, it being plainly much the same absurdity to put up with a mathematician who tries to persuade instead of proving, and to demand strict demonstrative reasoning of a rhetorician.' (*Nicomachean Ethics*, 109b, 30ff; cfr. 1104a, 1–5). Cf. Aristotle's remarks on the distinction between 'ethical', 'natural' and 'logical' propositions in *Topics* 105b, 21–9. 25 *From Morality to Religion*, pp. 1, 37–44, 55–7. 26 pp. 117–32, 140–3; cf. 55–8. He accepts of course the intuitionist doctrine of 'ought' as self-justifying and as permitting of and needing no reasons. He quotes Price in this connection. (pp. 57–8).

completely to the state in which it does duty by inclination and without struggle.[27] But the paradox is that if morality were brought to this state of perfect realisation, it would have abolished itself. 'If the contradiction were overcome ' and the ideal realised, morality would no longer exist as morality.[28] If aspiration after the ideal were fully and always present, there would be no place left for moral action.[29] If I do a moral act because I desire to do it, then its morality is annulled, it has been replaced by inclination.[30] Therefore the ideal and the actual are parted by a gulf that ethics cannot bridge.[31]

These are not the only antinomies of ethics. There is also the contradiction between the reality of evil and our conviction of the ultimate triumph of good. There is the problem of how the will can be free if it is necessitated by the Good.[32] But at the base of all these antinomies is the irreconcilable dualism of the ethical principles: 'do duty' and 'pursue good'.[33] De Burgh concludes that alike by its inner contradictions and by the other-worldly references implicit in its principles, 'ethics points beyond its own borders to the fields of metaphysics and religion'.[34] The final explanation of duty, the final reconciliation of duty with good, is that morality is the expression of the will and intention of God.[35]

Again we must protest that most of what de Burgh calls 'contradictions in ethics' are instead intuitionist confusions about ethics. As we have already argued, it is not true that there is a 'fundamental dualism of ethical principles', that duty and good are irreconcilable. Duty is action justified and required by good reasons; and good reasons are reasons showing that the action in question is good and that to omit it would be evil. It is true that duty presents itself to me as something objective, authoritative, having the right to command me and to judge me. It appears as something transcendent. Its commands cannot be perfectly fulfilled, because in all virtuous action I am conscious of my imperfection. Whatever I do or am, I am always certain that I could have done and could be better.[36] These

---

27 pp. 49–50, 53–6, 67. 28 p. 69. He tells us that 'in proclaiming the universal transcendence of the moral principle, Kant was virtually heralding the euthanasia of the moral life.' 29 p. 87. Laird quotes a similar passage from McTaggart about the abolition of virtue in an ideal universe 'when the righteous was *ipso facto* the real' (*An Enquiry into Moral Notions*, p. 111). H.D. Lewis draws an interesting parallel between the views of de Burgh and those of the neo-Lutherans, who also criticise the 'ethics of obligation'. He quotes from Brunner, *The Divine Imperative*: 'Duty and genuine goodness are mutually exclusive. Obedience due to a sense of unwilling constraint is bondage, and indeed the bondage of sin. If I feel I ought to do right, it is a sign that I cannot do it. If I could really do it, there would be no question of "ought" about it at all. The sense of "ought" shows me the Good at an infinite, impassable distance from my will. Willing obedience is never the fruit of a sense of "ought" but only of love' (*Morals and the New Theology*, Gollancz, London, 1947, p. 30; cf. W.G. Maclagan, *The Theological Frontiers of Ethics*, Allen and Unwin, London, 1961). There are evident analogies also with much that is being written nowadays, under the auspices of 'the New Morality' and elsewhere, about the alleged antinomies of love versus law, conscience versus authority, etc. 30 p. 118. 31 pp. 67, 123, 127. 32 pp. 110, 186. 33 p. 188; cf. p. 159. 34 p. 110. 35 p. 188. 36 H.D. Lewis overlooks this aspect of morality when he says that the 'belief that ideals must be always "beyond our reach", that they would cease to be our ideals if we could fulfill them, is a mischievous confusion'. See his paper 'Obedience to Conscience', reprinted in *Morals and Revelation* (Allen and Unwin, 1951), p. 73. He elsewhere writes that 'moral guilt and merit . . . depend,

features of moral experience certainly require for their explanation a dualism of matter and spirit in man and an ultimate recourse to God as author and as term of the moral law.[37]

But de Burgh's presentation and analysis of these features of the moral life are mistaken. His mistake is the mistake of all rationalism and idealism, so well exposed by Wittgenstein, that of isolating words and ideas from their setting in reality. De Burgh is not thinking of the real experience of living men who have tried and who try to be saintly. He is reasoning from an abstract definition of what sanctity ideally would be or should be if it was not men who had to achieve it. Real saints have never thought they were finding virtue easier or fulfilling their duty more perfectly, the more they loved and wanted both. They never entertained a thought so foolish as that loving God was something distinct from doing His will. They were saints, not by passing beyond morality, but by realising more and more fully its claims upon them.

2.2 Rules versus 'Creative Morality': L.A. Reid

A different kind of plea for the surpassing of the ethics of rules or duties is that made by L.A. Reid, in his book *Creative Morality*.[38] He rejects a number of intuitionist views on ethics, particularly the separation of motive from duty.[39] But he accepts, somewhat inconsistently it would seem, the view of Ross and Prichard that moral goodness is entirely a matter of our 'trying, aiming or intending' to do the right or good act, not of our succeeding in doing so. We can perhaps never know what really is right or good: 'part of right falls on the objective side, and events in the objective world pass beyond our cognizance and control'.[40] The 'objects' of morality, therefore, that is the states of affairs which morality aims at

not on what would be possible under special conditions, nor on what may become possible eventually, not even on what we could see to be possible here and now if our judgment and our moral imagination were sharper, but *solely on the individual's loyalty to the ideal that presents itself to him.* And it is because of its proneness to obscure this elementary ethical truth that the term 'impossible ideal' should be used very cautiously—if at all' (*Morals and the New Theology,* p. 131). But it is precisely the 'ideal as it presents itself to me' which 'always pronounces my fulfilment of it inadequate and myself imperfect. It is '*my* ideal' but it cannot come from me because it is 'my *ideal*' not my reality. The day that I think I have fulfilled my ideal perfectly, I have been a prig and instead of acting virtuously, have incurred the vice of pride; and St Augustine said the greatest of all vices is pride in virtue.　37　A much sounder account of the relation of ethics to religion (though it too is marked by idealist faults) is that of A.E. Taylor in his 1926–8 Gifford Lectures, *The Faith of a Moralist,* 2 vols. (Macmillan, London, 1931). Taylor denies the disjunction of value and fact, finding value embodied in fact and fact as revealing value. (v. I, pp. 28–62). But he recognises the transcendence of value, and therefore the aspiration of man towards an ideal which is incessantly ahead of and above his actual achievement. This, together with our sense of sin and guilt, and the sense of morality as being the service, in love, of a Person who draws us by love and aids us by grace—these are for Taylor the 'traces of God' in moral experience. What he calls for is not a suicidal surpassing of morality by itself towards religion but a transfusing of morality by religion. (See v. I, pp. 152–5, 208–58; cfr. v. II, pp. 55–6, 68 ff.)　38　Allen and Unwin, London, 1936.　39　Op. cit., pp. 58–66, 75–80.　40　pp. 52–8. This is the same error as de Burgh's, criticised in the last section.

producing, 'lie outside morality's sphere'.[41] This obviously is another form of the quasi-naturalistic fallacy we have already encountered.

This leads Reid to accept the Prichard-Ross thesis that morality is exerting-ourselves-to, setting-ourselves-to do our duty.

It is reasonable to aim at doing right; in all probability many actions are actually right, and the fact that we do not always (or perhaps never do) know that our actions are right does not mean that we should abandon skilful aiming. The alternatives are not absolute right or absolute wrong; we may make a pretty good shot, and it is always worth trying to do the best we can.[42]

We can only 'act up to our lights' and duty cannot oblige us to do more than we can.[43] But neither can we know that we are acting fully up to our lights. It seems in the end as though Reid's theory implies that morality is doing our best to do our best.

The content of duty must be redefined as *trying* to act up to our lights, or (alternatively) acting up to our lights as far as we reasonably can, *trying* to do the best we know, or (alternatively) doing the best we know up to the limits of our capacity, trying to summon up good motives if we can, summoning them up to the limits of our abilities. . . .[44]

We are by now familiar with the epistemological fallacies involved here. We need only note the unfortunate, if unintentional, laxism involved in this language. It is strange that Reid, and other moralists who spoke so much of 'doing the best we can',[45] did not reflect that in ordinary usage the phrase is more often used pejoratively and taken to mean failure through *lack* of effort.

Reid's characteristic contribution to ethics, however, is his notion of the 'larger good' which lies beyond conventional morality, the 'living morality' which is 'the quality of an "inspired" human being'.

---

41 pp. 54–1, 81–5. It is in this context that he introduces the notion of a perfectly morally good act (conscientious posting of a borrowed book) being rendered objectively not-good by the burning of the Post Office. He agrees with Prichard that the morally good action involved in moving my limbs can only be the setting myself to move them, because 'some physiological disturbance might make it impossible' to move them (p. 75). This is all wrong, as we have argued above against Ross.   42 pp. 53–4; cf. 57–9.
43 pp. 57–9.   44 p. 66. Reid has more valuable things to say about moral knowledge in a later chapter, in which he insists that morality has its own kind of valid knowledge, proof and reason, and that individual moral judgments are validated by reference to a system of values which imposes itself upon us because of its inherent worth. Value judgments are personal but objective. 'To assert the importance of individuality is not to deny the objectivity of the larger objective order. All moral conduct in the end involves a submission of oneself and one's conduct to what one believes to be this objective order' (p. 178). See the whole chapter on 'Value, Truth and Reality', pp. 166–84.   45 e.g. Laird, *A Study in Moral Theory*, p. 60; *An Enquiry into Moral Notions*, p. 295. In an article, "On Doing One's Best", in *Journal of Philosophical Studies* (later *Philosophy*), V.VI, 1931, pp. 56–71, Laird points out that Bradley held there was no moral law which could not in some conceivable or imaginable circumstances be morally broken, 'except of course the universal law to do the best we can in the circumstances'. (See *Ethical Studies*, Oxford, 1927, p. 157, and note.)

The vast majority of human beings are tyros and remain tyros. They never reach moral adolescence. Morality to them means the obedience to the conventional rules of duty. . . . And because both in art and in morals, obedience to such rules tends to conventionality and unreality, of living, 'morality' is accounted by the plain man a dull thing. . . . The morally wise man who, like the true artist, is exceptional, is on the other hand an individual who does individual things and who is not a type working from formulae. He takes rules for what they are worth as valuable bits of generalised experience, which must not be traversed without good reason, but which are general guides, warning signs, signs which keep him from bias and undue egoism. They are to be taken, realised, absorbed and forgotten in the creative business of living.[46]

Moral rules, he says, are mainly negative, mainly prudential and utilitarian. An 'imaginative and inspired life' tends more and more to dispense with them. 'Rules, when the imagination of the morally wise man is working at its best, are unnecessary.'[47] Such a life has a 'spontaneity and beauty' transcending 'duty, which make of it a kind of 'living poetry', in contrast to 'the routine of formalised living'.[48] Using the formula of Bergson, which has by now become a cliché, Reid speaks of the morality of rules as a 'closed morality' and of the morality of 'inspired living' as 'open morality'.[49] He also contrasts the morality of rules with the spirit of the Sermon on the Mount.[50] Although, however, it is usual for moralists in this line to contrast duty with love, Reid regards this as mistaken. Love does not supersede duty, it 'embodies duty in the fullest sense', and transforms rules and routine into a life of poetry and beauty.[51]

This last remark is valid; but the general thesis will not bear examination. The pseudo-Nietzschean rhetoric of this sort of writing used to have a certain power to mesmerise. Later on, when repeated by every spokesman of the Beat Generation and the Angry Young Men, it became a boring jargon. We have only to think of the 'conventional rules of duty' 'we should be just, beneficent, loyal, truthful'[52] to see what a morality would be which would *really*, and not just rhetorically, find them 'unnecessary'. The same reflection will show us that an 'open morality' is one which is open *to* and not outside or beyond traditional morality. Moral perfection is progress within moral rules and not away from them. Some of the novels of Aldous Huxley should provide sufficient corrective of the aestheticism of 'super-moral' morality, which many of L.A. Reid's pages seem to favour.[53]

---

46 pp. 100–1; cf. 136–7.　47 p. 103; cf. 134–7.　48 pp. 103–4, 109–10; cf. 255.　49 p. 107.　50 pp. 244–5.　51 pp. 115–6, 123, 131–46.　52 p. 102.　53 See pp. 99–101, 117–19. The analogy between art and morals is one of his main themes: see in particular chapters 6 and 7, on ' "Creative" Art and "Creative" Morality', and 'Duty and Expressiveness'.

2.3 'The two moralities': A.D. Lindsay

In the first months of the Second World War, A.D. Lindsay published *The Two Moralities*.[54] Despite the criticisms we shall make of it, we hold that this little book says some of the best things that have been said by a British philosopher about Christian morality and about the role of the Christian and of Christianity in society.[55]

The main purpose of this book is to distinguish 'the morality of my station and its duties, or "playing the game"', from 'the challenge of perfection or the morality of grace'. An alternative formula is the contrast between 'the demands of ordinary morality' and the 'challenge of the Sermon on the Mount'. The critique of 'ordinary morality' is by now familiar. This morality is described as tribal or nationalistic, conservative, hostile to those not of the group.

> A world where the only morality is the morality of my station and its duties is a world of closed and often hostile societies, at variance or at war with one another. . . . War is [its] negative aspect.[56]

This morality is self-interested, contractual, ungenerous as between man and man. Its terms 'obligation', 'duty', 'right', betray an anxiety not to exceed the just minimum, not to give except to him who has a right to receive and in the founded hope of receiving back a merited recompense.[57]

Furthemore ordinary morality is 'necessarily imperfect, relative, changeable'. It represents not what the best of us, or any of us at our best, is capable of doing and becoming, but the sort of conduct 'ordinary decent people of our sort' can be relied on to observe. In this part of his argument, Lindsay slips into identifying ordinary morality with that embodied in the laws of our society. Now laws, he says cannot require specially virtuous or ideal behaviour; they must be 'rules which most people approve and are on the whole prepared to obey'; they cannot prescribe conduct higher than that which the 'decent average man is prepared to act up to'. Morality as embodied in laws must change with changes in social conditions and mentalities; it accommodates itself to people rather than moulding people to itself.[58] We must quarrel, however, with the amalgamation of morality and law on which part of this critique rests. Surely ordinary men are usually clear about the distinction between 'legal' and 'moral'. In practice, indeed, they often confuse the two; but this is surely because they feel that laws ought to conform to morality and not because they think morality should or could be adjusted to law.

54 Eyre and Spottiswoode, January 1940; the sub-title is: 'Our duty to God and to Society'. Our edition is a reprinting of July 1940. Compare his *The Moral Teaching of Jesus* (Hodder and Stoughton, London, 1937). 55 On Lindsay as a man and as a philosopher and educator, see W.B. Gallis, *A New University. A.D. Lindsay and the Keele Experiment* (Chatto and Windus, London, 1960). Chapter III, 'Lindsay as Philosopher', is an admirable succint statement and appreciation of Lindsay's philosophical position. 56 Op. cit., pp. 18–20. 57 pp. 43–6. 58 pp. 20–32; cf. 96–7.

Ordinary morality, Lindsay holds, is a 'closed morality'. But 'into the closed world of our ordinary accepted duties' there sometimes comes a call to a larger, morality, a 'morality of grace or of challenge'. This morality invites us to go beyond 'the world of claims and counter-claims',[59] to go beyond what is expected or owed; to give without hoping to receive.[60] Instead of calculating what I must do, this morality asks what can I do; it seeks 'to be inventive, to create, to discover something new'. It is sensitive, imaginative; it is moral artistry.[61] This morality is 'open', seeing all men as brothers. It is not a morality of *doing* so much as of *being*.[62] 'Its primary appeal is not to duty and obligation but to love and admiration.' Its spirit is religious rather than moralistic. It puts the spirit before the letter.[63]

The morality of grace, which is Christian morality, never permits of smugness or pharisaism, as ordinary morality too often does; for its standard of perfection is God, and this standard we can never claim to have attained.

No one who accepts the teaching of Jesus about perfection can ever sit down and say, 'Well, now I am good. I have attained perfection'. . . . A Christian is a man who is always trying to be something better than he is.

The saint is he who is deeply conscious of his own imperfection.[64]

Lindsay, however, recognises that the 'two moralities' are usually 'not conflicting but complementary'. We are to do what law and moral rules demand, but more—going in love beyond the letter of the law. His best thought is:

If the rules are to serve their purpose, their purpose must be served also by the spontaneity and creativeness and freedom shown within the rules. Of course, love is the fulfilling of the law. The law provides a framework which love fills up; is the dry bones into which love breathes life.[65]

With this, as with much of what Lindsay has to say in this book, we are in agreement. And yet we find that, as is usual with thinkers in this line, his critique of ordinary morality or of moral rules tends to become forced and artificial. It is certainly possible to be conformist, unreflecting and pharisaical in observing

---

59 Lindsay quotes this as Bosanquet's description of ordinary morality (p. 43). 60 pp. 416. 61 pp. 46–9; cf. 98–9. 62 pp. 50–1. 63 pp. 51–7. 64 pp. 58–63, 92–3. 65 pp. 97. In a short chapter on 'A Consideration of St. Paul's Teaching on Slavery and of its Implications', Lindsay has admirable things to say about how Christianity acts on and in society. 'Institutions go back to how men think about one another. Unless we can somehow change the way men think about one another, we cannot change the institution at all—whatever we may legally do if we are in earnest about social reform, about changing the standard of "my station and its duties" we must display in our own lives the ideals which we wish to see embodied in that standard' (p. 83). He quotes Bishop Gore: 'Bad dwellings, inadequate wages, inadequate education, inability to use leisure,—these are stones upon the graves of men spiritually dead. We must take away the stones. Only we shall not exaggerate what merely external reform is likely to accomplish. The real obstacle to social advance is selfishness and sin. No external reform will remove this. Nothing but the conversion of souls from self to God. Real social reform, then, will proceed, not by the method of majorities, but from small groups of sanctified men. . . ' (p. 87). Compare Lindsay's *The Moral Teaching of Jesus*, pp. 18–68.

moral rules; but this is precisely because we have become insensitive to their nature as *moral* rules. Every moral rule is, or is connected with a rule which enjoins *love* of other persons, respect for, attention to or concern for others as persons. One cannot keep moral rules passively, unreflectively, effortlessly; just because one cannot *attend to* persons without thought;—attention to others is thoughtfulness. Furthermore, the claims of morality are, as we have seen, transcendent claims; if we feel smug and self-satisfied about fulfilling them, we have failed to fulfil them—or to realise what they claim. It is not values that fail; it is we who fail them and make them seem stale and hollow by the shallowness and hypocrisy of our lives which are supposed to embody them. Lindsay quotes, in criticism of ordinary morality, Plato's definition of justice as 'doing one's business'. But this is very unfair to Plato. Plato meant doing our business of *being men.* That is what morality is; and it is as such *open*; and progress towards perfection consists in being open to it. It is *within* 'my station and its duties' that the saints have found 'the challenge to perfection'.

Yet, insofar as the philosophers we have considered in this paper were criticising intuitionism, we have sympathy with them. For intuitionism was on the whole as wrong-headed a moral theory, and suggested as conformist and smug a moral practice as one could invent—and produced as dull books as it could ever be one's *prima facie* duty to read.

Because it is rare to find philosophers in the British tradition in the period under review who take the religious question seriously or who think it has any relevance to moral philosophy, it may seem strange that the present writer should be critical of philosophers like de Burgh, Reid and Lindsay. There is certainly very much that is of value in the thought of such writers and much with which we are in sympathy. The relationships between religion and morality are indeed many and are of profound importance. They are overdue for exploring. But this exploration requires for its starting point a more profound philosophy of morality than that which these writers took over from intuitionism. There are within moral experience undeniable intimations of the transcendent: for instance, our experience that our best moral actions always fall short of our own moral standards and ideals; our awareness of a moral obligation to strive to be and to do 'better than we can'; our humbling awareness that our most unselfish actions prove in retrospect to have been tinged with egoism; our repeated sense that our virtues are never fully up to the measure of what we know virtue should be. Familiar phrases from the Gospels express these paradoxes: 'We are unprofitable servants; we have done only what we ought to do'; 'Be ye perfect, as your Heavenly Father is perfect.' Surprisingly, Sartre expresses this feature of morality well when he calls moral obligation the 'necessary impossible'; but Sartre's one-dimensional philosophy provided him with neither means nor incentive to pursue the paradox further. De Burgh, Reid and Linsday perform a valuable service in calling attention to this dimension of morality. Their writings are an invitation to others to explore it in greater depth.

CHAPTER FIVE

Cambridge Intuitionism

Oxford intuitionism can hardly be said to have survived the Second World War; its advocates did not face up to the criticisms of the younger generation of philosophers; they did not try to re-think or re-state their doctrine in terms of the new-style philosophy which was introduced by Wittgenstein in his second period. They did not speak its language; they remained largely silent in the new discussions. As Carritt and Ross were writing their books, the revolution which was to unseat then was gathering strength at Cambridge. Wittgenstein returned to philosophy and to Cambridge in 1929. Thereafter, the book-posting and the fiddle-string-replacing discussions of the Oxford moralists were taking place in a house that had been set on fire. We have pointed out, however, and shall have occasion to repeat, that some of the features of the new ethics—including features that the intuitionists most strongly deplored—were possible, and indeed legitimate developments of intuitionist doctrines.

At Cambridge itself, intuitionism and objectivism partly survived the revolutionary period and sought to adapt themselves to the new regime. The possibility and the form of this adaptation shed a further light upon the nature of intuitionism. We shall look at some rather special features of the pre-Wittgenstein intuitionism professed at Cambridge by C.D. Broad and by A.C. Ewing; and then at the modified post-Wittgenstein intuitionism of Ewing.

1 C.D. BROAD

Broad's main contributions to ethics was his book, *Five Types of Ethical Theory*, published in 1930.[1] This book takes the form of studies of the ethics of Spinoza, Butler, Hume, Kant and Sidgwick.[2] The point of departure is a critique of naturalism similar to Moore's, and an affirmation of the indefinability of ethical terms. A certain nuance of non-naturalism appears in Broad and in the early Ewing, in that they hold that ethical predicates denote 'non-natural properties' of objects. This they hold to be a consequence both of the fact that, as against emotivism, ethical judgments are propositions and can be true or false; and of the fact that, as against subjectivism, ethical propositions are statements about the nature of objects and not about the psychological reactions of people. True,

1 Kegan Paul, London. Our edition is a reprinting of 1944. 2 The essays on Spinoza, Hume and Kant formed the Donnellan Lectures which Broad delivered in Trinity College, Dublin, in 1929.

110

fact-stating propositions must be indicative sentences ascribing properties to objects. But what sort of properties do ethical propositions ascribe to objects?— it obviously is not empirical or natural properties, for these, they hold, are non-ethical. Therefore it must be non-empirical or 'non-natural' properties. Goodness and rightness are therefore non-natural properties of objects'.[3]

This is of course only another terminology for the doctrine of Moore, for whom goodness is a 'simple, indefinable, unanalysable' property of objects; a property which differs from all natural properties, but which results necessarily from the natural properties of objects; a property which does not exist in time and therefore, in Moore's sense of 'exist', does not exist at all. The same concept pervades the doctrine of Prichard, Carritt and Ross. It becomes more systematic in Broad and especially in Ewing. Criticism of this concept is very important in later developments of British ethics.

Broad, closely following Sidgwick, for whom he professes the strongest admiration, holds 'ought' to be a 'logically primitive' and 'unanalysable', 'unique and peculiar' term; an *a priori* concept, which is grasped by an immediate act of mental apprehension.[4] 'Ought' is 'indefinable', in the strict sense of the term 'definition'. Yet it can be translated into verbal equivalents which have the merit of showing the relation of 'ought' to other terms, and of helping to explicitate its meaning. These equivalents must, of course, be non-naturalistic. Broad proposes to translate 'ought' and 'right' in terms of the 'fittingness' or 'appropriateness' of certain responses in face of certain situations. To say that we ought to be grateful to our benefactors means that 'there is an intrinsic relation of fittingness between [the emotion of gratitude] and the latter kind of object.[5] About 'right', Broad says:

It seems to me that, when I speak of anything as 'right', I am always thinking of it as a factor in a certain wider total situation, and that I mean that it is 'appropriately' or 'fittingly' related to the rest of this situation. When I speak of anything as wrong, I am thinking of it as 'inappropriately' or 'unfittingly' related to the rest of the situation. . . . What I have just asserted is not, and does not pretend to be, an analytical definition of 'right' and 'wrong'. It does bring out their relational character, and it correlates them with certain other

3 The argument we have outlined is not found in so many words in Broad, but it underlies his whole ethical thought. See, in particular, passages such as the following: *Five Types of Ethical Theory*, pp. 112–5, 162–5, 170–1, 176–7, 277–81; the paper, 'Some of the Main Problems of Ethics', first published in *Philosophy*, 1946, and reprinted in *Readings in Philosophical Analysis*, eds. Herbert Feigl and Wilfred Sellars (Appleton-Century-Crofts, New York, 1949), pp. 550ff.; and the article, "Review of Huxley's Evolutionary Ethics", first published in *Mind*, 1944, and reprinted in the same collection, especially pp. 582–6. 4 *Five Types of Ethical Theory*, pp. 145–6, 170–1, 281. Cf. Readings in Philosophical Analysis, pp. 547–8: '[When I say that something was *wrong* and *ought not* to have happened] what I assert is something unique and peculiar, though perfectly familiar and intelligible to everyone. It cannot be expressed by any form of words which does not contain the words 'right' or 'ought' or some others which are obviously mere verbal translations of them.' 5 *Five Types of Ethical Theory*, p. 128. The notion of 'fittingness' was prominent in seventeenth-century rationalist ethics, in Cudworth, Clarke, and particularly Wollaston. See A.N. Prior, *Logic and the Basis of Ethics*, pp. 54ff.

notions. But the kind of appropriateness and inappropriateness which is implied in the notions of 'right' and 'wrong' is, so far as I can see, specific and unanalysable.[6]

What is 'thought to be wrong absolutely' is being 'held to be unfitting to *all* situations'.[7] 'Good' is similarly 'indefinable'; though there is a 'synthetic, necessary and mutual relation' between 'good' and 'right', in the sense that a 'good' situation means a situation which on the whole I 'ought' to desire or promote, or to which an emotion of approval would be appropriate or fitting.[8]

There are several difficulties in this notion of 'ought' as 'fitting response to situation'. It is held to be an act of reason, but not to rest on reasoning.[9] 'Ought'-judgments are in the first place individual, intuitive responses to concrete situations. General moral rules 'are derived by intuitive induction from inspecting the particular cases which are described in the singular judgments'.[10] The primacy given to the singular act of inspection of the particular case seems already to be a form of subjectivism.

More serious is that the 'particular cases' to be inspected are described as non-ethical situations; and the moral judgments we pass on them are said to be 'necessary propositions connecting ethical with non-ethical characteristics', and 'seen to be necessary by inspection'.[11] We have frequently met this sort of idea before and called it a quasi-naturalism, because it derives moral conclusions from non-moral premisses. The fallacy is concealed from its authors because, as Broad himself said of Huxley, 'the notion of value is surreptitiously imported'[12] by them into the so-called 'non-ethical characteristics'. This is blatant in Broad. He says:

> Moral characteristics are always dependent upon certain other characteristics which can be described in purely neutral non-moral terms.[13]

The latter he calls 'right-making' or 'wrong-making' characteristics; or rather, he adds, since the moral judgment depends on the concrete situation, and what is right in one situation may be wrong in another, we should say 'right-tending' and 'wrong-tending' characteristics. But the examples he gives of these are 'relieving pain', 'being a breach of promise', 'being an act of courage', 'being a feeling of pleasure at another's misfortune'. How can Broad have thought it either true or merely good English usage to call, e.g. 'breach of promise' and 'act of courage', 'purely neutral non-moral terms'? As for relieving pain, this is never 'neutral' and 'non-moral'; it is either moral or, as in the case of euthanasia, immoral.[14] More

---

6 pp. 164–5; cf. 170–1. 7 p. 165. 8 pp. 176–7. 9 pp. 108–15, 145–6, 178–9. 10 pp. 145–6. 11 pp. 282–3; cf. 112. 12 See *Readings in Philosophical Analysis*, p. 585. 13 'Some of the Main Problems in Ethics' in op. cit., p. 551. 14 In *Five Types of Ethical Theory*, p. 282, he says: 'In any possible world painfulness would *pro tanto* make an experience bad. . . .' This is nonsense. *Bad* painfulness makes an experience bad; but there is good painfulness too, and nearly every worth-while experience in life, has it—as, for example, athletics, study, doing research, writing books, lecturing, rearing a family, praying. . . .

incredibly still, in his review of Huxley, Broad speaks of 'the non-ethical characteristic of being an act of promise-keeping . . . [or] of deliberate deception', which 'necessarily involve' the 'ethical characteristic of being right [or] wrong' respectively.[15] Broad quotes with gusto Butler's remark about Hobbes—that his theory that sympathy is selfish is the kind of mistake no one but a philosopher would make, namely forcing a fact to accord with a theory. Surely Broad's own language here is another example; only a preconceived theory could make any one speak of a deliberate lie as a non-ethical situation which 'necessarily involves the ethical characteristic of being wrong'. The serious thing about this mistake is that it leads inevitably to the conclusion that ethical judgments are non-objective and non-rational.

Another difficulty about the notion of moral rightness as 'fittingness to situation' is that it seems to imply that one and the same act may be right in one situation, wrong in another. Broad accepts this implication. It makes his ethical 'objectivism' largely nugatory. It is true that he speaks of acts as being 'unfitting to *all* situations'; but he does not give any indication of *why* any act should be such, or even of whether there are any such acts. Now it seems to be among our ordinary moral beliefs, to say no more, that there are acts which are absolutely and always wrong. How could this be so unless these acts were thought unfitting to the human situation as such? But what we miss in Broad is an analysis of the 'human situation' or of the human person, as the basis of moral distinctions.

He has, indeed, promising remarks about this, remarks of a kind rarely found in recent British philosophy. Referring to Kant's concept of *Achtung*, or moral awe, aroused by the contemplation of moral purity, Broad writes:

> On such occasions the [human] being, who from his mixed nature belongs both to the world of sense and to the supersensible world, is getting a peep, and the only direct peep which he can get in this life, into the latter. This glimpse humbles and even frightens him, in so far as his nature is partly animal and sensuous; yet it exalts him, in so far as his nature is fundamentally rational, by reminding him that he is a citizen of the supersensible world. Here . . . it seems clear that Kant is describing a genuine fact in terms that most of us can understand and accept in outline. . . .[16]

He rejects the Kantian account of the moral person, however, saying that it leaves 'the concept of a rational being . . . unanalysed in an atmosphere misty with the incense of adoration.'[17] This is less than just to Kant. Also Kant does not, as Broad says, 'claim to infer from the concept of a rational being the necessary and sufficient conditions which [categorical imperatives] must fulfil'. He finds in the

---

15 *Reading in Philosophical Analysis*, p. 580.   16 *Five Types of Ethical Theory*, p. 139. ' "Duty" and "obligation," ' he puts it in the same place, 'have meaning and application only to beings who are fundamentally, and yet not wholly, rational.'   17 p. 127.

experience of human beings categorical imperatives whose necessary and sufficient conditions cannot be found within the limits of spatio-temporal existence. They require that there should be in man a principle of freedom and spirituality transcending that in him which is material and subject to physical laws. The freedom by which we are able to be moral, the moral obligation by which we know that we are free, both of them reveal to us a principle within ourselves which we cannot fully understand but which we are; and they point to their origin beyond ourselves in a Principle which we cannot understand but with which we commune and whose authority over us we recognise. The last word of Kant's *Fundamental Principles of the Metaphysic of Morals* is the recognition of this two-fold mystery, in us and beyond us, which morality is and shows.

> While we do not comprehend the practical unconditioned necessity of the moral imperative, we yet comprehend its *incomprehensibility*, and this is all that can fairly be demanded of a philosophy which strives to carry its principle up to the very limit of human reason.[18]

But Broad is content to state the 'double nature' of man, without analysing it or seeming to see its full importance for ethics.

> The double nature of man remains a fact, whatever may be the right explanation of it.[19]

On the last page of his book, he is warning against 'cheap and easy' 'scientific' solutions of ethical problems; reminding us of

> the extreme complexity of the whole subject of human desire, emotion and action; and the paradoxical position of man, half animal and half angel, completely at home in none of the mansions of his Father's house. . . .[20]

But this remains only the statement of a fact about human experience, unaccompanied by any philosophical analysis of human nature. The lack of this analysis persists throughout most of the subsequent course of British ethics.

---

18 In T.K. Abbott, p. 84; see the whole section, pp. 65–84, and cf. *Critique of Practical Reason*, ibid., pp. 88, 117–9. 19 *Five Types of Ethical Theory*, p. 135. 20 Op. cit. p. 284. On p. 57, he says: 'Virtue consists in acting in accordance with the ideal nature of man'; but he does not develop the point, saying only that 'we can form the conception of a perfect watch, although no watches are perfect'; and that 'science makes great use of such idealised concepts as perfectly straight lines etc. . . . though there are no such objects in Nature' (cf. pp. 58–60) This, however, is not a helpful analogy. The 'ideal nature' of man, in an ethical context, surely means man as he knows he should be and could be if he lived up to the standards of morality that are embedded in his actual nature.

2   A.C. EWING

A.C. Ewing's first book on ethics, *The Definition of Good*, was published in 1947.[21] Though this was all after the inauguration of Wittgenstein's new way of philosophising, it was before the influence of the latter had been widely felt; and the thought of the book can rightly be called 'pre-Wittgenstein'. In 1959, Ewing published *Second Thoughts in Moral Philosophy*,[22] in which he re-examines his 'objectivist' position and explores the possibility of a rapprochement between it and what he calls the 'new subjectivism' of the neo-Wittgensteinian moralists. Dr Ewing has written many articles on ethics, many of them incorporated, more or less completely, in one or the other of these books.[23]   He has also published a more popular short book, *Ethics*.[24]

2.1   'The Definition of Good'

Ewing's earlier book remains one of the best presentations and ablest defences of ethical objectivism and intuitionism in recent British philosophy. Its critique of naturalism and of subjectivism is one of its strongest features. Naturalism, or the analysing of ethical propositions 'solely in terms of the concepts of a natural science', had indeed the laudable motive of seeking to give ethical statements an objective reference and justification. But naturalists did not see that their analysis quite simply abolishes ethical judgments entirely, replacing them by descriptive statements. What is missing from naturalistic analyses, says Ewing, is the notion of obligation, and this is precisely the most characteristic ethical concept.[25] The irrefutable answer to all naturalism is that

> Ethics is a branch of study on its own which cannot be reduced to or derived from any other. Good, right, obligation are not at all like non-ethical concepts and can't be reduced to them. They can be related to . . . but not identified with non-ethical concepts.[26] If all ethical concepts are analysable completely

21 Macmillan, New York and London.   22 Routledge and Kegan Paul, London.   23 Two of these are reprinted in *Readings in Ethical Theory*, eds., W. Sellars and John Hospers, namely, 'A Suggested Non-naturalistic Analysis of Good', from *Mind*, 1939 (op. cit., pp. 115–33); and 'Subjectivism and Naturalism in Ethics', from *Mind*, 1944 (op. cit., pp. 231–249). These are taken up substantially into *The Definition of Good*. The newer thought of Dr Ewing was first tried out in an article in *Analysis*, 13.2, December 1952, called 'A Middle Way in Ethics?' (pp. 33–8). It was also a feature of his paper 'Recent Developments in British Ethical Thought', printed in the Cambridge symposium, *British Philosophy in the Mid-Century*, Allen and Unwin, London, 1957, which article also presents a valuable survey and appraisal of the new post-Wittgensteinian developments in ethics.   24 Teach Yourself Books, English Universities Press, 1953.   25 *The Definition of Good*, pp. 56–62. The second chapter, pp. 36–78, is devoted to the critique of naturalism. Evolutionary ethics is examined, and shown to involve the vicious circle of first 'personalising' and 'moralising' biological evolution and then pretending to deduce morals from biological evolution. 'There can be no chance of defining "good" in terms of evolution unless . . . we mean by "evolution" "good change", and that would constitute a vicious circle' (pp. 73–4, and the whole section, pp. 41–74).   26 Op. cit., p. 111; cf. 33–4.

in terms of non-ethical, this will reduce ethics to something else and destroy its distinctive nature altogether.[27]

Ewing's objectivism involves the affirmation that ethical judgments are 'genuine judgments', that is fact-stating indicative propositions, not, e.g., 'exclamations, commands or wishes'; that they can be true or false, just as other factual statements can; and that they refer to objective facts, and not to the feelings or psychological states of the person who makes them.[28] This thesis was supported by a trenchant critique of subjectivism,[29] both in its older hedonistic forms, already criticised by Moore, Prichard and Ross, and in its newer expressions, emotivism and imperativism. Emotivism he called the 'exclamational view', and he pointed out that it makes it impossible for ethical statements to contradict one another, or to be true or false; and that it ignored the fact that, when we are trying to form moral judgments, we are not just arousing feelings but trying to find out the truth about something.[30] Imperativist analyses are likewise condemned because they ignore the assertive, truth-claiming element in ethical statements; because they cannot account for moral judgments about past events and about unfulfilled conditionals; and because they ignore the fact that commands themselves must be morally judged and cannot therefore be adequate analyses of moral judgments.[31] He finds that the imperativist theory has important resemblances with emotivism, and reduces ethical statements to exclamations.[32] All analyses of ethical statements into descriptions of human psychology are equally in error. 'We have an idea of ethical obligation [which is] not analysable without residuum in psychological terms.'[33]

There is obviously implied in all this a doctrine of the indefinability of ethical terms. By this he means the impossibility of 'reducing the central concept of ethics [i.e. 'good'] to non-ethical terms'. 'Good' is 'too ultimate and unique to be analysed in terms of anything else'.[34] This, of course, is pure Moorean orthodoxy. But Ewing, like Broad, recognises the legitimacy and the importance of 'defining' good non-naturalistically.[35] His book in fact gets its title from its author's proposed 'definition of good' in terms of 'ought', which in turn is, as in

---

27 p. 78. 28 pp. 3–6. 29 On p. 212, he writes: 'I think that it is an extremely important task, both practically and theoretically, to stem the tide of subjectivism and naturalism in ethics, for the development of such beliefs seems to me bound to weaken seriously the sense of moral obligation by taking away any rational basis for ethics.' 30 pp. 11–14. C.D. Broad called the emotivist view 'interjectional', because it analyses moral sentences into interjections, like 'Hurrah!' or 'Blast'. On the interjectional analysis, to utter a moral sentence in the indicative is like expressing a feeling of annoyance with so-and-so by exclaiming 'Damn you!' ('Some of the Main Problems of Ethics'. . . in *Readings in Philosophical Analysis*, pp. 548–9). 31 pp. 14–16, 70, 76. 32 It reduces ethical statements to the equivalent of: 'You are interfering with other people's wishes, damn you!' (p. 70). 33 pp. 33–4; cf. 62–8. 34 pp. 45–9. 35 p. 145–6. He holds that Moore would admit non-naturalistic analyses or 'definitions' of good; but, as we saw, this is just where Moore got tied up in his own peculiar epistemological knots and refused to let anything be said about 'good' except that it is 'good'. We admit however, that Moore was unable to stick consistently to this tautology, and himself analysed good in terms of 'worth having for its own sake'.

Broad, analysed in terms of 'fittingness'. 'Ought' is therefore the ultimate and irreducible ethical concept. Ewing's most characteristic doctrine is that

> 'the good' means 'what it is fitting to bring into existence for its own sake' or 'what ought to be brought into existence, other things being equal'. . . . When something is good, it is fitting that we should welcome it, rejoice in it if it exists, desire and seek it if it does not exist. . . . The various attitudes I have mentioned have something in common which is opposite to the common element in condemning, shunning, fearing, regretting., etc. The former may well be called pro-attitudes, the latter anti-attitudes. . . . What is good is a suitable object of pro-attitudes, what is evil a suitable object of anti-attitudes. What is intrinsically good is a suitable object of a pro-attitude for its own sake.[36]
> We may therefore define 'good' as 'fitting object of a pro-attitude'.[37]

This is, in general, a satisfactory analysis of 'good' and of the relation between 'good' and 'ought', and in fact it approximates to the Thomistic analysis.[38] However, as Ewing presents it, it has several weaknesses. He appeals to introspection to establish the uniqueness and 'non-naturalness' of ethical terms.

> Introspective analysis of one's state of mind is not always easy. All I can say is that when I try to see what I mean when I use ethical terms I find that I have present to my consciousness an idea generically different from any empirical psychological concepts.[39]

After Wittgenstein's criticism, it is doubtful whether this way of talking about 'introspecting one's state of mind' can be defended today. What is happening in such a case does not anyhow seem to be introspection but rather reflection upon linguistic usage and on the facts which determine correct linguistic usage.

Ewing appeals to intuition both for the truth of the general proposition that good means 'fitting object of a pro-attitude' and for the determination in particular cases of what is in this sense good. We have already seen many difficulties in this sort of appeal to intuition. Ewing's use of the concept escaped most of these difficulties; by intuition he meant the ultimate premises of moral reasoning.

> It is not only ethics but *all* reasoning which presupposes intuition. . . . Sooner or later we must come to something we see immediately (intuitively) to be true.

---

36 pp. 148–9.   37 p. 152; cf. 146–8, 175–6.   38 See *S. Theol.*, 1–2, 94, 2.   39 'Subjectivism and Naturalism in Ethics'. *Readings in Ethical Theory*, p. 123—a passage which is not verbally reproduced in *The Definition of Good*, though exactly similar phrases occur there. For example: 'I see that propositions about . . . "good" . . . are propositions which cannot be analysed adequately in psychological terms almost as clearly as I see that they cannot be analysed adequately in terms of physics or mathematics . . . I see that "good", "right", "duty", "ought", morality, are just not the sort of concepts which can ever be analysed completely in terms of psychology as I can see that sights cannot be analysed in terms of sounds' (pp. 43–4; cf. 48–50).

We cannot, whatever we do, get rid of intuition if we are to have any inference at all.[40]

Yet Ewing himself recognises the unhappy history and associations of the term 'intuition', and in his later volume he abandons it and proposes to speak instead of 'direct cognition' or 'immediate apprehension of something as true', which is presupposed by 'the possibility of reasoning itself'.[41] This way of speaking is preferable. It is close to that of Wittgenstein himself.[42]

A more serious defect of Ewing's theory arises frcm the old difficulty of the connection between 'ethical characteristics' and 'non-ethical characteristics'. It was in the interests of an uncompromising ethical objectivism that he asserted:

When we see that something is intrinsically good or some act morally obliga-tory, we also see that it must be so, its factual properties being what they are. Goodness, badness, obligatoriness and wrongness are not properties that could possibly be removed from an experience or action without the experience or action being in other ways different; and this impossibility is not merely the effect of causal laws. Hitler could not have done the actions which had the factual properties his actions towards the Jews possessed, and yet prevented the actions having the additional properties of badness or wrongness.[43]

Goodness and badness, rightness and wrongness are pronounced to be non-natural characteristics of things, necessarily connected with their factual or non-natural characteristics. They are declared to be as really *in* the things as the factual characteristics are. But goodness is analysed into 'fitting object of a pro-attitude'; and imperceptibly the emphasis shifts from the characteristics of the object to the attitudes of the subject.

These 'pro-attitudes' were described predominantly in terms of emotions and feelings—welcoming, rejoicing at, admiring, desiring, seeking; while 'anti-atti-tudes' are the emotional opposites, condemning, shunning, fearing, regretting etc.[44] It was indeed held that these feelings and emotions were objectively justified by the factual characteristics of the situation.

The ground [of the pro-attitude] lies, not in some other ethical concept, goodness, but in the concrete, factual characteristics of what we pronounce good. Certain characteristics are such that the fitting response to what pos-sesses them is a pro-attitude, and that is all there is to it.[45]

---

40 pp. 28–30.   41 *Second Thoughts in Moral Philosophy*, pp. 64–8. Cf. 'A Middle Way in Ethics', *Analysis*, 13.2, December 1952, p. 38: 'To say that we sometimes see by "intuition" what constitutes a good or bad reason in ethics is only to say that we can sometimes know or rationally think something to be a reason without having to give another reason why it is a reason, and that we can do this must be held by any view that gives any place at all to reasoning in ethics.'   42 See *Philosophical Investigations*, pp. 481–5; cf. II v; cf. A.J. Ayer, *The Problem of Knowledge*, Penguin Books, pp. 20–3, a passage referred to by Ewing in *Second Thoughts*, pp. 65–6.   43 *The Definition of Good*, p. 53.   44 Op. cit., p. 149; cf. *Second Thoughts*, p. 85: 'The term "pro-attitude" covers any favourable attitude towards something. . . . The most important are— choice, pursuit, approval, admiration, liking.'   45 *The Definition of Good*, p. 172.

But this language is not, after all, very different from that of philosophers who analyse ethical statements in terms of psychological states. It is highly instructive to compare the formulae of Ewing with those of two great American naturalists, John Dewey and R.B. Perry, and to see how closely they resemble one another. Dewey defines good as 'enjoyment plus authorisation'; the good is not merely enjoyed but enjoy*able*, not merely satisfying but satis*factory*.

To declare something satis*factory* is to assert that it meets specifiable conditions. It is . . . a judgment that the thing 'will do'. . . . It involves a prediction . . . it will *do*. It asserts a consequence the thing will actively institute; it will *do*. That it is satisfying is the content of a proposition of fact; that it is satisfactory is a judgment, an estimate, an appraisal. It denotes an attitude *to be* taken, that of striving to perpetuate and to make secure.[46]

There seems little difference between Dewey's 'satisfactory' and Ewing's 'fitting object of a pro-attitude'.
Perry defines value as 'any object of any interest'.

Any object, whatever it be, acquires value when any interest, whatever it be, is taken in it. . . . In other words, Aristotle was fundamentally mistaken when he said that, as a thing's 'apparent good' makes it an object of appetite, so its real good makes it the object of 'rational desire'. . . . Spinoza was fundamentally correct when he said that 'in no case do we strive for, wish for, long for or desire anything because we deem it to be good, but on the other hand we deem a thing to be good because we strive for it, wish for it, long for it or desire it'. The view may otherwise be formulated in the equation : x is valuable = interest is taken in x.[47]

This doctrine seems the opposite of Ewing's. But when Perry defends his interest theory against relativism, we find it hard to distinguish from Ewing's 'pro-attitude' theory. For Perry, 'interests' are 'objective' because they have 'a content or object other than themselves'; and value judgments are about these objects, not about the acts of judgment themselves.[48] It is not, therefore, surprising that Ewing in his 'second thoughts' should confess: 'I think I erred in giving my account on the whole primarily in terms of feelings.' He now feels that it would be better to speak of a

conative attitude which would lead one, if occasion arose, to pursue a certain policy in thought and action. . . . Clearly what matters is not whether we feel

---

46 From the chapter 'The Construction of Good', from *The Quest for Certainty* (1929), reprinted in *Readings in Ethical Theory*; see p. 276.   47 From the chapter, 'Value as Any Object of Any Interest', from *General Theory of Value* (1926), reprinted in *Readings in Ethical Theory*; see 292–3.   48 Ibid., pp. 297–8.

a desire for something good in the sense of an uneasy feeling proportionate to its goodness, whether we strive for its attainment.[49]

This way of speaking is preferable; it is also, incidentally, closer to that of Aquinas.[50] Ewing also now feels that the term 'fittingness' is objectionable, because it 'suggests too much analogy between ethics and aesthetics'. He wishes to replace it by 'reasonableness'.[51]

The fundamental difficulty remains, namely that of thinking of 'good' as a 'non-natural property' necessarily connected with natural properties. It was both the unacceptability of this thesis as it stands, and the sort of development which it logically suggested, which led Ewing to a compromise between objectivism and subjectivism. But Ewing's 'second thoughts' were called forth primarily by Wittgenstein's 'philosophical revolution'. This we are to examine in the final chapter. The section which follows is not therefore, in its proper chronological place; but this cannot be helped, and the development of Ewing's thought is intelligible and significant apart from explicit reference to Wittgenstein.

2.2 'Second Thoughts'

Ewing tells us that, when he wrote *The Definition of Good*, he had not thought that any intermediate position could exist between objectivism and subjectivism. Gradually, however, through reflection on the writings of philosophers who had been influenced by Wittgensteinian ideas, or what they took to be such—among whom he names Toulmin, Barnes, Hare, Miss Macdonald, Paul Edwards— Ewing came to think that 'a middle way in ethics' was possible. He makes the suggestion first in an article in *Analysis* in December 1952. The neo-Wittgensteinian slogan, 'Every statement has its own logic' is central in the argument of the article. He begins by referring to

> the suggestion coming from various sources that, when we do what is ordinarily called making ethical judgments, we are doing something which is, strictly speaking, neither judging nor expressing our emotions nor giving commands but which has points of similarity with all three and has, so to speak, a logic of its own, so that, though we are not making judgments which could strictly be called true or false the attitudes we take in questions of ethics can be right or wrong and have valid or invalid reasons.[52]

Ewing has become convinced that the competing theories each erred by giving a one-sided description of ethical judgments. Objectivism erred by assimilating

---

49 *Second Thoughts in Moral Philosophy*, pp. 88–9, 92–3.   50 *S. Theol.*, 1–2, 94, 2; *bonum est faciendum et prosequendum, et malum vitandum.*   51 *Second Thoughts*, pp. 93–5.   52 *Analysis*, 13.2, December 1952, p. 33; cf. p. 37. A similar statement of the 'intermediate view' is found in Ewing's paper in British Philosophy in the Mid-Century; see pp. 92–5. Cf. *Ethics*, p. 135.

them too closely to descriptive statements. This is open to two objections; first, in making 'goodness' a 'property' of objects, it seems to assimilate value too closely to fact; second, it makes ethical judgments too intellectualist, ignoring their emotional and practical character. Subjectivism erred by assimilating ethical judgments too closely to mere expressions of unreasoning emotion, ignoring their nature as assertions and their claim to truth and objectivity. The question becomes one of determining in what sense ethical judgments are 'judgments' and are 'objective' and are 'true', and what are the 'reasons' justifying their claim to truth.

Objectivism was too intellectualist about all these points. But Ewing sees the subjectivist danger in the new ways of speaking; and he protests that all that is required is to admit that

> 'true', 'valid', 'property' as applied in ethics, are not being used in the same sense as when applied elsewhere, not that they cannot be applied in ethics in any sense at all.[53]

He thinks that the truth of both positions could be preserved and their errors avoided by holding that ethical judgments are practical judgments which can have valid reasons and which can therefore be true or false in a special ethical sense of true or false. He says a danger, however, also in the latter suggestion; for, if we leave the ethical sense of terms like 'true' and 'property' indefinable,

> have we not put ourselves in a position in which we can say nothing about ethics except that it is what it is and is not what it is not?[54]

The thought of this article is repeated in Ewing's *Second Thoughts in Moral Philosophy*. One has the impression that Ewing is not too happy in his new intermediate position, and one feels that the objectivism he still wishes to defend emerges from it weakened. There is nothing that Ewing, both in his second and in his first thoughts about ethics so much wishes to repudiate as subjectivism.[55] Yet there is an undeniably subjectivist ring about many passages in his *Second Thoughts*. Ewing has now definitely repudiated the doctrine that 'good' is a 'non-natural property' of objects. This was the great bulwark of his initial

---

53 *Analysis*, 13.2, p. 34. 54 *Analysis*, 13.2, p. 37. 55 He regards 'subjectivist theories as dangerous practically' (*Second Thoughts*, pp. 57–8, 123). He reaffirms objectivism in many passages. 'The subjectivist overlooks the fact that in an ought judgment we are not merely expressing a conative attitude but asserting it to be justified and indeed imperatively required by the facts' (p. 77). 'Theoretical judgments express a primarily cognitive attitude and claim this to be justified (imposed on us) by the facts; ought judgments express a primarily conative attitude and assert the conation to be justified (imposed on us by the facts in a different way). The claim that the attitude is justified is at the very same time for both, also a claim that every other rational being ought to adopt it in a similar situation. That sounds intolerant, but it is inescapable from the nature of judgment' (p. 78). 'In so far as the value judgment claims that the pro-attitude is not merely there in fact but is rightly based on the nature of its object, it is a judgment about the object' (p. 86). Cf. pp. 20–2, 43–7, 54–5, 59–63, 70–4.

objectivism. This removed, he seems caught in a wave which bears him towards subjectivism.[56]

But there was, in Ewing's very objectivism a built-in propensity towards subjectivism. We have called attention to it in every objectivist or intuitionist since Moore. It has two elements: first, the assimilation of ethical judgments to immediate unreasoned responses which have many of the features of emotional responses or psychological reactions; second the proposition that these responses are called forth or justified by the factual, that is, the non-ethical qualities of the real. Ewing, as we saw, deplored, in his second book, the fact that in his first, he described 'pro-attitudes' too much in terms of feelings. But, he still does so, more often than not in his second book.[57] He has himself sometimes recognised that his language of pro-attitude is not so different from that of 'new subjectivists' who deny that ethical judgments are propositions, or can be true, at all.[58]

The second proposition has met us constantly in the course of this study and will be with us until the end. It is that ethical judgments are 'dependent for their truth on "natural properties" ',[59] that moral reasons, or 'reasons for adopting a favourable attitude',[60] are constituted by descriptions of the empirical or factual nature of the situation to be judged. In *The Definition of Good*, 'ethical predicates' were held to be 'non-natural characteristics' necessarily connected with 'natural characteristics' of objects. In *Second Thoughts*, there are no longer allowed to be 'non-natural characteristics', and ethical predicates are held to be 'attitudes justified by' the natural or non-ethical characteristics of objects. A big step has been taken towards overt subjectivism. But implicit subjectivism is equally present in both formulations.

---

56 See pp. 50–3. 'I am now going to make a very important concession and one which may even seem to some philosophers to destroy most of my view. . . . While I am sure that ethical words do not just describe 'natural' qualities or relations, I have now realised, thanks to those recent developments in ethics, . . . that it is dangerously misleading to say that they describe other, 'non-natural' qualities or relations. The trouble about this way of speaking is that it still treats these judgments as if they *described* something. It was realised that they did not give the same kind of information as do ordinary factual judgments, so it is supposed that they described something else of a peculiar kind, non-natural properties, and I, like many others, assumed that I could not maintain the objectivity and autonomy of ethics if I did not take this view. But the oddness and elusiveness of these 'non-natural' properties cast grave doubts on the objectivity of 'ethical judgments' and inclined people to say that they asserted nothing, whereas they should have said that they did not assert anything directly or at least primarily about the factual nature of the real . . . but only about the right way of action or evaluation. . . . What then [are] the non-natural concepts of ethics? Simply ways, I should now say, of regarding experiences, states of mind and actions which . . . in so far as they are right, express favourable or unfavourable attitudes which are justified by the facts. . . .' Cf. p. 83. 57 See p. 118: 'It would be a mistake to think of 'good' as ascribing another quality besides the factual qualities and not rather as signifying only a way of regarding the latter for which objective validity is claimed.' Cf. pp. 50–3, cited in the preceding note; also pp. 73–4, 85–6, 105. 58 See *Analysis*, 13.2, p. 35. These philosophers, he says, maintain that ethical statements 'express certain attitudes and maintain the rightness or validity of these attitudes;' while, in *The Definition of Good*, he himself had maintained 'that the assertion that something is good is to be analysed as saying that we ought to take a certain attitude towards it'. 'On both views', he continues, 'ethical statements may be said to prescribe attitudes and actions rather than give descriptions. . . .' Cf. *Ethics*, pp. 118–9. 59 *Second Thoughts*, p. 47. 60 Op. cit., p. 63.

There is, of courses a quasi-naturalistic fallacy committed here. Ewing has an unhappy conscience about it. He protests that a doctrine is not naturalistic unless it *reduces* ethical propositions to merely factual ones, or holds they can be deduced *formally* therefrom.[61] But this is special pleading. A doctrine is naturalistic if it holds that ethical judgments depend exclusively on non-ethical situations and that moral reasons are found in non-moral facts; and Ewing's does. But, like all naturalistic or quasi-naturalistic theories, this one is camouflaged, so that even its author cannot recognise it, by the surreptitious importing of ethical values into the alleged 'natural' facts. Ewing thinks that

the ethical proposition, I ought not to do A, follows directly from the factual proposition that to do A will hurt another person.

It quite certainly does not, unless A is 'wrongfully hurting another person'; and this is not a factual proposition. Ewing says it is the 'factual nature of lies and their consequences' that make them wrong;[62] but lies are morally wrong actions, not non-moral facts; and their wrongness will not be altered even if in particular cases their factual consequences are good. The confusion of moral with non-moral predicates, which is the heart of the naturalistic fallacy, is here obvious.

The basic error of all this way of thinking is that it makes a radical separation between 'fact' and 'value'. It is because they all define 'fact' as 'non-ethical state of affairs' that British moralists can find no justification for ethical judgments except non-ethical descriptions. It is this prejudice that precludes for them the question which to our mind is basic for ethics, namely: Are there facts which not merely 'justify', or 'give valid reasons for', values, but also incarnate and indeed *are* values? The answer to this question will require a philosophy of man, the moral person. The existentialists rightly speak of man as the 'bearer of value'. Sartre says man is 'the being by whom values exist'.[63] He intends this in a subjectivist sense. But this is to distort our whole experience of value as transcendent. The point we wish to retain is that man cannot exist without value existing in him and in the things that are related to him as objects of his action. But the world of facts is the world of man's moral and moralising action. Man cannot exist in the world without facts receiving value in themselves from his presence. In man, and because of man, nature is also value.

Ewing at times seems to be groping after something like this. He speaks once of values as radicated in 'persons and states of persons'.

We are under obligations to take favourable and unfavourable attitudes to certain objects and on certain occasions because of the objective factual nature

61 Op. cit., p. 48. Cf. p. 99: 'The mistake of naturalism as such is not that it supposes normative propositions to follow from factual but that it reduces normative propositions to factual.' For the assertion that ethical judgments depend on the factual nature of the situation, see pp. 46–8, 60, 63, 68–70, 77–8, 86–7, 118. 62 p. 48. 63 *Being and Nothingness*, E. trans., p. 627.

of these. The 'objects' to which I refer are indeed not just physical, they are persons or states of persons, but this does not contradict what I have said. Human beings are part of reality, and to say that all ethical judgments refer to persons and their states is not to say that they just depend for their validity on the wishes or arbitrary judgments or feelings of the speaker or are made true by these. . . . The objectivity of ethics [can be] used as a starting-point in metaphysical argument. At any rate reality must be such that ethical and evaluative judgments can be legitimately made . . .[64]

But his distinction of 'fact' from 'value' would probably lead him to maintain that persons too and their states are factual and not 'moral'. The same prejudice, and an inveterate repugnance towards metaphysics, will be found later to prevent Mayo and Hampshire in their turn from deriving much profit from their project to reintegrate ethics with philosophy of man. Still, to have posed a question, to have seen a need, is progress in philosophy.

Before leaving Ewing, it is only fair to say that, despite the criticisms we have offered, he seems to us to have said, on the whole, more wise things and true things about ethics than most writers in English since Moore.

---

64 *Second Thoughts*, p. 69.

CHAPTER SIX

Logical Positivism and Ethics

The first of the two schools of thought which claimed Ludwig Wittgenstein as their progenitor but which Wittgenstein repudiated was logical positivism. This movement exercised a certain influence on British philosophy and ethics, and enjoyed a brief notoriety, chiefly through the early work of A.J. Ayer. Before examining the ethical theory of Ayer, it is necessary to have some idea of the philosophical and ethical positions of the logical positivists.

1 THE 'VIENNA CIRCLE'

The name 'logical positivism' was first attached to the doctrines of the group known as the 'Vienna Circle', which was founded by Moritz Schlick in 1929. Schlick had been appointed in 1922 to the professorship in the philosophy of the inductive sciences which had been created for Ernst Mach in 1895. The best-known members of the Circle were Rudolf Carnap, Otto Neurath, Herbert Feigl, Karl Menger, Hans Hahn, Kurt Gödel. It worked in close collaboration with the 'Society of Empirical Philosophy' at Berlin, among whose members were Hans Reichenbach and F. Kraus. During its short period of collective existence the Circle displayed impressive energy. It published from 1930 on a journal called *Erkenntnis*, edited jointly by Carnap and Reichenbach; also a series of monographs called *Einheitswissenschaft* (Unified Science).[1]

But by 1938 the Circle had largely ceased to exist as a group, mainly because of the exiling of its members by Hitler. Schlick had himself died tragically in 1936, being shot on the steps of the University by a demented pupil whose thesis on ethics he had failed. Hahn had died. Carnap, Feigl, Menger, and Gödel, as well as Reichenbach, had gone to university chairs in the United States. Neurath took refuge in Holland, and died in England early in the War. Waismann went to Cambridge, where he became an important influence in philosophy, though his thought moved far away from logical positivism. Popper taught at the London School of Economics from 1946 on, and then became Professor of Logic and Scientific Method in the University of London.[2]

---

1 Not all contributors to the latter series were members of the Circle; it was in this series for example, that Karl Popper's *Logik der Forsshung* (The Logic of Scientific Discovery) first appeared. Though Popper shared the scientific-rationalist optimism of the Circle, he was a critic of many of its philosophical theses.
2 See A.J. Ayer, 'The Vienna Circle', in '*The Revolution in Philosophy*', ed. Gilbert Ryle, pp. 70–87; also the volume *Logical Positivism*, edited by A.J. Ayer, in the series: J.Passmore, *A Hundred Years of Philosophy*, pp. 369–93; J.R. Weinberg, *An Examination of Logical Positivism* (Kegan Paul, London, 1936).

The positivism of the circle was a continuation of the nineteenth century positivist tradition at Vienna, and was particularly influenced by Mach. Its ambition was to complete Mach's programme of purging science, and therefore knowledge, of the last vestiges of the 'occult qualities' and other 'sham ideas of the old metaphysics'.[3] This was accompanied by a rather nineteenth-century sort of confidence in progress through science and in the moral betterment of mankind through the application of scientific method to social and moral problems. This spirit ensured that the members of the Vienna Circle, when dispersed, found themselves quickly at home in the universities of Britain and America, where an even older empiricist tradition had been accompanied by a similar radicalism and a somewhat romantic rationalist optimism in the sphere of morals.

The presence of the term 'logical' in the designation of these philosophers, marks, however a significant twentieth-century addition to the older positivism. Empiricism had always been embarrassed by the problem of how to account for the necessary and *a priori* truths of mathematics and logic. John Stuart Mill had been forced into the impossible position of maintaining that they were empirical generalisations. The failure of his attempt left the problem intact of explaining how there can be necessary truth if all knowledge comes from sense particulars. It was the new logic of Frege, Russell and Whitehead, and Ludwig Wittgenstein which seemed to offer the explanation required by empiricism. Mathematics was shown to be reducible to logic; and mathematical and logical propositions were interpreted as being necessarily true because tautologously true; they belong to the structure of language and tell us nothing of the nature of reality. They show us to what we are necessarily committed by the requirement of consistency with the definitions which we adopt as initial axioms; but the definitions themselves are conventions; and internal consistency with them tells us nothing about the world.

This explanation of *a priori* truth seemed to remove all obstacle to the development of a total empiricism. A first principle of this is that there are no propositions which are at once necessary and factual; there is nothing corresponding to what Kant called synthetic a priori propositions. There are two and only two classes of meaningful proposition: fact-stating propositions and necessary propositions.

The former are empirical hypotheses, comprising the statements of common-sense observation and, more importantly, the propositions of the empirical sciences. The latter are the tautologies of logic and mathematics. The only propositions which can provide any new knowledge or give any knowledge of the world are the propositions of the sciences. These are obviously empirical in nature and must stand the test of empirical verification. All logical positivists accept some form of a principle of empirical verification, according to

3 See J. Passmore, op. cit., pp. 322–4.

which no proposition can be both factual and meaningful unless sensory observations[4] are somehow 'relevant to the determination of its truth or falsehood'.

All other propositions are meaningless. In particular, the propositions of metaphysics are meaningless. They are multiply so; for they claim to be both necessary and factual, or to be about the world, without being empirically verifiable; or they claim to be about metempirical entities which, by definition are unknowable and hence non-existent, because all knowledge of entities is empirical. The foundation manifesto of the Vienna Circle declared its aims to be: 'first to provide a secure foundation for the sciences; and second to demonstrate the meaninglessness of all metaphysics'.[5] As for philosophy, its role cannot be to discover or enunciate facts; for only the sciences can do that. The only possible role for philosophy is to be the logical ancilla of scientific research, to study the logic of the language of science.[6] Philosophy is, therefore, second-order knowledge; its concern is with words, not with facts; it is logical analysis of the words employed in science.[7]

We shall see that there are points of convergence between this doctrine and that of Wittgenstein's *Tractatus*. The Logical positivists' explanation of *a priori* truth was taken over from Wittgenstein; their logical 'elimination of metaphysics' came mainly from him and from Russell. It was natural that they should look on Wittgenstein as a kindred spirit. Schlick in particular sought Wittgenstein out and established connexions with him during the time he was preparing the foundation of the Vienna Circle. The problem of the relationship of the *Tractatus*-Wittgenstein to positivism is not a simple one. The *Tractatus* 'eliminated' metaphysics as sayable or as science—but kept its great themes as the 'unsayable', 'the Mystical'. The *Tractatus* says nothing about the origin of ideas; it has no empiricist—or other—theory of knowledge; yet its logical theory of meaning seems to require an epistemology and a psychology, and only an empiricist epistemology or psychology would seem to fit in with the logic. Wittgenstein quite casually identified 'the total natural science' with 'the totality of true propositions', and 'the propositions of natural science' with 'what can be said'.[8] He had no 'principle of verification'; yet his doctrine that a proposition cannot have factual meaning

---

4 This is the vague formulation finally arrived at by Ayer in the first edition of *Language, Truth and Logic*, p. 38. It was modified in the Introduction to the second edition; see p. 13. 5 See Weinberg, op. cit., p. 1. 6 See Carnap, *Syntax of Language* (Routledge, London, 1937), p. xiii (quoting from a letter he wrote in 1934): 'In our 'Vienna Circle', as well as in kindred groups (in Poland, France, England, U.S.A., and, amongst individuals, even in Germany), the conviction has grown and is steadily increasing that metaphysics can make no claim to possessing a scientific character. That part of the work of philosophy which may be held to be scientific in its nature,—excluding the empirical questions which can be referred to empirical science,—consists of logical analysis. The aim of logical syntax is to provide a system of concepts, a language, by the help of which the results of logical analysis will be exactly formulable. Philosophy is to be replaced by the logic of science, i.e., by the logical analysis of the concepts and sentences of the sciences, for the logic of science is nothing other than the logical syntax of the language of science.' 7 See Carnap, *Philosophy and Logical Syntax* (London, 1935), pp. 69–71, 83–5; cf. Ayer, op. cit., pp. 43ff., 151–3. 8 *Tractatus* 4.11, 6.53.

unless we know what factual difference its being true or false would make, had a superficial resemblance to the positivist verification theory of meaning.[9] The *Tractatus* regards philosophy as second-order knowledge, as 'not a theory but an activity' of 'logical clarification of thoughts', of elucidation.[10] But the *Tractatus* still maintained that 'even if all possible scientific questions be answered', we would be no nearer to a solution of the problems of human existence.[11] Parts of the *Tractatus* could undoubtedly be developed in a positivist direction. It would seem that the mind of Wittgenstein around 1929 had moved nearer to logical positivism than at any other period.[12] But the influence was not unilateral; Waismann was to move from positivism to positions more and more reminiscent of the mystical metaphysics of the *Tractatus*.[13]

2 LOGICAL POSITIVISM AND ETHICS

Moral judgments obviously posed a special problem for the logical positivists; since they claim to be both necessary and factual. For Kant, they were an outstanding example of synthetic *a priori* judgment. But all such propositions are ruled out by logical positivist definitions. Whatever moral judgments may be, they cannot be propositions. Wittgenstein, in the *Tractatus*, drew the conclusion that there 'can be no ethical propositions'; but maintained the absoluteness of value by locating it in the sphere of the Mystical. But for positivists there can be no mystical. Hence moral judgments must either be somehow reduced to empirical propositions; or analysed as non-propositional, or non-fact-stating and non-truth-claiming sentences.

2.1 *Rudolf Carnap*

Carnap, in the first of three lectures which he delivered in the University of London in 1934, with the aim of 'explaining the main feature of the method of philosophising of the Vienna Circle,'[14] interpreted value judgments as 'norms' or

9 4.024: 'To understand a proposition means to know what is the case, if it is true.' Cf. 2.201–2.225, 4.021–2, 4.46–4.4661. Passmore writes: 'According to Wittgenstein, the positivists misunderstood remarks he had let drop in conversation. "I used at one time to say," he is reported as remarking, "that, in order to get clear how a certain sentence is used, it was a good idea to ask oneself the question: How would one try to verify such an assertion? But that's just one way of getting clear about the use of a word or sentence. . . . Some people have turned this suggestion about asking for the verification into a dogma. . . ." ' (*A Hundred Years of Philosophy*, p. 371). 10 4.112. 11 6.52. 12 See G.H. Von Wright, in Malcom, *Memoir*, pp. 12–14. On the relation of the *Tractatus* to empiricism, see G.E.M. Anscombe, *An Introduction to Wittgenstein's* Tractatus, pp. 25–31, 49–50, 150–1. We have discussed the question in an article called 'New Light on Wittgenstein', in *Philosophical Studies*, X (Maynooth, December 1960). 13 See, e.g. his paper, 'How I see Philosophy', in *Contemporary British Philosophy*, ed. H.D. Lewis (Macmillan, London, 1956), pp. 447–90. 14 Published as *Philosophy and Logical Syntax*, Psyche Miniatures (Kegan Paul, London, 1935). Carnap was then Professor of Philosophy at the German University of Prague.

'rules' whose correct form of expression would be sentences in the imperative mood. 'Killing is evil' is only an alternative way of saying, 'Do not kill'. But it is a misleading alternative. It has deceived most philosophers into thinking that ethical judgments are assertions, which can be true or false, which can be reasoned about and can be matter for argument or proof. In fact, these judgments are merely expressions of wishes; they are commands 'in a misleading grammatical form'. They are neither true nor false. They do not assert anything and can neither be proved nor disproved. Ethical judgments are not empirically verifiable, and they are not tautologies either; hence they have no meaning. But this does not destroy their point; for their point was not to have a meaning in the sense of conveying information or giving knowledge, but to express a wish or issue an order.

> The propositions of normative ethics, whether they have the form of rules or the form of value judgments, have no theoretical sense and are not scientific propositions (taking the word 'scientific' to mean any assertive proposition).[15]

Carnap, therefore, does not adopt a strictly emotive theory of ethical judgments. He has, however, a doctrine of the emotivist or expressive use of language, which he uses to explain the significance of metaphysics. He distinguishes the representative from the expressive of language. Representative language informs us about what is the case in the world. Expressive language merely manifests our feelings, as laughter does, or as interjections do. Whole regions of discourse such as poetry, have no representative functions, but only an expressive one: their aim is to express certain feelings of the writer and excite similar feelings in us. Carnap declared that the Vienna Circle's thesis was that metaphysics belonged to the same region of language as lyric poetry.

> Metaphysical propositions are neither true nor false because they assert nothing; they contain neither knowledge nor error; they lie completely outside the field of knowledge, of theory, outside the domain of truth or falsehood. But they are, like laughing, lyrics and music, expressive.[16]

Yet metaphysics is not harmless, as poetry is, for it *seems* to make assertions and claims to be informative and true. Danger lies in the fact that metaphysics is deceptive: 'It gives the illusion of knowledge without actually giving any knowl-

---

15 Op. cit., pp. 24–5. The crude empiricism of the theory of meaning on which this rests is shown by the following: 'From the sentence 'killing is evil', we cannot deduce any proposition about future experiences. Thus the sentence is not verifiable and has no theoretical sense and the same is true of all other value sentences.' 16 pp. 27–30. What metaphysics expresses is 'not so much temporary feelings as permanent emotional or volitional dispositions'. For example, monism may express an even and harmonious mode of life; dualism, the emotional state of one who sees life as an eternal struggle; ethical rigorism may be expressive of a strong sense of duty or perhaps of the desire to rule severely; realism may express extraversion, idealism introversion.

edge. That is why we reject it.'[17] The emotive theory of ethics is simply the application to ethics of the analysis here made of metaphysics.

2.3   *Hans Reichenbach*

The ethical theory of Hans Reichenbach is similar to that of Carnap.[18] His starting point is the familiar positivist dogma that knowledge is either synthetic or analytic, finding expression either in the propositions of the sciences or in the tautologies of logic and mathematics. No part of knowledge can be moral, and morality can have no cognitive content or backing. Knowledge is never normative; morality is never cognitive. The great mistake of traditional philosophy was to confuse cognition with ethics.[19] It also supposed that ethical judgments are necessary judgments; but this too is a mistake, for only analytic or tautologous propositions can be necessary. The basic error has been to suppose that ethical expressions are statements. They are not statements of any kind, but 'directives', commands disguised as statements, wishes which we entertain in order to guide our own behaviour or which we express with the intention of influencing the behaviour of others.[20] Moral words do influence others because 'our fellow men are conditioned to respond to (such) words as instruments of our will'. The sense of obligation accompanying these 'volitional decisions' is explained naturalistically as deriving from the pressures of the social group. For it was the human group which originally set up these norms and conditioned us to conform to them.[21]

Reichenbach does not seem very consistent with this when he goes on to say that we must each take and stand by his own volitional decisions. A man's moral judgments are, in fact, merely the expressions of his own personal wishes and attitudes here and now.[22] We feel indeed that our moral judgments are 'true' for all men; but that is only because we wish that all men should conform to our moral directives. In a democratic society

> everybody is entitled to set up his own moral imperatives and to demand that everyone follow these imperatives.[23]

He may, of course, only use democratic means in trying to 'steer the group in the direction of his own volitions'.[24]

Reichenbach argues that ultimate moral principles are unarguable and unjustifiable. Justification of one value judgment could only be by another one which

---

17 p. 31. Cf. pp. 15–21.   18 See *The Rise of Scientific Philosophy* (University of California Press, (1951) 1958), pp. 50–73, 276–302. Reichenbach became Professor at the University of California; he died in 1953.   19 His fourth chapter is entitled: 'The Search for Moral Directives and the Ethico–cognitive Parallelism'. On p. 277, he says: 'The modern analysis of knowledge makes a cognitive ethics impossible.' It is, of course, only logical positivist definitions that make cognitive ethics impossible by so defining 'knowledge' that there could be no ethical knowledge.   20 Op. cit, pp. 280–1.   21 285–6.   22 pp. 287–90.   23 p. 295.   24 p. 300.

would be equally unjustifiable. We can influence or persuade others to adopt our goals; we cannot prove the validity of our goals. There are no true or absolute goals. Reasoning in ethics can only concern internal consistency with chosen goals; it cannot validate the goals.[25] The argument here is exactly parallel to the logical positivist account of reasoning in logic and mathematics.

The doctrine that moral judgments are individual decisions which each man must make for himself is held to be the only moral doctrine compatible with democracy and moral progress. Absolute ethics is opposed to change and progress., refuses the democratic process of reform by discussion.[26] It is the ethics of the fanatic and the anti-democrat.

> The person educated in an empiricist approach to ethics is better prepared than the absolutist to become an adjusted member of society.[27]

To look for truth or proof or certainty in ethics is a failure of nerve, a surrender of liberty of conscience into the hands of some authoritarian master. But democratic man is his own master. We must trust our own volitions because they are our own volitions.

> Human will is its own progenitor and its own judge. . . . There is no more purpose or meaning in the world than you put into it. Ethics comes from within: it expresses an 'I will' not a 'there is'. . . . There is no escape from the commitment to one's own volitions into an objective morality. . . .[28]

In accordance with the logical positivist conception of philosophy as 'second-order thinking', or as logical analysis, Reichenbach holds that ethical philosophy is neutral in respect of value-judgments; it is not concerned with 'moral issues' but with 'the nature of morality.'[29] The most interesting thing about Reichenbach for us, however, is the ease with which he can graft his logical positivist thesis into a certain American tradition. We speak of one rather predominant version of American liberalism, which, while it has largely rejected Protestant religion, retains some of the reflexes of what we may call sociological Protestantism. It identifies authority or the claim to certainty in religion or morals with political authoritarianism. It conjoins belief in progress, in science and in democracy, with an anti-clericalism, which is mainly an automatic response to the associated emotional stimuli, 'medieval', 'inquisition', 'Galileo'. This tradition associates ethical relativism with tolerance, with political liberalism and with moral progress.[30] Its expression in Britain, which we shall encounter frequently in future chapters, has been called 'moral protestantism'. Paradoxically, its positions fre-

---

25 pp. 280, 314–5, 320. **26** pp. 297–301, 305; cf. 64–6. **27** p. 300. **28** pp. 292, 302, 306, 318; cf. 301, 323. **29** p. 295; cf. 312. **30** Santayana has amusingly remarked that, for most of his readers, 'Naturalism and humanism meant no popery, the rights of man, pragmatism, international and cosmopolitan culture' (see Passmore, *A Hundred Years of Philosophy*, p. 290). We shall meet this mentality again in Paul Edwards.

quently have a remarkable similarity to those of Sartre, himself above all a romantic rationalist.

3 BRITISH PRECURSORS OF AYER

Logical positivism in Britain received its classic formulation in A.J. Ayer's early book, *Language, Truth and Logic*.[31] But its doctrines both in general philosophy and in ethics, were fully in line with the long empiricist tradition in British philosophy, and had been anticipated, with remarkable closeness, both by some nineteenth-century positivists and by two twentieth-century students of language.

The division of meaningful propositions into empirical hypotheses and tautologies, on which logical positivism mainly rests, is found already almost *ad litteram* in Hume. All that positivists were to say about the meaninglessness of metaphysics was already in the last paragraph of Hume's *Enquiry Concerning Human Understanding*:

> When we run over libraries, persuaded of these principles, what havoc we must make? If we take in our hand any volume; of divinity or school metaphysics, for instance; let us ask, *Does it contain any abstract reasoning concerning quantity or number?* No. *Does it contain any experimental reasoning concerning matter of fact and existence?* No. Commit it then to the flames: for it can contain nothing but sophistry and illusion.

Towards the end of the nineteenth century, scientists like W.K. Clifford and Karl Pearson were popularising ideas similar to those of Mach, whom they admired; and these ideas have a strong resemblance to those of the logical positivists.[33] Ayer's thought was anticipated also, on many points, by the typically nineteenth-century materialist-agnostic-radical, Leslie Stephen.

3.1   *Ogden and Richards*

Closer precursors of Ayer, both in time and in ideas, were the two Cambridge scholars, C.K. Ogden, a psychologist, and T.A. Richards, student of literary criticism and of language. Already from 1910 onward they had been working together on a philosophy of language and meaning. They were publishing many of their ideas in periodical form during 1920–2. Finally their famous book, *The*

---

31 The first edition was published by Gollancz in 1936; a second edition, with a new Introduction, appeared in 1946.   32 Section xii, part iii; Selby-Bigge edition (1902) 1951, p. 165. Ayer proclaims his affinity with Hume in the Preface to his first edition.   33 See Passmore, *A Hundred Years of Philosophy*, pp. 324–6; Pearson's *Grammar of Science*.

Meaning of Meaning, appeared in 1923.[34] Much of what Ayer was to say in 1936 about meaning, about metaphysics and about ethics, had already been said by Ogden and Richards in 1923.

Ogden and Richards distinguish two uses of language, the symbolic or referential and the emotive. The former is the 'reflective, intellectual use of language', which coincides with its use by the sciences. Only this makes statements, conveys information, imparts knowledge. Only this use of language has factual meaning, and its meaning is the facts which its symbols are used to refer to or represent. Only of language so used is it meaningful to ask whether it is true or false; this is the same as to ask, whether the facts it refers to or 'stands for' have empirical existence or not. The test of whether a given use of words is symbolic or not will be the question: 'Is this true or false in the ordinary strict scientific sense?'[35]

Contrasted with this is the emotive use of language which is 'the use of words to express or excite feelings and attitudes'. Words thus used function like interjections. Ogden and Richards always stress the two functions of emotive language, the 'suasory and the emotive'; or 'the expression of emotions, attitudes, moods, intentions etc. in the speaker, and their communication, i.e. their evocation in the listener'; or again, the use of words as 'expressions or stimulants of attitudes'.[36] With regard to the emotive use of words 'no question as to their truth in the strict sense can directly arise'. Their purpose is not truth-stating, that is, scientific, but attitude-evoking. 'Provided that the attitude or feeling is evoked' this use of language has fulfilled its purpose and any information or truth incidentally conveyed has a purely subordinate role. The only question one can raise about emotive language concerns 'the character of the attitude aroused' and the successfulness of the language in having this attitude accepted by others.[37] The question of the 'truth or falsity of the statements is of no consequence'; 'it is not necessary to know what things are in order to take up fitting attitudes towards them'.[38]

This distinction was first conceived by Ogden and Richards as a means of contrasting science and poetry. A psychologist and a literary critic had obvious competence in these two domains. The distinction is thus far plausible.[39] But the two authors stray from their specialism to apply the same distinction to philosophy and religion. They find that the metaphysical and the religious uses of

---

34 Published by Routledge, London. A second edition appeared in 1926, a third in 1930, a fourth in 1936 and an eighth in 1946, each with a short additional Preface. Our edition is the tenth (1949). It is odd that Warnock should say that 'Ogden and Richards published their famous book' and 'first introduced the word "emotive"' in the same year (1936) that *Language Truth and Logic* was published (*Ethics since 1900*, p. 84). 35 Op.cit., p. 150, and pp. 10–11, 149, 159 , 238–9. 36 pp. 123, 149, 151. They instance 'Hurrah'!; or 'Poetry is a spirit' or 'Man is a worm'. 37 pp 150, 239. We may speak metaphorically of the truth of emotive language, where we mean the appropriateness or genuineness of the attitudes it evokes; but this 'truth' (the authors call it 'Truth') is totally different from the genuine truth of statements or symbolic language ('Truths') (p. 241). 38 pp. 239,159. 39 They quote Professor Mackenzie as saying that when Shelley wrote: 'Hail to thee blithe spirit, thou never went', 'he did not mean to deny that the lark belongs to the class Avis' (p. 238).

language are sheerly emotive, but that both are guilty of deceit in pretending instead to convey truth. Their first encounter with metaphysics and theology is in their second chapter, on 'The Power of Words'. This is, in part, an anthropological essay on the magic power of the word and the name among primitive peoples; and in part a theory about the survival of this primitive belief among philosophers and divines. The writers enjoy themselves in pursuing 'the history of spells, verbal magic and verbal medicine, whether as practised by the Trobriand magician . . . or by the modern metaphysician'.[40] They have the support of Rignano and Ribot in finding in scholasticism and idealism—for these for them are one—nothing but 'verbomania'; their formulae mean nothing and strictly say nothing, but they have 'effective resonance', or 'bombic capacity'; they are noises which, like music, arouse 'harmonious series of emotional echoes'.[41] The same is true of the philosophies of Plato and Aristotle, of the whole philosophy of Being, of Hegelianism, of modern logicians like Russell[42] and modern 'mystics' like Whitehead. Until recent times, apart from William of Occam, Bacon and Hobbes, civilised mankind has slept for two thousand years under the enchantment of words.[43]

Not much follows from this except that Ogden and Richards do not like metaphysics or religion. A more serious attempt to justify their dislike is made later when they try to convict metaphysics of logical mistakes. Their thought is essentially the same as that of Russell's Theory of Descriptions and Wittgenstein's *Tractatus*. The mistake of traditional philosophy has been

> the mistaking of symbolic machinery for referents . . . (the) invention of non-existent entities in order to account for the systematic use of symbols.[44]

It is thus that Universals, Subsistent Entities, Being, Relations, have been invented, and with them metaphysics. At their origin is the error of thinking that words like 'all', 'is', 'or', 'if', must stand for something, whereas they are only 'symbolic conveniences', 'corrective structural machinery.[45] Metaphysics is simply 'grammatical mistakes hypostatised; its concepts are 'phantoms due to linguistic misconception'.[46] At its source is a desire for the impossible, a desire to know the *why* of the world, whereas we can know about the world only what science tells us, that is to say, the *what*. The best, and the worst that can be said about metaphysics is that it is poetry masquerading as science.[47] The same is true of religion. If it recognised its role as being the same as that of poetry, as being, not to give knowledge, make statements, be true or false, but simply 'to induce a fitting attitude to experience', religion would be harmless. But instead religions

---

40 p. 39.   41 pp. 40–3.   42 They speak of the Russell of the Meinong-ian or so-called 'Platonic' period, before the promulgation of the Theory of Descriptions. These references to Russell are survivals from early versions of the text.   43 pp. 29–35.   44 pp. 94, 96; cfr. 133–4, 246.   45 pp. 93–103. On p. 97, they write: 'No argument about the world is valid if based merely upon the way a symbol system behaves.' The thought is the same as Wittgenstein's, that 'logical constants do not represent'—except that Ogden and Richards have an explicitly empiricist theory of meaning.   46 p. 250; cf. 248. They call on p. 135 for a 'Eugenics of language'.   47 p. 82 and note.

profess to give true knowledge; they confuse their emotion and rhetoric with science, and exploit this confusion.[48] They must therefore be pronounced 'unmistakably pathological growths'.

The emotive theory is next applied by Ogden and Richards to ethical terms. These are 'symbolically blank but emotionally active'. In view of what we have several times said about the ease of the transition from intuitionism to emotivism, it is significant that our authors explicitly begin from Moore's thesis that good is 'a unique, unanalysable concept'. It is indefinable, they go on, precisely because it does not state anything; it 'stands for nothing whatever and has no symbolic function'. When we say 'this is good', we are merely referring to *this*, and the phrase 'is good' makes 'no difference whatever' to our reference.

> It serves only as an emotive sign expressing our attitude to *this*, and perhaps evoking similar attitudes in other persons or inciting them to actions of one kind or another.[49]

Traditional ethics has been built on the mistake of thinking that moral judgments are statements and that there must exist moral realities corresponding to them. We can escape from its confusion and its bogus entities only by realising the emotional character of moral judgments. Only thus can we hope also to take the temper out of moral discussions. Where our moral disputes turn on questions of fact, let us appeal to science; where they turn on emotional differences, let us resort to persuasion or agree to differ. Only then will ethics, and conversation, be scientifically conducted.[50]

Thus we have, in Ogden and Richards, an almost complete anticipation of the doctrine of Ayer, without a mention of the term logical positivism. The 'elimination

---

48 pp. 158–9. 49 pp. 124–5. 50 pp. 120–4, 126–38, 250. A similar hope seems still to exist at Cambridge; e.g. John Wilson, in *Language and the Pursuit of Truth* (Cambridge University Press, 1956), agrees with Ogden and Richards that 'only the empirical sciences can give us genuine information about facts' and says 'this is why people place more faith in scientists than in moralists, philosophers, politicians and men of religion:—the scientists produce results, the others do not'. Contrasting with the progress of science is the stagnation and the unsettlable controversies of metaphysics and ethics. We are not even agreed about what the propositions of the latter mean or how they could be verified. But agreement is *per se* possible here too, if we had similar experiences and if we found agreement useful or advantageous. The problem is: can people be got to share experiences of a kind which would make it useful for them to agree on the meaning and verification of metaphysical and ethical propositions? With regard to value judgments, the question is: Can people be got to accept the same set of criteria? There is no logical way of getting them to do so. But there could be psychological ways; and recent progress in psychology and the human sciences justifies the hope that people can, eventually, by their aid, be got to agree in value-judgments. 'Then we shall all hold the same set of criteria for all values . . . and shall be able to say what is true and what is not true in ethics with certainty.' At any rate what is certain is that 'only a scientific approach to our problems of value can help to solve them.' For metaphysics, the case is more difficult, for the nature of the experiences which might verify its claims is more elusive. But 'it may be possible to discover or to notice experiences of a special kind which we might use as a basis for the verification of metaphysical statements.' There does seem to be a basic 'metaphysical experience common to religion, to mysticism and to natural euphoria or 'feeling in tune with the world'. If this were investigated, it might become a basis for metaphysics and might enable us to give a meaning to the sentence, 'God exists'. Op.cit., pp. 70–4, 81–97.

of metaphysics' and the emotive theory of ethics need no ancestry other than the long tradition of British empiricism and the spirit of rationalist utopianism which so strongly pervaded nineteenth- and early twentieth-century Cambridge and which we found so characteristic of the entourage of Moore.

3.2 W.H.F. Barnes

The first statement of the emotive theory of ethics by a British philosopher was made as a suggestion by W.H.F. Barnes, in two papers of 1933.[51] Seldom can so drastic a theory have been presented in so few words as Barnes's 'Suggestion about Value', which occupied hardly more than a page of the first number of *Analysis*. Value judgments, he suggested, should be regarded as not being strictly judgments at all. They do not *state* anything, not even that I approve of A. They *express* my approval of A. Their origin must be sought in 'the expressions of approval, delight and affection which children utter when confronted with certain experiences'. They can have meaning, therefore, only within societies whose members, having been similarly moulded, are 'agreed on what things [they] approve'. And even then, their meaning is the empirical nature of the objects they are used to appraise, and not any 'non-natural quality' of these objects. Ethical terms simply express my approval of empirical states of affairs, this approval resting on the empirical, that is non-ethical, qualities of the said states of affairs.

It would follow from this that there can be no strictly ethical argument. Barnes recognises the difficuty. He remarks: 'Many controversies arising out of value judgments are settled by saying, "I like it and you don't", and that's the end of the matter.' We are content with this position in matters such as those of food and drink. But we are not satisfied with it in matters of moral value. The reason for the difference is, Barnes thinks, that living in society calls for continual adjustment of conflicting attitudes in moral judgments. It creates the necessity for language designed to effect transfers of approval between opposing individuals and groups. This is what moral language is. When I say 'A is good' and my interlocutor says 'A is bad', I am not really contradicting him and my arguments are not designed to prove that he is wrong. They consist simply in pointing out to him feature after feature of A in the hope that, in the end, he will come to react to it as I do, 'A is good'.

> But what I have done is not really to gain his assent to a proposition but to change his attitude from one of disapproval to one of approval towards A. All attempts to persuade others of the truth of value judgments are thus really attempts to make others approve the things we approve.

51 'A Suggestion about Value', published in *Analysis*, 1, 1933, and reprinted in *Readings in Ethical Theory*, eds., Sellars and Hospers, pp. 391–2; and 'Ethics Without Propositions', published in the Aristotelian Society's *Supplementary Volume XXII*.

CHAPTER SEVEN

The Emotive Theory: A.J. Ayer

Although Ayer was saying nothing very new when he published *Language, Truth and Logic* in 1936,[1] he nevertheless said it with such verve, such confidence, such clarity and vigour of language, that his book remains a classic of logical positivism. Ayer was only 25 when the book appeared. It is rare for a philosopher to attain fame so young. But it is, as he later said himself, 'in every sense a young man's book'. Ayer has long since abandoned most of its tenets and largely shed its self-assured manner. As Passmore puts it speaking of the Introduction to the second edition, which was written only ten years later, 'where once he blasted, he now discreetly recommends'.[2]

1 LOGICAL POSITIVISM IN BRITISH PHILOSOPHY

Logical positivism is now repudiated universally by British philosophers.[3] Yet, as Ayer himself has remarked, although logical positivism is 'in a way, a thing of the past . . . , many of its ideas live on'.[4] In particular there lives on a certain positivism of desire, a presumption against metaphysics and the metempirical. Even if all the stones from the young Ayer's sling are admitted to have been badly aimed, it is generally taken for granted that the Goliath of metaphysics died anyhow. We should remember, however, that metaphysics, for most modern

---

1 Gollancz, London. Our edition is that of June 1950. 2 *A Hundred Years of Philosophy*, p. 392. In the same Introduction, Ayer significantly remarked that he had, in the ten years intervening since the first edition, 'come to see that the questions with which [the book] deals are not in all respects so simple as it makes them to appear'. He regretted also the book's youthful passion and harshness of tone. 3 In his contribution to the broadcast symposium published under the title,, *The Revolution in Philosophy*, in 1956, G.J. Warnock said: 'I should like to say in very plain terms that I am not, nor is any philosopher of my acquaintance, a Logical Positivist. This is worth saying . . . because there has seemed to be a current belief that Logical Positivism is somehow the official doctrine of contemporary philosophy. There is, in fact, no such official doctrine; and it is even more certain, if possible, that Logical Positivism is not it . . . Contemporary philosophy is not a dogmatic, restrictive body of doctrines at all, but a common pursuit of illumination in certain fields. . . . Let us avoid inflicting on the present the obsolete classifications of the past . . . I suppose the most immediately striking feature of Logical Positivism was its iconoclasm, its short and apparently lethal way with the ponderous enigmas of metaphysicians. . . . It happens to be true that the restrictive iconoclasm of Logical Positivism is quite alien to the spirit of philosophy today. In particular, its exclusive respect for science, mathematics, formal logic and very plain facts is now generally admitted to be unwarranted. If any one thing is characteristic of contemporary philosophy, it would be precisely the realization that language has *many* uses, ethical, aesthetic, literary and indeed metaphysical uses among them' (pp. 124-5). Cf. Warnock's, *English Philosophy since 1900* (Home University Library, Oxford University Press, 1958), pp. 43-51, 55-61, 167. 4 In his contribution to *The Revolution in Philosophy*; see p. 73.

137

British philosophers, means a certain sort of idealism, typified for them by the British Hegelians. This they project back into the past and identify with platonism, scholasticism, cartesianism, spinozism, all of these being lumped together and called 'classical philosophy'. In so far as British idealism and continental rationalism are concerned, the criticisms are frequently valid, and the obituary notices authentic.

There is a second, and a better sense in which logical positivism may be said to survive. This is that the enquiries carried on by the logical positivists and the controversies they aroused, have helped to clarify concepts such as those of meaning, verification and truth; and have shed new light on the nature of philosophy and its distinction from the sciences. A new interest has had to be taken in the relation of thought to language and the different uses of language.

The very violence of the positivists' attacks on metaphysics have led metaphysicians to devote more attention to the nature of metaphysical knowledge, the precise character of explanation and proof in metaphysics, the relation of metaphysics with experience and the logic of metaphysical (and religious) language. Metaphysics has thus been given the possibility of emerging from the conflict stronger than before.

This, however, was no part of Ayer's thoughts in 1936. He was quite confident then that he had proved metaphysics to be 'literally senseless' and shown that the labours of the learned men who expounded it 'have all been devoted to the production of nonsense'.[5] His case need not here be examined in detail. It differs from the standard arguments of the logical positivists only in the relentlessness of his refusal to allow any merit, even a literary or inspirational merit, to metaphysics.[6] He has the further interest of showing how easily logical positivism can be made to fit into the tradition of Humean empiricism.[7] It is now generally recognised that Ayer's 'proof' that metaphysics was 'meaningless' consisted in so *defining* 'meaning' that only 'tautologies' and 'empirical hypotheses' can be

---

5 *Language, Truth and Logic*, pp. 34, 44–5 *et saepe.* 6 We have noted that Carnap, in his London lectures of 1935, allowed metaphysics a certain expressive or emotional value, like that of poetry or music. C.A. Mace in an article called 'Representation and Expression', in the Journal *Analysis* in 1934, had defended a similar view, quite independently of theViennese philosophers and solely under the influence of Ogden and Richards. Ayer replied in the next number of the same Journal, in an article called, 'The Genesis of Metaphysics'. He protested, with vehemence, that the comparison of metaphysician with poets is not fair to poets. Nor can metaphysicians be excused on the ground that they are mystics. The vast majority of metaphysicians have let themselves be caught in linguistic traps: and it takes more to make a mystic than the commission of logical mistakes . . . The metaphysician produces plain nonsense in the attempt to give straightforward information. In this article, Ayer retracted an earlier epigram in which he had proposed that metaphysical writings should be published in the *London Mercury* (a literary journal) rather than in *Mind*. This, he had since come to think, might be taken to imply that metaphysics made some sort of sense; which he did not. Both Mace's and Ayer's articles are reprinted in *Philosophy and Analysis*, ed. Margaret Macdonald (Blackwell, Oxford, 1954), pp. 15–25. Cf. *Language, Truth and Logic*, pp. 44–5, 118–20. 7 In the Preface to the first edition, Ayer writes: 'The views which are put forward in this treatise derive from the doctrines of Bertrand Russell and Wittgenstein, which are themselves the logical outcome of the empiricism of Berkeley and David Hume.' He goes on to equate his distinction between

'meaningful'. From this, all that follows is that metaphysics has not the same kind of meaning as mathematics or empirical science.[8] A metaphysics like the thomist, which has always repudiated any claim to be an *a priori*, deductive system, and which has reflected on its difference from empirical science, is quite unaffected by Ayer's critique.

2 ETHICS IN 'LANGUAGE, TRUTH AND LOGIC'

Mary Warnock says that the chapter on ethics in *Language, Truth and Logic* is 'superbly short, less than twenty pages'. This is to be less than fair to its record for brevity; for the chapter contained also Ayer's philosophy of aesthetics and of theology and religion. There are in all eleven pages on ethics, one on aesthetics and six on theology and religion. It must be added that the pages are written with an admirable economy of words and a total absence of qualification, doubt or hesitation.

As we saw in the case of Schlick, Carnap and Reichenbach, ethics presented a challenge to logical positivism by its claim to give true factual knowledge, while being neither tautologous nor empirical. Ayer's emotive theory is his attempt to meet this challenge and reconcile the existence of ethics with his positivistic theory of meaning. He presents the theory primarily as being a way of answering an objection against the logical positivist theory 'that all synthetic propositions are empirical hypotheses'.[9] Perhaps this was to put the theory in too unfavourable a light, for it was to be defended for many years, in one form or another, on its

---

'tautologous' and empirical propositions with Hume's distinction between propositions concerning 'relations of ideas' and those which concern 'matters of fact'. In his paper, 'The Vienna Circle', in the *Revolution in Philosophy*, he notes: 'It is remarkable how many of [the] most radical doctrines [of the Viennese logical positivists] are already found in Hume' (p. 73). 8 Ayer, in the Introduction to the second edition, meekly admits that his principle of verification was 'a definition, though not supposed to be entirely arbitrary; and that the force of it is to show that unless a statement 'satisfied the principle of verification, it would not be capable of being understood in the sense in which either scientific hypotheses or common-sense Statements are habitually understood'. But he owns that it is very unlikely that any metaphysician would claim this sort of meaning for his propositions. There cannot therefore be a global 'elimination of metaphysics'; there must be 'detailed analyses of particular metaphysical arguments'. pp. 15–16. We have examined Ayer's positivistic philosophy (other than his ethics) in an article entitled, 'A.J. Ayer: The Positivist Phase', in the *Irish Theological Quarterly*, January 1957, pp. 32–75. 9 *Language, Truth and Logic*, p. 102: 'It will be said that . . . the existence of ethics and aesthetics as branches of speculative knowledge presents an insuperable objection to our radical empiricist thesis. In face of this objection, it is our business to give an account of "judgments of value" which is both satisfactory in itself and consistent with our general empiricist principles. We shall set ourselves to show that in so far as statements of value are significant, they are ordinary "scientific" statements; and that in so far as they are not scientific. they are not in the literal sense significant, but are simply expressions of emotion which can be neither true nor false.' On pp. 106–7, he speaks of the need, in order to escape from an impasse 'which would undermine the whole of our main argument', of finding a theory which is 'wholly compatible with our radical empiricism'. In the Introduction to the second edition he wrote: 'I do not deny that in putting forward this theory I was concerned with maintaining the general consistency of my position.' Iris Murdoch

own merits and long after people had forgotten where the 'principle of verification' was buried.

In fact, one of the most interesting things about the emotive theory is how naturally it seems to grow out of the British ethical thought which preceded it. It appears as a logical development of the ideas of Moore and the intuitionists. All of Ayer's premisses are Moorean. It is by means of Moore's 'naturalistic fallacy' argument that Ayer refutes naturalism, the first alternative to his own theory. This is the attempt, associated with subjectivists and utilitarians,to translate ethical terms into non-ethical terms.[10] Moore had refuted naturalism by pointing out that, of all such proposed translations of 'good', one could always ask, with significance, whether what is named by the 'translation' is itself good. It was then that Moore showed that 'this is good' or 'this is right' cannot be translated into 'this is pleasant', or 'this is approved by someone—whether myself or the majority of men'. In exactly the same fashion, Ayer argues that all empirical translations of ethical terms fail,

> because it is not self-contradictory to assert that some actions which are generally approved of are not right, or that some things which are generally approved of are not good. . . . A man who confessed that he sometimes approved of what was bad or wrong would not be contradicting himself. . . . It is not self-contradictory to say that some pleasant things are not good or that some bad things are desired.[11]

The validity of ethical judgments is, therefore, 'not empirically calculable'; Ayer concludes that it must be 'absolute' or 'intrinsic'.[12]

This was precisely the reasoning which led Moore, and after him the intuitionists, to speak of 'goodness' or 'rightness' as intrinsic, non-natural properties of objects. Obviously Ayer cannot follow them here. It is a basic principle of his 'radical empiricism' that there are no non-empirical properties or predicates. Some years later, Ayer was to write:

> With regard to statements of value, the one thing which was excluded by the verification principle was the metaphysical view that they are descriptive of a realm of values, which somehow exists on its own independently of the natural world.[13]

The rejection of what Ayer calls the 'absolutist theory' of intrinsic values is,

observes: 'The emotive theory of ethics was not created as the result of a patient scrutiny of ethical propositions. It arose largely as the by-product of a theory of meaning whose most proper application was in other fields'. See her paper, 'Metaphysics and Ethics', contributed to the broadcast symposium, *The Nature of Metaphysics*, ed. D.F. Pears (Macmillan, London, 1957), p. 102.   10 Ayer does not think it important to decide which, among ethical terms, is the fundamental one: he takes ethical terms globally and seeks an explanation of that in them which is specifically ethical (p. 104).   11 pp. 104–5.   12 p. 105. 13 'The Vienna Circle', in *The Revolution in Philosophy*, p. 77.

therefore, part of his rejection of metaphysics. F.P. Ramsey's statement at Cambridge in 1925 has often been quoted: 'Theology and Absolute Ethics are two famous subjects which we have realised to have no real objects.'[14] We have noted, however, that all that the anti-metaphysician is entitled to say is that God, the soul, values, are not 'real' and are not 'objects' in the sense in which empirical science or common-sense observation use the terms 'real' and 'object'.[15] But metaphysicians—at least the only metaphysicians we are interested to defend— have always insisted that God, the soul, and values are not realities of the same sort as empirical objects and that terms cannot be predicated univocally of them and of empirical objects. The analogical nature of metaphysical language is the corner-stone of thomist metaphysics.

Ayer's actual refutation of the 'absolutist theory', however, shows how close that theory, in Moore and the intuitionists, came to emotivism. Ayer thinks it enough to say of it that it makes value judgments 'unverifiable', for the deliverances of its 'mysterious intellectual intuition' are notoriously subjective and 'what seems intuitively certain to one person may seem doubtful, or even false, to another'. The fact that people claim to have intuitions of this sort is merely an interesting psychological fact, but it 'has not the slightest tendency to prove the validity of any moral judgment.'[16] Ayer goes on to say that a theory which makes moral judgments unverifiable and moral concepts unanalysable, as absolutism does, should logically conclude that ethical sentences are not propositions at all.

We begin by admitting that the fundamental ethical concepts are unanalysable, inasmuch as there is no criterion by which one can test the validity of the judgments in which they occur. So far we are in agreement with the absolutists. But, unlike the absolutists, we are able to give an explanation of this fact about ethical concepts. We say that the reason why they are unanalysable is, that they are mere pseudo-concepts. The presence of an ethical symbol in a proposition adds nothing to its factual content.[17]

14 It is quoted by Ayer himself in his paper, '*On the Analysis of Moral Judgments*' (1954) which we are to examine in our next section. 15 Compare R. Jolivet, *L'home métaphysique* (Je sais, Je crois, Arthème Fayard, Paris, 1958), pp. 33–4, 94–5: 'Neither being nor God are 'objects' . . . God, in the thomist tradition is not an "object". . . . There are no particular objects except sense objects. . . . In fact, there is only one 'object', the world, and metaphysics is from beginning to end knowledge of the world; its aim is not some 'extra-mundane object' dreamt up by the anti-metaphysicians, but the *meaning of the world*. Cf. F.C. Copleston, *Aquinas* (Penguin Books, 1955), pp. 36–7, 40, 42–3, 68, 110, 142. 16 *Language, Truth and Logic*, p. 106. Ayer makes the same points against intuitionist theories of knowledge in his later book, *The Problem of Knowledge* (Penguin Books, 1956), pp. 14–26, 41–68. It is doubtful, however, whether he is fair to intuitionism in either book; for intuitionism does not claim that 'knowing consists in being in a certain state of mind' or that 'from the fact that someone is convinced that something is true, it follows logically that it is true' (*Problem of Knowledge*, pp. 14, 19.) Their position is rather that all reasoning must start from some statements immediately known to be true—and this, as Ewing pointed out (*Second Thoughts in Moral Philosophy*, pp. 64–6) is precisely the view of Ayer himself in op. cit. pp. 14–26. We must recall, however, that most intuitionist moralists went much further than this, making each moral judgment the work of a separate, unreasoned intuition; it is this which is vulnerable to Ayer's attack. 17 *Language, Truth And Logic*, p. 107.

When I say, 'You acted wrongly in stealing that money', I seem to be stating some further fact over and above the fact (which Ayer treats as a non-ethical fact) stated in the sentence, 'you stole that money'. But Ayer denies that I am stating any further fact. What, then, is the force of the ethical predicate, 'wrongly'? It is simply 'to evince my moral disapproval' of the act.

It is as if I had said, 'You stole that money' in a peculiar tone of horror or written it with the addition of some special exclamation marks. The tone, or the exclamation marks, adds nothing to the literal meaning of the sentence. It merely serves to show that the expression of it is attended by certain feelings in the speaker.[18]

Generalised moral judgments such as 'Stealing money is wrong', are simply words written or spoken in such a way as to express my moral disapproval of the state of affairs they refer to.

It is as if I had written 'Stealing money!!', where the shape and thickness of the exclamation marks show, by a suitable convention, that a special sort of moral disapproval is the feeling that is being expressed.

It follows that, since moral judgments are not propositions and do not state anything, they cannot be true or false. People who make opposite moral appraisals of the same situation are not contradicting one another. To contradict another person is to state something incompatible with what he states. But

in saying that a certain type of action is right or wrong, I am not making any factual statement, not even a statement about my own state of mind. I am merely expressing certain moral sentiments. And the man who is ostensibly contradicting me is merely expressing his moral sentiments. So that there is plainly no sense in asking which of us is in the right. For neither of us is asserting a genuine proposition.

In order to make it plain that ethical judgments could not meaningfully be said to be true or false, Ayer is careful to distinguish his emotive theory from ordinary subjectivism. A subjectivist admits that ethical judgments are propositions; he denies only that they state 'unique non-empirical' facts, and affirms instead that they state facts about the feelings of the speaker. This would make ethical judgments empirically verifiable, capable of being true or false, and contradict-able. But Ayer denies that ethical judgments are propositions at all. They do not make any statements, even about my own feelings. They simply express or 'evince'

---

18 The language here is very close to that of Ogden and Richards, *The Meaning of Meaning*, p. 125: 'When we use [the word 'good'] in the sentence '*This* is good', we merely refer to this, and the addition of 'is good' makes no difference whatever to our reference . . . ; it serves only as an emotive sign expressing our attitude to this . . .'.

my feelings, and thus incidentally serve to arouse corresponding feelings in others.

> We can now see why it is impossible to find a criterion for determining the validity of ethical judgments. It is not because they have an 'absolute' validity which is mysteriously independent of ordinary sense-experience, but because they have no objective validity whatsoever. If a sentence makes no statement at all, there is obviously no sense in asking whether what it says is true or false. And we have seen that sentences which simply express moral judgments do not say anything. They are pure expressions of feeling and as such do not come under the category of truth and falsehood. They are unverifiable for the same reason as a cry of pain or a word of command is unverifiable—because they do not express genuine propositions.[19]

Ayer realised that his theory was open to an objection that had been urged by Moore against subjectivist theories, namely that they make it 'impossible to argue about questions of value'. So, notoriously, does Ayer's. But Ayer was not the young man to weaken before such a difficulty. He defiantly maintains that 'one really never does dispute about questions of value'. This, he agrees, seems 'very paradoxical'. We do resort to argument with people who disagree with us on moral issues, and we do so in order to win them over to our way of thinking. But, Ayer says, if we reflect upon what we are doing when we are engaged in moral argument, we find that what we are arguing about is not the rightness or the wrongness of our 'ethical feelings', but the accuracy or inaccuracy of our information about the 'facts of the case'. We argue that our opponent is mistaken about the motive with which the act in question was done or about the effects of the action, or is unaware of some special circumstances. But all these are empirical, non-ethical facts. What we expect, therefore,

> is that we have only to get our opponent to agree with us about the nature of the empirical facts for him to adopt the same moral attitude towards them as we do.

In fact, he goes on, the expectation is usually justified, because most of the people we argue with have received broadly the same moral 'conditioning' as ourselves and live in a similar society, so that by and large they will make the same moral response in face of what are seen as the same facts. But if, after we have reached agreement about the facts, my opponent persists in disagreeing with my moral judgment on the facts, I do not continue to argue. At the very point when the argument might be supposed to be becoming purely moral, discussion is found to become impossible. The disputants, instead of arguing, begin to express

19 pp. 107–10.

unfavourable moral judgments about one anothers and in the end 'resort to mere abuse'.

In short, we find that argument is possible on moral questions only if some system of values is presupposed. . . . Given that a man has certain moral principles, we argue that he must, in order to be consistent, react morally to certain things in a certain way. What we do not and cannot argue about is the validity of these moral parinciples. We merely praise or condemn·them in the light of our own feelings.

This being so, Ayer concludes, the fact that the emotive theory makes purely ethical argument impossible is not, as Moore thought, an objection to the theory, but rather an argument in its favour.[20]

Ayer speaks usually of ethical terms as expressing feelings. But this is only a condensed way of referring to a whole range of emotive functions which ethical terms fulfil. 'They are calculated also to arouse feeling and so to stimulate action.' Indeed they can function also as commands or suggestions. The sentence, 'It is your duty to tell the truth', both expresses the speaker's 'ethical feeling about truthfulness' and conveys the command, 'Tell the truth.' The sentence, 'You ought to tell the truth', conveys the same command, but less emphatically. In the sentence, 'It is good to tell the truth', 'the command has become little more than a suggestion.'[21] Ayer thinks that 'duty', 'ought' and 'good' can thus be distinguished from one another on the basis both of the feelings they express and the 'responses which they are calculated to provoke.'

The last two pages of Ayer's discussion of ethics draw the conclusions which his theory entails as to the nature of ethical philosophy. This can be briefly stated. Ethical philosophy consists wholly and solely in showing that ethical terms have the function of expressing and evoking feelings. The task of identifying the feelings that the different ethical terms are used to express and the reactions they customarily evoke, is a task for psychologists. The investigation of the moral habits of individuals and groups within which all moral argument must be conducted, is a task for sociologists.

It appears, then, that ethics, as a branch of knowledge, is nothing more than a department of psychology and sociology.[22]

Psychological research will, for example, immediately enable us to account for the Kantian and hedonistic systems of ethics. It is a psychological fact that much of people's moral behaviour is caused by fear, conscious or unconscious, 'of a

---

20 pp. 110–12. This is very close to the analysis of moral argument made by Ogden and Richards. 21 p. 108. This was all anticipated by Ogden and Richards, who, if they did not speak explicitly of ethical terms as words of command, did nevertheless assign to them the function of 'expressing our attitude and perhaps evoking similar attitudes in other persons or inciting them to actions of one kind or another'. They spoke of emotive words as 'expressions or stimulants of attitudes' (op. cit., pp. 125, 151). 22 p. 112.

god's displeasure', and fear of the hostility of society. This is why 'moral precepts present themselves to some people as "categorical" commands', and why, incidentally, Kant's theory had some plausibility. It is a further psychological and sociological fact that the precepts and prohibitions of society are in part determined by that society's beliefs 'concerning the conditions of its own happiness.' Hence the utilitarian component in moral codes—and hence the plausibility of utilitarian or hedonistic theories of ethics. But both theories confuse the psychological genesis of ethical feelings with the definition of ethical terms, and thus miss the central truth of ethical philosophy, which is that ethical concepts are indefinable.[23]

We can thus make a radical reclassification of the contents of traditional ethics. These fall into four main classes.

> There are, first of all, propositions which express definitions of ethical terms . . . . Secondly, there are propositions describing the phenomena of moral experience and their causes. Thirdly, there are exhortations to moral virtue. And lastly there are ethical judgments.

Much confusion has been caused by the failure of philosophers to distinguish these classes of propositions from one another and to be clear about 'what it is that they are seeking to discover or prove'. But philosophers need be confused no longer. The propositions of the second category, as we have seen, belong to psychology or sociology. Exhortations to moral virtue, the third group, 'are not propositions at all, but ejaculations or commands' designed to influence the behaviour of the reader. 'Accordingly they do not belong to any branch of philosophy or science.'

Ethical judgments themselves form no part of ethical philosophy. They are expressions of the speaker's or writer's own moral feelings; and it is no part of the business of the philosopher as such to express his moral feelings or to make moral judgments. His only function is to analyse the language which people use to express moral judgments.

> A strictly philosophical treatise on ethics should therefore make no ethical pronouncements.

> That is to say, the concern of ethical philosophy is solely with the first class of propositions named above, that is, propositions defining ethical terms or rather showing them to be indefinable but pointing to their emotive function. Thus moral philosophy, like the rest of philosophy, is exclusively 'activity of analysis'.[24]

---

23 pp. 112–3.   **24** pp. 103–4.

Ethical philosophy consists simply in saying that ethical concepts are pseudo-concepts and therefore unanalysable.[25]

The search for a 'true' system of morals is vain; the question whether any ethical system, or any ethical proposition, is true or false, is indeed senseless.

As ethical judgments are mere expressions of feeling, there can be no way of determining the validity of any ethical system and indeed no sense in asking whether any such system is true.[26]

Such, then, is Ayer's celebrated emotive theory of ethics. Before attempting an assessment of it, let us acknowledge the brilliance of Ayer's performance. Into eleven pages he concentrated the essence of almost every ethical theory that was to be defended in Britain over the succeeding twenty years. The 'persuasive' theory of ethics, the 'imperative' theory, the various 'decision' theories, the many 'commending-or-approving-with-reasons' theories of ethics, all of them are anticipated in these pages. The thesis that moral reasoning can only be either a matter of internal consistency within an unarguable system of values, or is an appeal to non-ethical facts recurs in almost every subsequent British philosopher for the next two decades. The doctrine that ethics is 'neutral', making no value judgments and having nothing to say as to the truth of any value judgments, became a dogma with all Ayer's successors. Each of these theories is mistaken, each of these theses fallacious; but it was a brilliant *tour de force* to have anticipated twenty years of ethical literature.

3 ASSESSMENT OF THE EMOTIVE THEORY

It is important also to notice how naturally the emotive theory grows out of the British ethical tradition. The ethical thought and even the language of Ayer is strongly Moorean. When Ayer says that 'ethical philosophy consists simply in saying that ethical concepts are pseudo-concepts and therefore unanalysable', we seem to hear Moore saying (in answer to 'the most fundamental question in all ethics' namely, 'how "good" is to be defined'): 'My answer is that good is good and that is the end of the matter. . . . My answer is that it cannot be defined, and that is all I have to say about it.'[27] When Ayer speaks of how philosophers fail to distinguish different classes of ethical propositions or to get clear 'what it is that they are seeking to discover or prove', it is the echo of Moore's voice lamenting that 'the difficulties and disagreements of which [the] history [of ethics] is full are mainly due to a very simple cause; namely to the attempt to answer questions, without first discovering precisely *what* question it is which you desire to answer.'[28]

25 p. 112. 26 Ibid. 27 *Principia Ethica*, pp. 5–6. 28 Op. cit., Preface.

Ayer divides the questions of traditional ethics into two groups, those which are properly ethical, and which are answered by saying that ethical terms are unanalysable and ethical judgments unverifiable; and those which are factual or verifiable, and which belong to empirical science. This is again Moore's teaching, that there are two questions in ethics, one, the strictly ethical question, 'What things are good?', for the answers to which question 'no relevant evidence whatever can be adduced'; and the second the question, 'What actions are right?', the answers to which are given by 'the method of empirical investigation, by means of which causes are discovered in the other sciences'.[29]

Moore did not himself teach that ethics is purely an 'activity of analysis'. But the general trend of his theory and method in philosophy was that philosophy is not discovery or information or knowledge, not proof or justification, but clarification or analysis of what is already otherwise known.[30] The force of Moore's famous papers, 'The Refutation of Idealism' (1903), 'The Defence of Common Sense' (1925), 'The Proof of an External World' (1939), was to spread the idea that philosophy can neither disqualify nor justify our common-sense convictions; it can only analyse what we mean when we state them. Philosophy cannot improve on our ordinary language; it can only analyse its meaning.[31]

The trend of Moore's ethical philosophy was surely in the same direction. His ethical writings come from comparatively early in his development, and he thinks in them that ethics can establish certain or probable propositions. It can establish with certainty, by intuitive inspection, what things are good. It can establish, with greater or less probability, by inductive reasoning, what actions are right. But only the former propositions are strictly ethical. And they are incapable of proof or of explication or of analysis. In fact, it does not seem that they are anything more than statements of how, according to Moore, we use ethical terms. We *mean* by the term 'good', just 'good', and nothing else whatever can be said about the meaning of good. But we *use* the term 'good' to refer to 'the pleasures of human intercourse and the enjoyment of beautiful objects'.[32] There is only one step from here to the contemporary slogan that ethics is the logical analysis of the language of morals.[33]

29 Ibid. and p. 146. 30 J. Wisdom, *Philosophy and Psycho-analysis* (Blackwell, Oxford, 1953), p. 121, writing of 'Moore's technique', says: 'Students came for guidance in the profound enquiry as to whether what they had always regarded as unquestionable is unquestionable. Moore tries to make their profound questions seem ridiculous by telling them that what they really want is an analysis of what it is that they hold to be unquestionable.' 31 See G.J. Warnock, *English Philosophy since 1900*, Home University Library (Oxford University Press, 1958), p. 29: [Moore's practice] naturally tended to give rise to the idea that the business of philosophy is clarification, not discovery; that its concern is with meaning, not with truth; that its subject matter is our thought or language, rather than facts'; cf. op. cit., pp. 12–29, 55–61. Cf. W.H.F. Barnes, *The Philosophical Predicament* (A. and C. Black, 1945), pp. 31–45; J.O. Urmson, *Philosophical Analysis. Its Development between the two World Wars* (Oxford, 1956), pp. 115, 140ff.; J. Passmore, *A Hundred Years of Philosophy*, pp. 212–6. 32 *Principia Ethica*, p. 188. 33 Cf. M.J. Charlesworth, *Philosophy and Linguistic Analysis*, p. 31: Due to the influence of Moore's Naturalistic Fallacy argument, 'Ethics, as a reasoned examination of what things are good, simply disappears, and its place is taken by logic, that is, an examination of the logical status of ethical propositions and ethical terms.'

Moore's influence, therefore, joined that of Wittgenstein (in both his philosophical periods as we shall see in a later chapter), that of the logical positivists, and that of Russell, different though all these were, to impose on contemporary British philosophy the axiom that philosophy is a 'second-order' activity of analysis of 'first-order' knowledge; that it deals with meta-problems or logico-linguistic problems about problems, and not with problems of reality or truth; and that therefore philosophy has no doctrines and no doctrinal commitments. It is virtually taken for granted by the majority of subsequent British philosophers that philosophy is neutral in respect of all beliefs and moral philosophy neutral in respect of all value judgments. Ayer's philosophy in this respect owes much to Moore.[34]

It is only when we set Ayer's emotive theory in its context in British ethics that we see its true significance. It is essentially an attempt to answer questions raised by non-naturalism. At the basis of it is Hume's distinction of 'ought' from 'is', or of 'facts' from 'values'. From this non-naturalists concluded that the meaning of ethical judgments must be irreducibly different from the meaning of any propositions describing 'what is the case' or 'stating facts'.[35] Ayer's problem began from here. His question was: What, if anything, can ethical judgments 'mean'? Or, since they cannot 'mean' what is their function? Being young, and in a hurry, he could not see anything for them to be except expressions of emotion, instruments of psychological persuasion. He could not envisage any other way of saving the autonomy of ethics. He could not think of 'ought' as being radicated in the 'is' of man, which is not just an empirical 'is' but also an 'ought-to-be'. This is partly because the author of *Language, Truth and Logic*, like so many modern British philosophers, leaves the study of man to the psychologists, and these are empirical scientists. But it is above all, because, as Wittgenstein would put it, they are so 'bewitched' by the distinction of 'fact' from 'value', 'descriptive' from 'normative', that they cease to question it; or have become so 'calloused' by doing philosophy within a tradition that they cease to be critical of the tradition.

---

34 See Preface to the first edition of *Language, Truth and Logic*, where Ayer acknowledges Moore's influence while pointing out that Moore does not share his 'thorough-going phenomenalism', nor does he have quite the same view of the nature of the analysis which philosophy is. See also Ayer's paper, 'Does Philosophy analyse Common-Sense', in the Aristotelian Society's *Supplementary Volume XVI*, 1937, pp. 162–76; and his paper 'Verification and Experience', in *Aristotelian Society Proceedings*, 1936–7.   35 In his broadcast paper on 'The Vienna Circle', Ayer said: 'The view which has come to be associated with logical positivism in this country . . . is that statements of value are emotive: they are not descriptive of anything; whether natural or non-natural; they express the speaker's feelings, or define his attitude. Consequently, they are neither true nor false, any more than commands are either true or false, though reasons can be given for them. This thesis has aroused considerable opposition, partly owing to the crudity of certain early formulations of it. It has been thought, quite mistakenly, that the seriousness of morals and aesthetics was somehow being impugned. In fact, it came to little more than development of the perfectly respectable logical point that normative statements are not derivable from descriptive statements, or, as Hume put it, that you cannot deduce "ought" from "is". Laying down a standard is not reporting a fact: but it is none the worse for that.' (See *The Revolution in Philosophy*, p. 78.)

We turn now to examine some errors of detail which are special to Ayer's emotive theory. We need not repeat the well-known arguments which call attention to the fact-stating, truth-claiming character of moral judgments; to their inherent claim to have necessary and universal validity; to their appeal to reasons and justifications and to reasoning of a moral kind[36]—all of these features being written into the ordinary language of morals, which the theory generally claimed to be analysing.[37] We shall rather concentrate on some inner inconsistencies of Ayer's theory, many of which persist unnoticed in subsequent British ethics.

Ayer believed that the emotive theory was the logical working out of Moorean non-naturalism. Yet the theory is itself riddled with naturalistic fallacies. There is first the comparatively crude and overt naturalism of his psychological-sociological 'explanations' of Kantianism and utilitarianism; for Ayer is not just setting out to 'explain' these ethical theories, but professing to 'explain' the ethical phenomena of the sense of categorical obligation and of the duty to be altruistic, which these theories tried to account for. The explanation effectively reduces these ethical concepts to 'statements of empirical fact'.

A more subtle form of the naturalistic fallacy is involved in Ayer's doctrine that ethical judgments are expressions of feeling which are called forth by non-ethical situations or descriptions. This we have called a quasi-naturalistic fallacy, for in fact it bases a moral judgment on non-moral determinants. But, as usual, the fallacy is camouflaged from its author by the fact that he first imports moral factors into the supposedly non-moral facts. Ayer proceeds as though a man's motives in acting or the special circumstances of his action were 'empirical facts', whereas these are clearly moral facts.[38] He speaks of the effects of the action as if these were non-ethical facts; whereas moral reasoning has continuously to distinguish moral from non-moral effects; and failure to distinguish these is simply the 'naive and artless' naturalistic fallacy which Moore found in Mill.

But the best example of how a philosopher's mind can become blinded to plain

---

36 The intuitionists did good service in this respect in their critiques of emotivism, though we have argued that emotivism was not so far removed from their own theory. See W.D. Ross, *Foundations of Ethics*, pp. 31–41; E.F. Carritt *Ethical and Political Thinking*, pp. 29–38, and his paper, 'Moral Positivism and Moral Aestheticism', first published in *Philosophy*, 1938, and reprinted in *Readings in Ethical Theory*, eds. Sellars and Hospers, pp. 405–14; C.D. Broad, 'Some Reflections on Moral Sense Theories in Ethics', first published in *Aristotelian Society Proceedings*, 1944–5, and reprinted in *Readings in Ethical Theory*, pp. 363–88; A.C. Ewing, *The Definition of Good*, pp. 10–16, 70–76. Cf. C.A. Campbell, *On Selfhood and Godhood*, pp. 186–9, 203.   37 In his 1949 paper, on 'The Analysis of Moral Judgments', which we shall examine in the next section, Ayer, admits that ordinary language is against his non-propositional theory (*Philosophical Essays*, p. 233). But in *Language, Truth and Logic*, he thought it a refutation of utilitarian and subjectivist theories that they were inconsistent 'with the conventions of our actual language' (p. 105). This ambivalence of attitude towards 'ordinary language' is not uncommon among analytic philosophers, who seem to appeal to ordinary language as an escape from metaphysics, until ordinary language is itself found to be metaphysical, when they rapidly appeal from it to suitably corrected language.   38 Aquinas speaks of the morality of actions as being determined by the nature of the act, the motive, the circumstances; but in all cases he is speaking of the *moral* nature of act, motive and circumstances. See *S. Theol.* 1–2, 18, 2–4, 6–11; cf. ibid. 7.1–4.

facts by a dazzling theory is provided by Ayer's telling us, in all good faith, that 'stealing' is a merely descriptive, ethically neutral word, and that 'You stole that money' is a neutral description of 'ordinary empirical facts'; and that the note of wrongness is communicated to these utterances by the tone of horror in which I say them or the exclamation marks I add when I write them. But surely it is too obvious to need saying, that before I decide to call a certain set of facts 'stealing', I have already morally appraised them. The term 'stealing' is a *moral description* of a situation, and I justify its use by pointing out that the empirical transfer of money in this case, from this person's possession, by this other person, was an immoral transfer of money, a transfer which ought-not-to-have-been-done. The transfer, in other words, is stated not to have been simply an empirical fact but an ethical fact; a fact which can be completely described only by the use of ethical predicates. The ethical predicates are not projected by me on to morally feature-less facts; they are found by me in the facts.[39]

Another form of naturalistic fallacy, similarly concealed, is contained in Ayer's central affirmation, that moral concepts are expressions of feeling. His thesis is that moral utterances are expressions of feeling exactly like exclamations of horror or cries of pain—and this is the basis of his main conclusion, that they are not statements and cannot be true or false. But he cannot ignore the difference between 'moral feelings' and non-moral feelings of pleasure or dislike: he has just rejected hedonism because it reduces ethical concepts to non-ethical feelings. Hence he must suitably qualify the term 'feelings' when he means by it 'moral feelings'. All through, therefore, he speaks of 'a *peculiar* tone of horror', '*special* exclamation marks', '*certain* feelings', 'a *certain sort of ethical* feeling'; when he does not speak simply of 'a special sort of moral disapproval', 'moral sentiments', 'reacting morally'. This conclusion that moral utterances are emotive or exclama-tory is plausible only when we forget the qualifying terms, 'ethical', 'special' etc., and think only of the 'feelings' member of the above phrases. But then the specifically moral differentia, that which makes moral utterances *moral*, has been lost.

The same dilemma faces all feeling-theories or moral-sense theories of ethics. Hume sought to prove that moral judgments must rest on some 'impression or

---

39 Aquinas, in the passages referred to in the preceding note, repeatedly emphasises that the 'object', 'motive', and 'circumstances' determining moral judgment are not the 'physical', 'object' etc., but the 'object' as consciously and deliberately performed by a man, i.e. the object made a moral object by being embraced by a human will and incorporated into the life of a human person: for everything willed and lived by a human person is moral. 'Physical acts have a moral character only as deliberately willed by someone' (1–2. 18. 6.) Sexual intercourse is the same physical or empirical act as performed by married partners or as performed by adulterers; but the act has a specifically different moral character in the two cases (1–2. 18–5.). The object, motive, circumstances which determine moral judgment, are those which are 'right', or which 'ought to be present' or which are 'rightly related to the situation', i.e. they are *moral* determinants. (See 1–2. 18. 2–5.)

sentiment', some 'feeling or sentiment . . . agreeable or . . . uneasy'. But he too had to qualify the term 'feeling' by the term 'moral' or its equivalent.

An action or sentiment or character is vicious; why? because its view causes a pleasure or uneasiness of a particular kind. . . . To have the sense of virtue is nothing but to *feel* a satisfaction of a particular kind from the contemplation of a character. The very feeling constitutes our praise or admiration. . . . We do not infer a character to be vicious, because it pleases: but in feeling that it pleases after such a particular manner, we in effect feel that it is virtuous. . . . Nor is every sentiment of pleasure or pain, which arises from characters and actions, of that *peculiar* kind which makes us praise or condemn . . .[40]

Now, as Moore showed against Mill, all such reasoning either commits the naturalistic fallacy or is a set of tautologies. Either moral concepts are identified with non-moral feelings, and this is the elimination of ethics; or else 'particular', 'peculiar' etc. in the above passage are simply 'synonymous for 'moral', and then we are merely being told that moral feelings are moral feelings and not any other sort of feelings—and this is the abolition of the feeling-theory.[41] Thus, when Hume seeks to give content to the vague terms 'particular', 'peculiar', etc., it becomes plain that what makes moral judgments 'a peculiar kind' of 'feelings' is that they are not feelings at all; for he now speaks of 'universal principles', 'general ideas of human conduct and behaviour', which are such as to 'comprehend all human creatures', and claim the general agreement of mankind.[42] This is to abandon the theory of 'moral sentiment' and return to a doctrine of rational moral judgment.[43]

---

40 *A Treatise of Human Nature*, III sect, ii (ed. Selby-Bigge, pp. 470–1; cf. p. 517). The italics are, of course, ours.   41 See Moore, *Principia Ethica*, pp. 66–7, 72–3, 78–9.   42 *Enquiry Concerning the Principles of Morals*, sect. IX i (ed. Selby-Bigge, pp. 272–4): 'The notion of morals implies some sentiment common to all mankind, which recommends the same object to general approbation, and makes every man, or most men, agree in the same opinion or decision concerning it. It also implies some sentiment, so universal and comprehensive as to extend to all mankind. . . . When a man denominates another his *enemy*, his *rival* . . . he is understood to speak the language of self-love ' and to express sentiments peculiar to himself. . . . But when he bestows on any man the epithets of vicious or odious or depraved, he then speaks another language and expresses   sentiments in which he expects all his audience are to concur with him. He must here, therefore, depart from his private and particular situation and must choose a point of view, common to him with others; he must move some universal principle of the human frame, and touch a string to which all mankind have an accord and symphony. . . . The sentiments which arise from humanity, are not only the same in all human creatures, and produce the same approbation or censure; but they also comprehend all human creatures. The distinction, therefore, between these species of sentiment [i.e. self-centred and moral] being so great and evident, language must soon be moulded upon it, and must invent a peculiar set of terms, in order to express those universal sentiments of censure or approbation, which arise from humanity or from a general view of usefulness and its contrary. Virtue and Vice then become known; morals are recognised; certain general ideas are framed of human conduct and behaviour; such measures are expected from men in such situations. This action is determined to be conformable to our abstract rule; that other, contrary. And by such universal principles are the particular sentiments of self-love frequently controlled and limited.'   43 Cf. E.F. Carritt, *Ethical and Political Thinking*, p. 36. Hume, of course, was determined not to call moral judgments rational, because 'rational'

Exactly the same dilemma confronts Ayer's emotive theory, or theory of ethics without propositions. It is indeed remarkable how close to Hume Ayer remains in ethics. If Ayer is to explain what precise sort of feelings are the 'certain sort' of feelings which are ethical, he will in fact have to abandon the language of feeling and the theory of emotivism. For he will have to say that ethical 'feelings' claim to be necessary, universal, obligatory, to be justified and required by the facts of the case, to be binding on all men, to state truths that should be recognised by all men and can, by rational discussion, win the general agreement of mankind. Carritt points out that to

show by a suitable convention that a special sort of moral disapproval is the feeling that is being expressed.[44]

is not 'expressing a feeling' at all, but is

a deliberate attempt to *show* or convince my audience of something by a *suitable verbal expression*, i.e. to tell them something, true or false.[45]

Thus, inescapably, the emotive theory lands us back into an ethics *with* propositions, stating facts that must be true or false.

The subsequent development of the emotive theory, particularly in the hands of C.L. Stevenson, was, though unwittingly, to reveal to all an unpleasant side of the emotive theory itself, of which most people, and Ayer himself, had not been conscious. Stevenson showed that philosophical descriptions or redescriptions of classes of facts or propositions are often not exercises of reasoning but essays in persuasion or in redirection of emotional attitude. Applying this to emotivism we can see that to say of some statements, like the statements of science, that they alone are 'genuine propositions', and are 'verifiable', 'meaningful', 'true or false' this is not to prove anything, or even to argue, but simply to confer 'laudatory titles' on science and to discredit other propositions. To say of 'ethical utterances' that they are not 'genuine propositions', 'are not, in the literal sense, significant' are 'mere pseudo-concepts', are 'unverifiable', that 'there is no sense in asking whether [they are] true or false', that they 'have no validity', but are like 'a cry of pain'—this is not to *reason* about ethics, but simply to attach 'derogatory titles' to it and thus discredit it.[46] This is, in fact, an example of propaganda, not of philosophical reasoning. And the 'damning by definition' which we have found in the ethics of Ayer, characterises the whole of his logical positivist doctrine. The

---

for him meant what the rationalists and rationalistic moralists had made of it. And the latter, in the seventeenth century and in Hume's time, had represented moral reasoning as if it were a species of abstract geometrical reasoning. (So, as we have seen, did their twentieth century intuitionistic followers.) Such reasoning, Hume protested, has nothing to do with *living*, and morals is good living. What Hume was seeking, as we have pointed out before, was a concept of *practical* reason. 44 *Language, Truth and Logic*, p. 107. 45 *Ethical and Political Thinking*, p. 32. 46 See Stevenson's paper, 'Persuasive Definitions', in *Mind*, 1938, pp. 331–50. We examine Stevenson's ideas in the next chapter.

commendatory definiton of 'meaning' and the consequent pejorative definitions of 'meaningless', 'senseless', 'nonsense', on which the whole edifice of *Language, Truth and Logic* rested, were 'persuasive definitions' and the book was, from this point of view, a sustained exercise in propaganda.[47]

4 AYER'S LATER ETHICAL THOUGHT

He later departed very little, if at all, from his early emotive theory of ethics; he merely became more sophisticated in the enunciation of it. Ten years after the publication of *Language, Truth and Logic*, in the Introduction to the second edition, he declared that he still believed 'the emotive' analysis of moral judgments to be valid on its own account. He admits, however, that the theory was very summarily presented, and needs to be 'supported by a more detailed analysis of specimen ethical judgments' than he had made any attempt to give. He makes only two concessions to criticisms. The first is to admit that he had failed to take account of the fact that 'the common objects of moral approval and disapproval are not particular actions so much as classes of actions'. But the rectification this makes to his theory is minimal. He goes on:

> This point seems to me important because I think that what seems to be an ethical judgment is very often a factual classification of an action as belonging to some class of actions by which a certain moral attitude on the part of the speaker is habitually aroused.

So Ayer persists in the preposterous opinion that such terms as 'theft', 'murder', 'lying', 'adultery', are 'factual classifications' of actions, needing to receive their moral categorisation from the attitude they habitually arouse on the part of the speaker.

There is a modification, slight but significant, in Ayer's doctrine about ethical dispute. He still maintains that 'what seem to be disputes about questions of value are really disputes about questions of fact'. But he now acknowledges:

> I should have made it clear that it does not follow from this that two persons cannot significantly disagree about a question of value, or that it is idle for them to attempt to convince one another.

But ethical disagreement is like 'any dispute about a question of taste' and does not entail that the disputants are making contradictory assertions. Discussion

---

47 See our article in *Irish Theological Quarterly*, January 1957, esp. pp. 52–3. In the light of what Ayer said about ethical utterances in *Language, Truth and Logic*, it seems that he was somewhat disingenuous to say, in 1955; 'It has been thought, quite mistakenly, that the seriousness of morals and aesthetics was somehow being impugned'.

here has not the character of argument and counter-argument and its purpose is not proof or disproof. Ethical discussion is entirely suasory. It is an

> effort to alter another man's opinions in the sense of getting him to change his attitude . . . to affect another person in such a way as to bring his sentiments on a given point into accordance with [one's] own.

There are various ways of doing this. One may 'call his attention to certain facts that one supposes him to have overlooked'—and much so-called ethical discussion is of this type. Or:

> It is also possible to influence other people by a suitable choice of emotive language; and this is the practical justification for the use of normative expressions of value.

Another way of influencing other people to change their attitudes—which Ayer does not mention—would be by one or other of the various psychological or chemical processes of 'conditioning' or 'brainwashing'. We mention them merely to show that Ayer has committed here a crass naturalistic fallacy about the nature of truth and of reasoning—as well as about the nature of truth and of reasoning—as well as about the nature of ethical judgment. A man can be brought to change his mind as a result of reasoned conviction as to which opinion is true. A man can be brought to change his mind also as a result of lies, fraud, fear, force or drugs. In both cases, there is a change of mind. But between the two lies the naturalistic fallacy—and Buchenwald and the former Soviet way of changing the mind of dissidents.

It is by sophisms like this that Ayer is able to persist in saying that

> there is no sense in asking which of the conflicting views is true. For, since the expression of a value judgment is not a preposition, the question of truth or falsehood does not here arise.[48]

Let us note how close this thought comes to the theory which was later to be called the persuasive theory of ethics and was to be associated with the name of C.L. Stevenson; though the two philosophers seem to have arrived at their positions independently.[49]

There are three papers on ethics in the volume of collected papers published by Ayer in 1954 with the title, *Philosophical Essays*.[50] Of these, it is the first,'On

---

48 The section on ethics in the new Introduction is found on pp. 20–2. 49 In a footnote on p. 20, Ayer notes that he has not been able to see Stevenson's book, *Ethics and Language*, (1945), but has a good indication of his argument from various articles published in *Mind* in 1937 and 1938. 50 Macmillan, London, 1954. The papers are: 'On the Analysis of Moral Judgments', first published in *Horizon*, 1949 (pp. 231–49); 'The Principle of Utility', first published in a book called *Jeremy Bentham and the Law*, in America in 1948 (pp. 250–70); and 'Freedom and Necessity', published in *Polemic*, 1946 (pp. 271–84).

the Analysis of Moral Judgments' which is much the most important and which will claim most of our attention. It maintains the essential thesis of the emotive theory—that 'ethical statements are not really statements at all . . . are not descriptive of anything . . . cannot be true or false'.[51] Ayer admits that this thesis is at variance with ordinary usage. But he has a new conception now of what philosophy is: it is 'laying down a usage of words', 'laying down a verbal convention', 'making a linguistic recommendation'—always of course, for the purpose of making necessary distinctions and clarifications, and always with the support of good reasons. This way of conceiving philosophy came from some ideas of Wittgenstein.[52] Philosophers worked it to death in the nineteen forties as a way of giving a function to philosophy, since philosophy could not discover truths or convey knowledge—only science being able to do this. Ayer remained strongly attached to this formula.[53]

In accordance with it, he announces that his purpose in the paper is to 'show that there are good reasons' for

laying down a usage, of the words 'proposition' and 'fact', according to which only propositions express facts and ethical statements fall outside the class of propositions.

The reasons are that ethical statements so differ from other statements that it is advisable to put them into a separate category altogether and say either that they are not statements or at least to say that they do not express propositions and consequently that there are no 'ethical facts'. Ayer protests that this does not mean that ethical statements are held to be false. It is simply a question of how widely or loosely we want to use the word 'fact'. 'My own view is that it is preferable to use it so as to exclude ethical judgments.' It is, he urges, a question of clarity.[54]

In proof of the contention that there are no ethical facts, Ayer asks us to consider a situation which calls for a moral judgment; for example, a murder. What are the facts of this situation? There are the 'police-court details', the expert

51 *Philosophical Essays*, pp. 232–3; cf. p. 246; 'Moral judgments are emotive rather than descriptive, persuasive expressions of attitude and not statements of fact and consequently . . . cannot be true or false . . . '. He still draws an analogy between ethical judgments and ejaculations and commands (p. 232).
52 See *The Blue Book*, pp. 57, 59, 70. 53 See *The Foundations of Empirical Knowledge* (Macmillan, London, 1940), pp. 18, 28, 113–4, 153; *The Problem of Knowledge* (Penguin Books, 1956), pp. 28–30, 86–7. Writing of Wittgenstein, we have pointed out the important element of truth which is contained in this formulation of the function of philosophy: see *Philosophical Studies*, X, December 1960.
54 *Philosophical Essays*, pp. 231–3. Everett W. Hall points out that this theory as to the nature of philosophical statements must in the end contradict itself. It assumes that philosophic statement, cannot be true or false, but are only proposals to use words in certain ways. It should treat the opposing theories of other philosophers as alternative 'linguistic proposals' which cannot be true or false either. But in fact these philosophers hold and try to prove that their opponents views are *false* and their own *true* because of some state of reality. (See *What is Value*, Routledge, London, 1952, pp. 218–21.) In fact, as we shall see, Ayer passionately maintains that his emotive analysis of moral judgments is true and that objectivist analyses are *false*, because *there are* no moral facts. Ayer, in other words; is claiming that philosophy can make and prove true statements about reality. But his theory of philosophical thinking excludes this.

witnesses' evidence—for example, the testimony of a psycho-analyst as to the accused's balance of mind; there is the question of a motive for the deed, of the attitude of the accused's conscience. These are all statements of fact, verified or falsified by observation. When these have been catalogued, 'there is a very good sense in which' a complete description of the facts has been given. To add that the perpetrator of the deed acted wrongly 'adds nothing to the description'.

> To say that his motives were good or that they were bad is not to say what they were. To say that the man acted rightly, or that he acted wrongly is not to say what he did . . . not to add a further detail to the story. It is for this reason that these ethical predicates are not factual; they do not describe any features of the situation to which they are applied.[55]

There are no 'ethical features' of a situation. If there were, they would have to have some relation, logical or factual, with the 'natural features'. But they cannot be *logically* connected with these: for two people may agree in their natural description of a situation and differ in their ethical evaluation of it without contradicting themselves. Nor can the alleged 'ethical features' be *factually* connected with the 'natural features' of the situation: this would make the 'ethical features' some sort of observable, verifiable facts; but this they precisely cannot be. There are no 'ethical designata' over and above factual ones. The goodness or badness of the situation is not 'something apart from the situation, something independently verifiable', for which the facts would provide evidence or reasons or proof. 'There is no procedure of examining the value of the facts as distinct from examining the facts themselves! In the scientific sense, there is no evidence, there are no reasons, for ethical judgments.'[56]

We can interrupt our exposition at this point to make some comments. The first is to call attention to the part played by both persuasive and circular definitions in the above passages. No reason is given for the assertion that people may differ in their ethical evaluation of a situation without contradicting themselves; in other words, that the statements, 'x is good' and 'x is bad', are not self-contradictory. Simply, a self-contradiction is tacitly being so defined that it can occur only between propositions, which in turn are being so defined that they do not include ethical statements. The 'proof' that ethical statements are not factual is that they are not descriptive; and the proof that they are not descriptive is that there are no ethical facts or features for them to describe. That there is no 'evidence' or 'proof' for ethical statements is 'proved' by disallowing any valid use of these terms except the use of them in the empirical sciences.

It is surprising how short a distance Ayer has moved here from the much-recanted crude logical positivism of *Language, Truth and Logic*. The whole of this,

55 *Philosophical Essays*, pp. 233–6.   56 Op. cit. pp. 236–7.

by his own confession, rested on the taking of *one* proper use of the word 'meaning' as if it were the *only* proper use of the word 'meaning'. In this simple, but gravely misleading way, metaphysics, theology and ethics were pronounced as 'meaningless' without qualification. Exactly the same procedure is still being followed in this article. One use of the words 'proposition', 'fact', 'description', 'verifiable', 'true', is being treated as the *only* legitimate use of these words—and on this device a whole theory of ethics as non-propositional and non-objective is being erected. Ayer has not analysed his own thinking in the light of his own theory of the *persuasive* force of language. His conclusions would not follow if the 'linguistic redescription' he recommends were *completely* successful. His conclusions follow only if the 'emotive meaning' of 'proposition' and 'fact' remain *unchanged*, while the 'descriptive meaning' only is, at Ayer's recommendation, changed. Ayer's whole argument would collapse if he introduced a quite new 'emotionally-neutral' name for ethical statements; if he called them, for example, *Kathekontorhemes*. For this would distinguish ethical statements from non-ethical ones without suggesting that they cannot be true, factual, propositional, in a different sense of true, etc. from that applicable to non-ethical statements. But this is not enough for Ayer's purpose. He wants to do two things at once: to distinguish ethical from non-ethical statements *and* to prove that ethical statements can not be *in any sense* true, propositional, factual, and must therefore be attitudinal.

Nobody would think that Ayer had succeeded if he had not kept the same words 'proposition', 'fact', 'true' etc. throughout his argument and exploited the divergence between their prestige-associations and their descriptive function. For these words keep their prestige-symbol-status even when a philosopher decides to alter their meaning. His public is inevitably confused by the new usage. Language being what it is, they cannot but conclude that statements which are not propositions, do not state facts, have no evidence, are nor provable, cannot be true, etc., . . . are quite simply arbitrary noises. But the above procedure is not philosophy, it is propaganda. Scientists can create new technical terminology because their entities are not part of ordinary experience or language. But philosophers are dealing with ordinary experience, using ordinary language, and they must respect the conditions and laws of ordinary language. One of these is that if you say something is not true, you are saying it is false; if you say something is not a fact, you are saying it does not exist or is unreal; if you say there is no evidence for some statement, you are saying that it is only a personal whim. Philosophers may not make words mean what they choose, because they cannot. Words are public; philosophers can only change them partially; when they do so, they have a duty to see that their public—and themselves—are not deceived by the partial nature of the change.

Ayer thought he had proved that there are no ethical facts, by challenging us to find the 'ethical features' in a case of murder. Few mistakes in philosophy can be at once such obvious 'howlers' and have had so long a run as this one. Ayer's argument is found almost verbatim in Hume's *Treatise*, in a paragraph immediately preceding the famous passage about the distinction between 'ought' and 'is'.

> Take any action allowed to be vicious: Wilful murder, for instance. Examine it in all lights, and see if you can find that matter of fact, or real existence, which you call *vice*. In whichever way you take it, you find only certain passions, motives, volitions and thoughts. There is no other matter of fact in the case. The vice entirely escapes you, so long as you consider the object. You never can find it, till you turn your reflection into your own breast, and find a sentiment of disapprobation, which arises in you, towards this action. Here is a matter of fact, but it is the object of feeling, not of reason. It lies in yourself, not in the object. So that when you pronounce any action or character to be vicious, you mean nothing but that from the constitution of your nature you have a feeling or sentiment of blame from the contemplation of it.[57]

A great part of the reasoning of contemporary British moralists is contained germinally in this passage.

But how can Hume, and Ayer after him, have convinced themselves that a situation which they begin by calling 'murder' is an non-ethical situation?; or that the 'passions, motives, volitions, thoughts' (Ayer adds, the state of the murderer's conscience), involved precisely in 'wilful murder', are 'facts' distinct from the 'vice' of the said murder and in themselves ethically neutral? We are still in the world of Oxford's professors' paralysed moral agents who set themselves to utter cries (or plant daggers) but have (theoretically) no control over the cries (or deaths) that then happen to result. But what *is* wilful murder except an action or the bringing to be of a state of affairs characterised by 'passions, motives, volitions and thoughts'? The immorality is not a further fact, whether a 'non-natural' fact 'apart from the situation', 'over and above the factual ones; or an 'attitude-fact' in the observer. The immorality is *in* the facts, because precisely they are facts embedded in an ethical situation; they are ethical facts and their adequate description necessarily includes their moral evaluation.

It becomes plausible to treat the 'facts' of a wilful murder as ethically neutral only if we, on the one hand, define 'facts' as the referents of scientific descriptions; and on the other, decide *a priori* to regard moral judgments as the expression of some kind of non-rational and emotionally coloured personal attitudes. The 'facts' of a wilful murder are indeed 'ethically neutral' for a psychiatrist, a criminologist, a social-statistician, etc. But that is because they, in the interests of particular scientific tasks, have abstracted from the ethical content of the facts. The morality of a situation is indeed what the sciences omit from their descriptions, but this

---

57 *Treatise of Human Nature*, Book III, i, sect. i (ed. Selby-Bigge, pp. 468–9).

not to say that the morality is non-factual in the sense of being non-objective or merely attitudinal.[58] All that Ayer's whole argument against ethical propositions and facts proves, is that ethics is not empirical science and that ethical realities are not physical objects.

His fallacy about ethics is in all respects parallel to his fallacy about metaphysics. His treatment of 'good' corresponds exactly to his treatment of 'being' and 'true', or to his treatment of the soul, in *Language, Truth and Logic*. He there, as it were, listed all the properties or predicates of an object; then challenged his reader to point to the further property or predicate which is the 'being' of the object. He put before us a true proposition and asked us to point to the 'something' in it which the word truth 'stands for'. He described all the perceptible properties of a man and asked us to say where, in the description, is the place for the 'something imperceptible inside' which is his soul. This is to be very naive about the nature of metaphysics. In every case, the answer is the same. 'Being' is *in* the predicates, as the precondition of all predicating. 'Truth' is in the being-true of the true proposition. The soul is that without which the human body is not a *human* body. Similarly, 'goodness' is a factual-moral situation which it was right for a man to bring about; 'badness' a factual-moral state of affairs which ought not to have been brought into existence. It is foolish to say that because there is no such 'thing' as goodness, therefore there is 'no such thing' as goodness.

Such are the fallacies on which Ayer erects his emotive persuasive theory of moral language. There are, he continues, no reasons, in the strict sense, for moral judgments.

> What are accounted reasons for our moral judgments are reasons only in the sense that they determine attitudes. One attempts to influence another person morally by calling his attention to certain natural features of the situation such as will be likely to evoke from him the desired response.

Similarly one reasons with oneself in order to settle on an attitude or come to a decision.[59] To say that an action is right is to give myself and others leave to imitate

---

58 As we have pointed out, and shall see in the sequel, very many contemporary philosophers repeat Hume's and Ayer's error. They seem to become so mesmerised by the science— model of a 'fact' that they can produce lists of obviously ethical predicates, yet blandly describe these as 'neutral' and as still requiring to receive their ethical value from the attitude of the speaker. Paul Edwards holds that a certain wicked American Senator's 'deliberate distortion of facts, his spite and desire for revenge' are non-ethical predicates; and that to call them 'evil' is to 'add a definite indication of the speaker's attitude'. See his *The Logic of Moral Discourse* (Free Press, Glencoe, Illinois, 1955), pp. 204–5. A later writer, Alan Montefiore, proposes to regard the description of someone as 'truthful, dependable, helpful, affectionate', not as a moral evaluation of that person, but as factual reasons justifying a moral commendation of him. See his *A Modern Introduction to Moral Philosophy* (Routledge and Kegan Paul, London, 1958), p. 116.　59 C.A. Campbell supposes that 'hortatory theories' of ethics would have to explain un-uttered moral judgments as exhortations addressed to oneself. He remarks: 'Whether any theorist has in fact even sponsored so fantastic a view, I do not know. I can only insist, that there is a limit, even in moral philosophy, to the hypotheses that deserve discussion, and give my opinion that this one passes well beyond that limit' (*On Selfhood and Godhood*, pp. 185–6). Ayer's position seems close to the hypothesis Campbell is discussing.

it in similar circumstances; or to 'show myself favourably disposed . . . towards actions of that type'. To pronounce an action wrong, is to express a resolution not to imitate it and to try to discourage others from doing so. I appeal to reasons in order to get others to adopt my attitude; and if I succeed in this, it is because others share with me a common set of moral attitudes.

Ayer thinks that, in earlier writing, his definition of moral attitudes in terms of feelings was too narrow. He should have spoken of 'patterns of behaviour' in which the moral judgment or expression of moral feeling is an element.[60]

He does not see any essential difference between his doctrine and that of Moore and the intuitionists. Perhaps, he suggests, 'intuition' is only another name for 'feeling of approval'. He still thinks that his doctrine is the logical working out of the distinction between 'ought' and 'is'. If ethical terms describe features of the world, they are *descriptive* terms and cannot be normative.

> But if the ethical term is understood to be normative it does not merely describe the alleged non-natural property ['good']; and if it does merely describe this property then it is not normative.[61]

A valuation is not a description. This is as simple as a dictionary. But it was against this kind of philosopher's revision of the dictionary that Wittgenstein recommended the return to ordinary language.

Moral deliberation, Ayer continues, is never concerned to find out what is true, but only to decide how to act.

> Talking about values is not a matter of describing what may or may not be there, the problem being whether it really is there. There is no such problem. The moral problem is: 'What am I to do? What attitude am I to take?' Moral judgments are directives. . . . There is nothing to be done except look at the facts, look at them harder, look at more of them and then come to a moral decision.

To the question, 'Is it a right decision, there can be no answer except to ask another: Are you prepared to stand by it?'[62]

Any attempt to justify moral decisions in the sense of proving them true, would make them into descriptive statements and take them out of the category of ethical terms. This was the mistake of the utilitarians and in particular of Bentham. But, if their moral philosophy was fallacious, their moral-reform programme was successful. It succeeded because the terms 'right' and 'wrong' retain their normative, that is to say their emotive-suasory force, even when their descriptive meaning is revised. People continued to want to do what was 'right', even when Bentham had redefined it as the socially useful. Unless the use of the words 'right'

---

and 'wrong' was primarily emotive, this aim would not be achieved.[63] This is a remarkably accurate analysis of how much modern campaigning to change people's moral beliefs is in fact carried on. It is a pity Ayer did not see its application to his own campaign to change people's beliefs about what morality is.

Ayer protests, however, that his theory is neutral both with regard to moral beliefs and with regard to beliefs about the nature of morality. The moral philosopher has no theories. His field is meta-ethics. Ayer's own theory

> is entirely on the level of analysis; it is an attempt to show what people are doing when they make moral judgments.[64]

But let us recall that Ayer began by saying

> as the English language is currently used—and what else, it may be asked, is here in question?

His analysis of moral language is, 'in an obvious sense, incorrect'. For the language that people use shows that they suppose that what they 'are doing when they make moral judgments' *is* 'making statements . . . descriptions . . . of facts which may be true or false.[65] Ayer is not analysing 'what people are doing' but prescribing what he thinks they ought to be doing or ought to think that they are doing, when they make moral judgments. His ethics is not morally neutral; it is a sustained 'moral recommendation' to think in a certain way about morals.

It is idle thereafter for Ayer to pretend to be giving 'no moral guidance'. How we think about morals is a moral matter and perhaps the most fundamental of all moral matters. Ayer says that a man's moral judgments have nothing to do with his moral philosophy. The former are stands, attitudes; the latter is analysis, reasoning. He himself is not saying that nothing is good or bad, right or wrong, or that it does not matter what we do. That would be 'expressing a moral attitude'; but a philosopher only analyses. He is not saying that what anyone thinks right is really right; that would be to range oneself on that persons's side. But the philosopher does not range himself on anyone's side; he only, we suppose, thinks.

Precisely, Wittgenstein was to say; and that is the philosopher's disease. The philosopher is too busy thinking theories to have any time to look at facts. Wittgenstein prescribed as remedy: Don't think but look![66] Look at how people use moral language, at how they think morally, at how variously we use the words 'true', 'fact', 'describe', 'know', 'proposition', 'reasons', 'proof'. Ayer has not done this. He has been 'bewitched' by a theory and followed it out of the land of living men.

---

63 pp. 242–5. 64 pp. 262–4; cf. p. 245. 65 p. 246. Cf. p. 235: 'The question for moral philosophy is not whether a certain action is right or wrong but what is implied by saying that it is right or wrong.' 66 *Philosophical Investigations*, 66.

One of Ayer's weaknesses is that he has learned very little from the Wittgensteinian critique of philosophers' thinking. He remains remarkably pre-Wittgenstein.

He ends his paper on a highly moral note. Is people's moral conduct affected, he asks, by their 'meta-moral' beliefs? It would take an empirical investigation to find out. But whatever about this, Ayer can at once affirm that he 'should dispute on moral grounds' any suggestion that a philosophical theory should be kept secret because it had evil consequences. There is a fine moralising fervour about his last sentence.

What I have tried to show is not that the theory I am defending is expedient, but that it is true.[67]

It looks as though one entry of Ayer's dictionary were: 'Emotivist—a lover of truth'; and another: 'Critic of emotivism—one who prefers expediency to truth'.[68] Our criticism has, however, intended to show not that Ayer, or his theory, is wicked; but that he is mistaken and it is false.

---

67 *Philosophical Studies*, p. 249. We have called attention (No. 689 above) to the inconsistency of this claim to truth with Ayer's theory of philosophy.   68 C.A. Campbell remarks, in a similar context: 'I should myself doubt whether any greater bias has been imparted to the writings of moral philosophers by the desire of some to reach agreeable results, than by the ruthless determination of others to be what they call 'tough-minded' at all costs. Assuredly, there is no duty laid upon the philosopher 'to think nobly of the soul'. But he has no duty to think *ig*nobly about it either. By all means let us be tough-minded. But it is well to remember that if one makes a fetish of tough-mindedness, the result is apt to be not too easily distinguishable from thick-headedness' (*On Selfhood and Godhood*, p. 181.)

CHAPTER EIGHT

C.L. Stevenson: Ethics as Persuasion

Charles Leslie Stevenson, who taught philosophy at the University of Michigan, though an American, has an important place in the evolution of British ethics in this century. It was in *Mind* that his first papers on ethics were published in 1937–8.[1] They had considerable influence in Britain in promoting the emotive-persuasive theory of moral language. The author of the theory that much of philosophy and ethics is persuasive rhetoric, was himself a plausible illustration of his own theory. His breeziness of style seemed to sweep difficulties out of the way. His papers had an unconventionality which appealed all the more to the younger generation of philosophers because it shocked the older. He seemed to discredit critics by not appearing able to understand the archaic language they are talking. The ideas of these early papers were taken up into a book, *Ethics and Language*, published in 1944.[2] The book is more ponderous and indeed somewhat pedantic. In it, Stevenson's ideas lose in freshness what they gain in professorial gravity.[3] But the impressive size of the book, the number and variety of the examples of moral argument which it discussed, the apparently wide range of the treatment, made the book for some time a sort of bible of emotivism. The book was also important as the first major study of ethics based on the neo–Wittgensteinian slogan that moral philosophy is the analysis of moral language.

Another reason why Stevenson merits a place in this survey is that his thought grows out of the British tradition. His theory was suggested to him by the page on ethics in *The Meaning of Meaning* by Ogden and Richards.[4] He remarks that 'of all traditional philosophers, Hume has most clearly asked the questions that here concern us and has most nearly reached a conclusion that the present writer can accept'.[5] His ethical theory is in an important sense an effort to develop the

---

1 These were, in order of publication: "The Emotive Meaning of Ethical Terms', published in *Mind*, 46, 1937 (reprinted in *Readings in Ethical Theory*, eds. Sellars and Hospers, pp. 415–29); 'Ethical Judgments and Avoidability', published in *Mind*, 47, 1938 (reprinted in *Readings in Ethical Theory*, pp. 548–59); "Persuasive Definitions", published also in *Mind*, 47, 1938, pp. 331–50. In addition to these, we note a paper called "The Nature of Ethical Disagreement", delivered at the Centro di Metodologia, Milan, and reprinted in *Readings in Philosophical Analysis*, eds. Feigl and Sellars, pp. 587–93. 2 Yale University Press, New Haven. Our edition is a reprinting of March 1950. 3 Mary Warnock says of it: 'The books seems to me to suffer from inflation and from a resulting failure of impact, compared with the articles. It is as if Stevenson had become over-self-conscious about Methodology and there is a good deal of reflexive consenting upon his own procedure, which add little or nothing to the actual ethical theory.' (*Ethics since 1900*, p. 106). 4 See footnote in 'The Emotive Meaning of Ethical Terms', where he says that the passage on ethics in Ogden and Richard's book 'was the source of the ideas embodied in this paper'. (See *Readings in Ethical Theory*, p. 422.) He quotes the passage (with one from John Dewey as frontispiece to *Ethics and Language*. 5 *Ethics and Language*, p. 273; in the Preface, he writes: 'Apart from my emphasis on language, my approach is not dissimilar to that of Hume.'

non-naturalism of Moore without involving any non-natural ethical concept. Stevenson, as we shall see, recognises the close dependence of the emotive and persuasive theories of ethics on the teaching of Moore.

We shall begin by outlining the doctrine of the early *Mind* articles.

1 'THE EMOTIVE MEANING OF ETHICAL TERMS'

Stevenson begins this paper in the Moorean manner by saying that the difficulty of ethical questions arises partly from the fact that we are not clear as to what questions precisely we are asking. 'The present paper is concerned wholly with this preliminary step of making ethical questions clear.' It sets out to make clear the meaning of the question, 'Is X good?' by substituting for it a question 'which is free from ambiguity and confusion'.[6]

Three conditions of substitutability are laid down. The terms substituted, in the interests of clarity, for the ethical term 'good' must not make ethical disagreement impossible; must not eliminate the 'magnetic' force which the term 'good' possesses, i.e. its power to move to action; and must not 'define' ethics in terms of science or reduce ethics to what is empirically verifiable. Hobbes-type theories, which define 'good' in terms of 'desired by me', are ruled out on the first count; for then two people who say respectively, 'This is good', 'This is bad', are not contradicting one another. Hume-type theories, which define 'good' in terms of 'approval by most people',[7] are ruled out on the second count, because the fact that most people approve of a thing need not give a man 'a stronger tendency to favour it'. All interest-theories and all merely empiricist theories, including Hume's are ruled out on the third count; for there is always some residual meaning in the ethical term 'good', which is not accounted for in empirical or scientific substitutes. 'Ethics must not be psychology.' Statements about what things are and how people react do not *make* people react, as the term 'good' does.

---

6 See *Readings in Ethical Theory*, p. 415.   7 This is a caricature of Hume, as is the remark (p. 417) that 'According to Hume's definition, one may prove ethical judgments (roughly speaking) by taking a vote.' C.D. Broad made the same point, saying: 'The logical consequence of his theory is that all such disputes *could* be settled, and that the way to settle them is to collect statistics of how people in fact do feel' (*Five Types of Ethical theory*, p. 115). This is not Hume's teaching, even 'roughly speaking'. Hume, as the quotation from the *Enquiry* shows, said that moral judgments *expect* and *claim* general consensus. This is said by way of giving part of the definition of what a 'moral sentiment' is, and by no means as a criterion for the verification of ethical statements. So far, Hume is surely right; though this characteristic of moral judgments precisely disqualifies Hume's own account of them as sentiments quite distinct from cognition and reasoning. Stevenson, in a footnote to the article as reprinted in *Readings in Ethical Theory*, remarks that the reference to Hume is not to be taken as applying strictly to Hume but 'to the general family of definitions of which Hume's is typical'. (He adds that the same may be true of the reference to Hobbes). He refers to *Ethics and Language* for a more adequate treatment of Hume's views. Here however (pp. 273–6) we find the same error, of treating Hume as though he were giving a criterion of verification for ethical judgments, instead of trying to show what makes ethical 'feelings' ethical and distinguishes them from non-ethical feelings.

Moore's method is still valid: of any set of 'scientifically knowable properties' which may be substituted for 'good', it is always possible to ask, 'Is the thing possessing these properties *good*?' Clearly, there is

> some sense of 'good' which is not definable, relevantly, in terms of anything scientifically knowable. That is, the scientific method is not sufficient for ethics.[8]

Stevenson next proceeds to state his own theory in outline. He claims for it that it can meet all three conditions of substitutability, without having recourse to any 'other-worldly' or 'mysterious' hypothesis such as 'Platonic Idea or . . . Categorical Imperative or . . . unique unanalysable property'. His theory is, he allows, a kind of 'interest-theory'. Traditional interest theories, however, made the mistake of interpreting ethical statements as though they described, or gave information about, the interests of people. But the distinctive feature of ethical judgments, Stevenson urges, is that they actively redirect, modify, or recommend interests. This is totally different from describing interests, or stating that they exist. Ethical judgments are quasi-imperative, not descriptive or cognitive. Ethical argument is simply an attempt to exert influence over another man's conduct; and reasons in ethics are simply means supporting this influence. The originality of Stevenson's theory is, he argues, that it calls attention to the power of words, and especially ethical words, to change attitudes by their power of suggestion. 'Ethical terms are instruments used in the complicated interplay and readjustment of human interests.' People's moral attitudes vary in function of the way words were used in their community.[9] Coming to more detail in the elaboration of his theory, Stevenson distinguishes two uses of words;

> on the one hand we use words (as in science) to record, clarify and communicate *beliefs*. On the other hand we use words to give vent to our feelings (interjection) or to create moods (poetry), or to incite people to actions or attitudes (oratory).

The first use he calls 'descriptive', the second 'dynamic'. The distinction depends on the purpose of the speaker. The possibility of using words dynamically is connected with the fact that, in addition to their 'propositional' meaning, words have also, as Ogden and Richard showed, an 'emotive' meaning; they carry an 'aura of feeling' created by long emotional associations; they have acquired tenacious 'tendencies to produce affective responses'.[10]

Now, Stevenson's theory goes on, ethical use of language is dynamic use of language. Previous attempts by empiricists to analyse 'This is good' in terms of 'I (or we) like this' have failed because they suppose the latter sentence to be a

---

8 *Readings in Ethical Theory*, pp. 416–8.   9 Op. cit., pp. 418–21.   10 pp. 421–3.

descriptive use of words. But 'We like this' has a function similar to 'This is good' only when it is used dynamically—to influence the likes of others by the suggestive power of the speaker's enthusiasm. 'This is good' is a statement to be *made* true by the success of the speaker's oratory. Yet no translation will exactly replace the ethical term or fully discharge its function. For example, the formula, 'I *do* like this; do so as well', has something like the same meaning as 'This is good'. But yet it has not the same effect or effectiveness. Its imperative part 'appeals to the conscious efforts of the hearer'. But this is its weakness; for a man 'can't like something just by trying'. The irreplaceable power of ethical words is that they work 'in a much more subtle, less fully conscious way'. Also they turn the hearer's attention 'not on his interests, but on the object of interest', and this extravert quality greatly facilitates suggestion.

When we apply the above analysis to strictly moral uses of 'good' we must, says Stevenson, keep in mind the distinguishing features of the latter. The moral term 'good' signifies 'a stronger sort of approval' than the non-moral term. When a person morally approves of something, he has 'a rich feeling of security when it prospers and is indignant or 'shocked' when it doesn't.'[11] Moral and non-moral expressions containing the term 'good' are both, therefore, in part statements *about* the speaker's 'favourable interest'; but their significance is not conveyed by any analysis which omits their emotive meaning and consequent suggestive force. It is the presence in them of the latter element which makes ethical terms strictly indefinable.[12]

Stevenson's theory fulfills his three conditions for any analysis of ethical terms. There is no need to point out that it allows for the 'magnetism' of moral words: that is the heart of the theory. Stevenson claims that it allows also for disagreement in moral judgments. But it puts ethical disagreement in its true light, as being, not disagreement in *belief* but disagreement in *interest*. Ethical dispute is not a matter of trying to discover or demonstrate what is the truth. It is not a clash of intellects but a clash of wills.

> When C says 'This is good' and D says 'No, it's bad', we have a case of suggestion and counter-suggestion. Each man is trying to redirect the other's interest.[13]

But disagreement in interest can arise from disagreement in belief, and can in some cases, be settled by appeal to facts, to empirical knowledge. But this must not cause us to forget the third of our conditions of valid substitution for ethical terms: namely, that ethics must not be reduced to empirical description. When, however, we examine the part actually played by empirical descriptions in moral argument, we find that they are not used as argument or proof but are wholly

---

11 pp. 423–5.   12 p. 425.   13 p. 426.

subordinate to the persuasive or suggestive force of the ethical words they support. The differences between persons which ethical discourse seeks to settle are not differences of opinion or of information, but differences of interest. But differences of interest are affected by states of fact. *Some* disagreements in interest are rooted in disagreement in belief; and in so far as they are, empirical statements are relevant to them. A man who prefers a symphony to the cinema on some occasion may do so because he is misinformed about the programme. His friend, who has begun to persuade him by saying that it would be *better* to go to the cinema may succeed in 'completing the redirection of interest' by giving fuller information about the competing objects of interest.

Thus the empirical method is relevant to ethics simply because our knowledge of the world is a determining factor to our interests.

But 'the empirical method' is far from being able to settle all our ethical disagreements. Many are rooted more deeply in differences of emotional temperament, social and class differences, etc. In these cases, the appeal to empirical facts is useless. When ethical disagreement is not rooted in difference of belief, there is in fact no *rational* way in which it can be removed. But there is a non-rational way; that is, by working on the temperaments and emotions of others through the contagion of one's own feelings. This is a valid way of obtaining ethical agreement; indeed it is the characteristically ethical way; and it is not to be despised because neither empirical nor rational.

Empirical statements, therefore, while they have their role in ethics, can never replace ethical utterances. Psychology can never replace ethics; for at most it can tell us how interests are directed; but ethics actually directs interests, and 'that's quite another matter'. The logic of G.E. Moore is still explicitly operative in all this. Stevenson says:

Whatever scientifically knowable properties a thing may have, it *is* always open to question whether a thing having these (enumerated) qualities is good.

But Stevenson supplies a reason why ethical terms are indefinable. It is a reason which, he claims, dispenses with myth and mystery; but it would surely have surprised Moore in 1903. It is that ethical terms are 'persuasive': the man who uses an ethical term is trying to influence others; the man who asks an ethical question is asking to be influenced.

For to ask whether a thing is good is to ask for *influence*. And whatever I may know about an object I can still ask, quite pertinently, to be influenced with regard to my interest in it.[14]

14 pp. 426–9.

Stevenson foresees that many will object that this theory misses the fundamental point about ethical judgments, namely their truth or falsehood. But when the objectors are pressed as to what they mean by the truth of ethical judgments, they will begin talking about the peculiarity of this truth, saying that it is 'an unique sort of truth . . . a truth which must be apprehended *a priori*'. Stevenson retorts:

> I can only answer that I do not understand. What is the truth to be *about*? For I recollect no Platonic Idea, nor do I know what to *try* to recollect. I find no indefinable property, nor do I know what to look for. And the 'self-evident' deliverances of reason, which so many philosophers have claimed, seem, on examination, to be deliverances of their respective reasons only (if of anyone's) and not of mine.

He strongly suspects that people who wish ethical terms both to be necessarily true and to be practically 'dynamic' are guilty of a great confusion. It is, he finds, the dynamic force, the 'power of influence' of ethical terms, which is their distinctive characteristic; and it is in virtue of this alone that they are irreducible to non-ethical terms.

It follows from all this that it is no part of the business of philosophers as such to make ethical judgments. Persuasion is not their profession.

> If 'X is good' is essentially a vehicle for suggestion, it is scarcely a statement which philosophers, any more than many other men, are called upon to make. To the extent that ethics predicates the ethical terms of anything, rather than explains their meaning, it ceases to be a reflective study.

Philosophy is reflection, thought, analysis. Ethics is living, and especially living with others, through the help of discussion, the great democratic medium of persuasion.

> Ethical statements are social instruments. They are used in a co-operative enterprise in which we are mutually adjusting ourselves to the interests of others. Philosophers have a part in this, as do all men, but not the major part.[15]

This article of Stevenson's seemed revolutionary in 1937. It is easier to see now how close it was to the established conventions reigning in British ethics since Moore. The heart of it is the non-naturalism of Moore, which in another form was anticipated by the non-naturalism of Hume. With the whole British empiricist tradition, Stevenson separates fact and value, and confines descriptive statement to the former. He thus makes value-utterances by definition non-factual and non-descriptive, and therefore, non truth-claiming. If they purported

---

15 See *Readings in Ethical Theory*, pp. 554–6. Note the resemblance with Reichenbach, who also, as we have seen, regards ethical discussion as part of the democratic process.

to describe facts or state truths, then, since these alleged facts or truths are by definition not empirical, they could only be 'platonic', that is non-terrestrial, non-verifiable, hence mythical. Again with the empiricist tradition, Stevenson gives two functions to reason: to enquire inductively into the 'causes' of matters of empirical fact; and to establish analytically or *a priori* the relations between ideas. In neither case does reason, in Hume's words, 'have an influence on the actions and affections'. Stevenson does not *prove*, any more than Hume, that reason cannot be practical, or as the former would say, dynamic. Simply, like Hume, he has no defined reason that it cannot be practical. From his definition of reason it similarly follows that there cannot be ethical reasoning; for the only kinds of reasoning there can be are empirical, or 'common sense' and scientific reasoning, on one hand; and deductive or logical and mathematical reasoning on the other. When we have allowed ordinary empirical reasoning its ancillary role in ethical discussion, we must still account for the residuum of what passes mistakenly for reasoning in ethics. Hume called it feeling or sentiment. Stevenson calls it persuasive rhetoric.

But the concept 'feeling' must be qualified before it can plausibly be substituted for *moral* feeling; and when the necessary qualifications are added it turns out in fact to be not 'feeling' but reasoned judgment. Ethical terms express 'interest' or 'approval'; but a 'stronger sort of approval' a 'rich feeling of security'. To give meaning to these latter vague terms, Stevenson would have to say that ethical terms express 'ethical interest' or 'moral approval'; and then his substitution turns out to be a tautology. In fact, Stevenson gives his own show away, when he says that ethical terms turn the hearer's attention 'not on his interests, but on the object of interest'; for what can this mean, except that ethical terms, instead of 'redirecting interest' by 'suggestion' really seek to convince the listener by valid reasons of the objective values of things; in other words of the objective truth of value judgments. When Stevenson suggests that nothing in objects correspond to value judgments except empirical, that is, non-ethical, states of affairs, he is committing the quasi-naturalistic fallacy now so familiar to us. These errors recur in his book, *Ethics and Language*, and will have to be referred to again in our examination of the book.

There is a pervasive naturalistic fallacy in the whole of Stevenson's paper. It is due to his ignoring the ambiguous character of terms such as 'persuade', 'influence', 'agree' on the one hand, and 'interest', 'favour', 'approve', on the other. One can 'persuade' others by rational discussion or by various forms and combinations of force, fear, demagoguery, propaganda, 'conditioning'. In all cases dissidents can be brought to 'agree' with the 'persuader'. But to confuse these methods with one another is to commit a crass naturalistic fallacy about the terms persuasion and agreement, reason and truth. It is, quite simply, to abolish truth. Similarly, I can have a 'favourable interest' in going to the cinema, 'winning the sweep', helping my enemy, becoming a monk. But to confuse these with one another, because all are instances of 'favourable interest', is to commit a gross naturalistic fallacy which simply abolishes ethics. Stevenson commits both these naturalistic fallacies; and his argument depends on committing them.

We shall return to some of these points when we examine the more laborious exposition of Stevenson's themes in *Ethics and Language*. But we have thought it better to begin by expounding the theory in the more simple, fresh and unsophisticated form in which it came first to the philosophical public in 1937.

2 'PERSUASIVE DEFINITIONS'

In a second article, 'Ethical Judgments and Avoidability', published in *Mind* in 1938,[15a] Stevenson, as he tells us himself, subjected his theory of the emotive meaning of ethical terms 'to an important test'. He set out to establish 'whether it permits us to make intelligible the relationship between ethical judgments and the "freedom" of the will'. We shall not dwell on his discussion of free-will, having already decided to omit this problem for our purview. We merely note that Stevenson's position closely resembles that of Moore and anticipates that of Nowell-Smith. He finds that indeterminism is neither required by nor consistent with ethical judgments and that its defenders are often forced, by the weakness of their case, to become 'unintelligibly metaphysical'. Why, then, he asks, should people have defended indeterminism? The answer is that they were deceived by the indicative-propositional form of ethical judgments into thinking that these referred to past behaviour and that they claimed to judge it exclusively in moral terms. The frame of mind in which moral judgments are uttered also favours indeterminism; when we 'moralise' we are adopting the judicial, condemnatory attitude, and we are impatient with any causal 'explanation' which might disqualify our self-righteous wrath against the conduct we are judging.[15b]

Ethical judgments do not presuppose indeterminism; they presuppose only avoidability. They assume only that the agent *could* have acted differently *if* he had chosen; but do not assume that the choice he did make was causeless. The reason why ethical judgments presuppose avoidability is precisely that these judgments are not cognitive but emotive, not descriptive or indicative but quasi-imperative. They 'look mainly to the future'. They attach praise or blame to someone's past conduct with a view, whether openly or implicitly, to influencing that person's future conduct. Moral judgments seek, therefore, above all, to be practically effective. But ethical judgments are negatived by the plea of

---

15a This paper is incorporated, 'though with many changes, omissions and additions', in the author's *Ethics and Language*, pp. 301–18. 15b *Readings in Ethical Theory*, pp. 550–4. Note the close resemblance between Stevenson's doctrine on free will and that of G.E. Moore (*Principia Ethics*, pp. 169–71; *Ethics*, pp. 188–9, 215–6, and the whole chapter on Free Will, pp. 196–222), as well as the later doctrine of Nowell-Smith (*Ethics*, pp. 294–306).

unavoidability. If the person being blamed can plead that his action was unavoidable, further blame is precluded. Here is the reason why ethical judgments presuppose avoidability. It is wholly a practical reason.

The relationship is not logical but psychological. It is a psychological fact that people are unwilling to make purposeless ethical judgments.[16]

Logical questions have, indeed, nothing to do with ethical judgments. These are exercises of influence and they can be rebutted only by counter-influence, not by logic. Empirical considerations, too, are relevant only insofar as they help to direct the other's interest or affect his beliefs about the efficacy of the influence he is trying to exercise.[17]

The last question Stevenson raises in this article is that of the status of the propositions about moral judgments which he has himself been making. They are, of course, philosopher's propositions. They have been answering the question, 'Why, *as a matter of fact, are* ethical judgments commonly limited to avoidable acts?' They have answered this question partly by giving definitions of the relevant terms, and partly by psychological enquiries. But the philosopher as such has nothing to say to the question, '*Ought* ethical judgments to be limited to avoidable acts?' This is an ethical question; it is a request to be persuaded or influenced in a positive or negative sense. Stevenson as a philosopher has no right to proffer influence. But Stevenson as a man has the same right as any other man to do so. And he answers that ethical judgments indeed ought to be limited to avoidable acts.

It must be understood that this statement is essentially persuasive. I use it in order to influence people to disapprove of judging unavoidable acts.

He gives a reason in support of his judgment, namely that judgments of unavoidable acts are ineffectual. But the reason is given only in support of 'influence', in order to make [his] influence permanent. If the reason does not succeed, the discussion can continue without reasons; for it was never a reasoned discussion anyhow.

In the end I might have to resort to persuasive oratory. But I trust that in the present case this will not be necessary.[18]

There is no essentially new element introduced here. The emphasis on the pragmatic character of ethics is even greater than before, and it is clear how much Stevenson has been influenced by American pragmatism and especially by William James. This leads Stevenson, as it frequently led James, to confuse the philosophical question (here, the question, 'Why do ethical judgments presuppose avoidability?'),

---

16 *Readings in Ethical Theory*, pp. 554, 559. 17 Op. cit., p. 554. 18 p. 559.

with a psychological question (here, the question 'How do people come to associate avoidability with their ethical judgments?'). This is another example of the naturalistic fallacy about 'reason' and 'truth' which we pointed out in dealing with the earlier article.

Stevenson's account of the status of philosophical propositions, or of philosophy itself, is still not clearly thought out. There was obviously both a temptation and a logical proclivity for him to extend to philosophical propositions and theories his emotive analysis of ethical expressions. This is what in fact he did, in a third article, entitled 'Persuasive Definitions', which he published, again in *Mind*, later in 1938.[18a]

He begins by saying what he means by a persuasive definition: it is one which gives a new conceptual meaning to a familiar word without changing its emotive meaning; and which is used with the conscious or unconscious purpose of changing the direction of people's interests.[19] The words which lend themselves best to persuasive redefining are words with vague conceptual meaning, but rich emotive meaning; for example 'culture'. The years since Stevenson wrote have provided us with all too many examples of propaganda by redefinition: his analysis fits perfectly the uses nowadays made of words like 'democracy', 'progress', 'market forces' or 'the market-place', etc. Stevenson quotes from Aldous Huxley's novel, *Eyeless in Gaza*, a passage which brilliantly exposed this propaganda technique. After remarking that everyone who wants to promote something obnoxious, is careful to call it the 'true' embodiment of its opposite; the die-hard conservative calling his creed 'true socialism'; the brewer singing the praises of 'true temperance'. . . ; Huxley's spokesman goes on:

> What's in a name? . . . the answer is, practically everything, if the name's a good one. Freedom's a marvellous name. That's why you're so anxious to make use of it. You think that, if you call imprisonment true freedom, people will be attracted to prison. And the worst of it is, you're quite right.

Stevenson makes it clear that he is not out to condemn the persuasive use of words, but only to call attention to it. It is a matter of recognising that language has dynamic as well as informative purposes. It is a question of distinguishing 'between persuasion and rational demonstration'.[20]

Philosophers have generally thought that their procedures belonged entirely to the domain of rational demonstration. Stevenson calls attention to the considerable place of 'persuasion' in philosophy. He suggests that Spinoza used the 'persuasive' or 'emotive' term 'God' in order to give a religious significance to his atheistic doctrine of substance. It is not that Spinoza was being hypocritical; he was quite sincerely redefining the term 'religion' so that his doctrine of impersonal

---

18a The paper is incorporated, 'though with many changes, omissions and additions', in *Ethics and Language*, pp. 210–26, 277–97. 19 *Mind*, 47, 1938, p. 330. 20 Op. cit., pp. 333–9.

Absolute Substance would be 'true religion', while the biblical doctrine of a Personal God would be 'irreligious'.

Stevenson finds a striking example of 'persuasive redefinition' in the use the logical positivists made of the terms 'meaningless', 'senseless', 'nonsense'. The positivists were doing two things: they were putting forward a theory of meaning, encapsulated in a definition of meaning, which confined 'meaning' to science and denied it to metaphysics; but they were also conferring a 'laudatory title', 'meaningful', on science, and a 'derogatory title', 'nonsense', on metaphysics. They were thus showing science in a fine light and metaphysics in a poor one. In fact, though they were not explicitly conscious of what they were doing, they were persuasively redefining 'meaning'. But Stevenson stresses that they were not being dishonest nor was their critique of metaphysics without philosophical point.

> It is of no little service to stress the ways in which metaphysics has been confused with science; to the extent to which positivists have done this, they have not been merely exhorting or persuading. But the persuasive force of their language is still paramount.[21]

Stevenson next turns to ethics, and there, as we should expect, he finds the role of persuasive definition paramount. All the definitions of virtues, obligations, moral rules, given by moralists are attempts to influence people to adopt certain patterns of conduct by ascribing laudatory titles to them; this is 'to take sides in a social struggle'. Moral philosophers have seriously erred about the nature of their subject by failing to recognise the element of persuasion involved. They tried to avoid rhetoric or preaching by giving definitions, as though they were engaged in purely intellectual analysis. But they did not see that their definitions themselves were not logical but rhetorical. Many philosophers have glimpsed the truth that in ethics there can be no certitude, no 'definitive method of proof'; but they have still persisted in looking for something in ethics corresponding to certitude or proof or truth. It is only when we recognise that ethics is *non-rational* persuasion that we can at last both theoretically grasp the nature of ethical disagreement and practically work out efficacious methods of resolving it.

The essential features of ethical arguments . . . are emotive meaning, dynamic

---

21 pp. 339–40. The 'emotive' force of the terms 'meaning' and 'nonsense', as used by logical positivists was being noticed about the same time by other philosophers, priorities and mutual dependence in such matters being hard to establish. See Max Black, 'The Criterion of Verification', in *Analysis*, 2, 1934; John Wisdom, 'Metaphysics and Verification', in *Mind*, 47, 1938 (an earlier number of the same volume of *Mind* as that which carried Stevenson's article)—the paper is reprinted in the author's *Philosophy and Psycho-analysis* (Blackwell, Oxford, 1953); Laserowitz, "The Positivistic Use of Nonsense", in *Mind*, 56, 1947, reprinted in the author's *The Structure of Metaphysics* (Routledge, London 1955). Cf. *Ethics and Language*, pp. 290–4.

usage, disagreement in interest and an important but not definitive role for the empirical method.[22]

We shall comment more fully on this analysis of ethics after we have looked at *Ethics and Language*. At present we offer one or two observations on Stevenson's analysis of philosophy. He has undoubtedly pointed to an aspect of philosophical discourse little, if at all, noticed in the past. It is perhaps natural that it should be left to an age of propaganda and mass-advertising to become self-conscious about propagandistic and advertising uses of language. Stevenson has certainly shown that philosophers do use langauge in non-rational ways to a greater extent than they or their readers recognised. His analysis can be extended to many domains besides those to which he has himself referred. Many erroneous theories and false problems in modern philosophy, as well as in the thinking of modern intellectuals generally, is due to the emotive-persuasive use of words like 'science' and 'scientific', 'reason' and 'rational', 'exact' and 'verifiable', 'proof' and 'truth'. We have ourselves more than once called attention to the importance, in modern ethical discussions, of the question-begging way in which words like 'fact' and 'value', 'descriptive' and 'emotive', 'cognitive' and 'commendatory', are defined. This has been particularly decisive in the ethical theories of the logical positivists and of Ayer. We could justly use Stevenson's phrase and speak of these theories as 'persuasive definitions'.

Stevenson's ideas helped to encourage the view, widespread in the 1940s, that philosophy is 'linguistic proposal', or 'redefinition' or 'redescription' of facts, as distinct from being cognitive or factual. In this Stevenson was undoubtedly influenced by the supposed ideas of Wittgenstein, then being orally diffused.[22a] One could profitably compare Stevenson's analysis of philosophy with Wittgenstein's. Stevenson suggests that what philosophers do is to narrow down or alter the conceptual meaning of a word while leaving the emotive meaning unchanged; with the result that the whole of the emotive meaning is 'captured' for a part of the former conceptual range of the term, or for a different conceptual content. Wittgenstein says that what philosophers do is to let themselves be 'mesmerised' by *one* definition of a term to such an extent that they become blinded to other uses and other definitions, and thus come to deny the existence of facts other than those allowed to exist by their definition. Wittgenstein was well ahead of Stevenson in recognising the 'persuasive' power of definitions.[23] Both philosophers are,

---

22 *Mind*, loc. cit., pp. 344–50.   22a He refers to Wittgenstein, as well as to Wisdom and Malcolm, in this connexion, in *Ethics and Language*, p. 290. He says that these philosophers have called attention to the role played in philosophy by definitions 'which can conveniently be called 're-emphatic' . . . [which] are usually syntactical in form, and have an effect in pointing out differences and analogies, and so an effect on interests in knowledge, by making use of a temporary element of paradox or surprise. He says that Wittgenstein 'gave much attention to the subject in his lectures at Cambridge during 1932–3'. This particular theme is, however, much more characteristic of Wisdom.   23 See *The Blue and Brown Books*, p. 48: 'When we look at everything that we know and can say about the world as resting upon personal

though in different ways, pointing to the presence of non-rational elements in philosophical thinking. But Wittgenstein's remedy for this is entirely rational; for Wittgenstein the only cure for 'emotive' philosophy is rational philosophy.[24]

Stevenson, on the other hand, seems to be caught in a dilemma like that of the Cretan liars. If all Cretans were liars, no Cretan could truly say that they were, or could tell the difference between lies and truth. Stevenson has not provided any criterion for distinguishing between philosophy which is rational and philosophy which is non-rational. He elsewhere suggests that moralists who speak of 'the *true* concept of justice' are really meaning *their* concept of justice. It often seems as though for himself rational philosophy meant *his* philosophy and any other is non-rational. Is he simply claiming to be the only Cretan who is not lying?

In fact, however, Stevenson claims to give *reasons* which show that his analysis of other philosophers is the *correct* analysis. He claims that those who reject his analysis of ethics are *wrong*, are guilty of *misunderstanding*.[25] But he has no defence against those who use his own weapons against him and accuse *his* definitions of being persuasive and *his* analysis of being emotive. Indeed, he cannot deny that the terms 'emotive' and 'persuasive' with the contrasting terms 'cognitive' and 'rational', have themselves a highly 'emotive aspect'. How can he deny that, in calling ethics 'emotive' and much of philosophy 'persuasive', while calling science 'rational', he is himself 'emoting' and 'persuading'; attaching 'laudatory titles' to science and 'derogatory titles' to ethics and to part of philosophy, exactly as he saw that the positivists were doing.

3 DISAGREEMENT IN BELIEF VERSUS DISAGREEMENT IN ATTITUDE

Stevenson's book, *Ethics and Language*, works over these ideas in more studious detail but marks no fundamental change of principle. It opens with a chapter on 'Kinds of Agreement and Disagreement'. This chapter reiterates the doctrine of the earlier papers, that disagreement in belief must be distinguished from

---

experience, then what we know seems to lose a good deal of its value, reliability, and solidity. We are then inclined to say that it is all 'subjective', and 'subjective' is used derogatorily, as when we say that an opinion is *merely* subjective, a matter of taste. Now that this aspect should seem to shake the authority of experience and knowledge, points to the fact that here our language is tempting us to draw some misleading analogy.' Cf. p. 57: 'We may be irresistibly attracted or repelled by a notation. . . . A change of clothes or of names may mean very little, and it may mean a great deal.' Cf. *Philosophical Investigations*, 88. 24 Cf. Rush Rhees in *The Listener*, 4 February 1960: 'If Wittgenstein spoke of 'treatment', it is the problem or the question, that is treated, not the person raising it. . . . What can 'cure' you in philosophy is discussion, is understanding.' 25 See 'Persuasive Definitions' (loc. cit., p. 344): 'Blindness to persuasion has fostered a misunderstanding of the kind of disagreement that motivates many (ethical) disputes.' He distinguishes his own philosophical statements, asserting ethics to be emotive or persuasive, from emotive or persuasive statements. Similarly, both in 'The Emotive Meaning of Ethical Terms', and in 'Ethical Judgments and Avoidability', he distinguishes his own philosophical propositions, asserting much of philosophy and all of ethics to be persuasive, from persuasive propositions.

disagreement in attitude, and that ethical disagreement belongs to the latter category.

> The former is concerned with how matters are truthfully to be described and explained; the latter is concerned with how they are to be favoured or disfavoured, and hence with how they are to be shaped by human efforts.[26]

The former arises in 'science, history, biography', and it is marked by statements which can contradict or be incompatible with one another, and is settled either by proof or by further information. The latter is, by contrast, not an apposition of opinions, but 'an apposition of purposes, aspirations, wants, preferences, desires and so on'.[27]

It is the difference in the kind of disagreement they involve which 'chiefly distinguishes ethical issues from those of pure science'.[28] The thinking of Stevenson is dominated by the dichotomy between science—knowledge—disagreement in belief—rational methods of obtaining agreement—cognitive language, on one hand; and ethics—attitudes—disagreement in attitude— non-rational methods of obtaining agreement—emotive language, on the other.[28a] That which is characteristically ethical in ethical disputes is disagreement in attitude.[28b] In ethics, beliefs about facts are relevant only in so far as they serve to influence attitudes.

> In normative ethics, any description of what is the case is attended by considerations of what is to be felt and done about it; the beliefs that are in question are preparatory to guiding or redirecting attitudes. Moral judgments are concerned with *recommending* something for approval or disapproval; and this involves something more than a disinterested description, or a cold debate about whether it is already approved or whether it spontaneously will be.[29]

Ethical disagreement is not, of course, the only kind of disagreement in attitude. Other 'matters of taste', give rise to this kind of disagreement also. But the distinguishing feature of ethical disagreement in attitude is that in moral

---

26 *Ethics and Language*, p. 4; cf. pp. 10–11. **27** Op. cit., pp. 2–3. **28** p. 13; cf. p. 16, 20–1, 26, 109; 138, 139ff. **28a** See "The Nature of Ethical Disagreement", in *Readings in Philosophical Analysis*, eds. Feigl and Sellars, pp. 587–93. Here Stevenson writes: It will be obvious that to whatever extent an argument involves disagreement in belief, it is open to the usual methods of the sciences. If these methods are the *only* rational methods for supporting beliefs—as I believe to be so . . . —then scientific methods are the only rational methods for resolving the disagreement in *belief* that arguments about value may include' (p. 590). 'It is possible that the growth of scientific knowledge may leave many disputes about values permanently unsolved. Should these disputes persist, there are non-rational methods for dealing with them, of course, such as impassioned, moving oratory. But the purely intellectual methods of science, and indeed, *all* methods of reasoning, may be insufficient to settle disputes about values, even though they may greatly help to do so. . . . In so far as normative ethics draws from the sciences, in order to change attitudes *via* changing people's beliefs, it *draws* from *all* the sciences; but a moralist's peculiar aim,—that of *redirecting* attitudes—is a type of activity, rather than knowledge, and falls within no science' (p. 592). On the contrast, cognitive —scientific: emotive—ethical, see *Ethics and Language*, pp. 117, 134, 163–4, 307. **28b** *Ethics and Language*, pp. 27–8, 130–1, 139ff. **29** Op. cit., p. 13; cf. pp. 16–17, 24–5.

matters we cannot just 'live and let live'; we cannot content ourselves with the maxim: 'Matters of taste are not to be disputed.' Not only are we psychologically impelled to seek to change others' moral attitudes into agreement with our own; but the requirements of social living compel us to try to secure uniformity of moral judgment. Ethical persuasion is an inescapable element in human life.[29a]

Most of classical ethics has made the mistake of thinking that ethics is concerned with disagreement in belief. Even the great pioneer of emotivism, I.A. Richards, falls into the error of the naturalists, in making ethical disagreement a matter of disagreement in beliefs about attitudes. All these theories turn ethics into psychology or some other natural science; in other words, they abolish ethics.[30] It must not be concluded, however, that beliefs and empirical descriptions have no place in ethics. They have indeed a place there; and

> the central problem of ethical analysis—one might almost say 'the' problem— is one of showing a detail how beliefs and attitudes are related.[31]

There is no need to point out the large part played in the above discussion by non-rational 'persuasion', through question—begging redefinitions of the key terms. 'Truthful', 'description', 'proof', 'knowledge', 'information', are so defined that they can occur only in science or history; ethics is, by definition, allowed to be only a matter of non-rational attitudes.

4 THE PERSUASIVE ASPECT OF ETHICAL TERMS

Stevenson had become more impressed, by the time he wrote his book, with the width of the range of uses of ethical terms, and, in particular, of the term 'good'. Richards, and probably also Wittgenstein, had made him wary of the 'one-and-only-true-meaning-superstition'.[32] He now recognises a whole spectrum of meanings of 'good', ranging from those that are 'peculiarly moral' to those that are strongly admixed with descriptive content.[33] But his fundamental contention remains, that the 'peculiarly moral' meaning of ethical terms is emotive and persuasive meaning.[33a]

29a pp. 111–2. The language of these two pages suggests that differences over food and wine and differences over moral principles are species within a common genus of 'matters of taste'; and that the urge to seek ethical disagreement belongs to the same psychological category as 'the advertiser's desire to sell his products [or] the clergyman's desires to meet his congregation in heaven. . . .' 30 pp. 8–11. 31 p. 11; cf. p. 87. 32 pp. 84–5; cf. 34–6, 81. 33 See pp. 16, 89, 206–9, 227–31.. 33a pp. 62–71, develop, rather laboriously, the distinction between descriptive and emotive meaning. The only observation we need make is that Stevenson's anxiety to find a common definition of meaning, which will cover both 'descriptive meaning' and 'emotive meaning', seems to result in prejudice to the objectivity and truth—claim of 'descriptive meaning'. 'Meaning' is a 'disposition to affect a hearer . . . caused by . . . an elaborate process of conditioning' (p. 57). 'Emotive meaning' is 'a meaning to which the response . . . and the stimulus . . . is a range of emotions' (p. 59). 'Descriptive meaning' is, approximately, 'the disposition

As a 'first approximation' to ethical (or 'extrascientific') meaning, or as a helpful 'working model', he proposes to translate ethical expressions containing 'right', 'wrong', 'bad', 'ought', 'ought not', into imperatives of the form 'I approve (disapprove) of this; do so as well'.[34] This sentence has two parts: a declarative part, asserting the attitude of the speaker; and an imperative part, seeking to influence the attitude of the hearer.[35] This analysis is partly true, he finds; for there is an imperative and hortatory element in ethics, and this element both explains why ethical disagreement is attitudinal, not cognitive; and enables us to distinguish ethics from science.[36]

But the analysis is inadequate: firstly because it underestimates the importance of descriptive or factual considerations in ethical discussion;[37] and secondly because it does less than justice to the infinitely subtle way in which ethical terms suggest and persuade. We return to the first point in a later section. Here we follow Stevenson's development of the second point. Imperatives are, after all, he says a crude way of exerting influence or seeking to obtain agreement. They arouse resistance, they bespeak authoritarianism. Ethical persuasion is rather a 'co-operative enterprise', where feelings and attitudes are reciprocally modified by a sympathetic contagion.[38] Ethical words are uniquely fitted for this enterprise because of the 'characteristic and subtle kind of emotive meaning' they have acquired through long conditioning. Interjections, poetry, various forms of laudatory or condemnatory speech, all possess emotive meaning; but ethical words have it in a more refined form.

> In virtue of this kind of meaning, ethical judgments alter attitudes, not by an appeal to self-conscious efforts (as is the case with imperatives) but by the more flexible mechanics of suggestion.[39]

The fact is that no non–ethical term can quite reproduce the emotive force of an ethical term. This is why, ethical terms are indefinable.

> The term 'good' is indefinable, if a definition is expected to preserve its customary emotive meaning. It has *no* exact emotive equivalent.

---

of a sign to affect cognition' (p. 67). The distinction between them 'depends largely on the kind of psychological disposition that a sign . . . is disposed to evoke' (p. 67). If this were taken strictly, all enquiry into the truth of descriptive statements would be replaced by psychological enquiries into the dispositions of those who make the statements or accept them; truth is abolished by a naturalistic fallacy. Stevenson's mistake seems to be that diagnosed by Wittgenstein, of looking for *one* central, common meaning wherever there is a common term; thus ignoring vital differences. Can one, strictly speaking, call the emotive purpose or effect of speech a *meaning* of speech? Is it not a confusion to speak of emotive meaning as parallel to descriptive meaning? It seemed very Wittgensteinian and progressive in the 1940's to speak of the plurality of meanings of 'meaning'; but a *little* Wittgenstein has proved dangerous for many philosophers in the past half century! 34 p. 21; cf. 81. 35 p. 22. 36 pp. 26, 32. 37 pp. 23, 27–31, 95–6. 38 pp. 22, 32. 39 p. 33; cf. pp. 57–61. For the analogy with interjections, laughs, groans, etc., see pp. 37–41, 82.

But there is no mystery about this; and ethical terms are not the only emotive terms which are, for the same reason, 'indefinable'.

This is a simple fact, which should occasion neither surprise nor complexity. The term is indefinable for the same reasons that 'hurrah' is indefinable.[40]

Let us note once more, in passing, the fidelity of emotivists to the heritage of Moore. It is an interesting evolution which leads from Moore's slogan, ' "Good" is indefinable, just like "yellow",' to the Ayer-Stevenson slogan, ' "Good" is indefinable, just like "hurrah".'

There is, indeed, Stevenson grants, an important place in ethics for empirical descriptions, facts, reasons,—we shall be dealing with this in the next section. But when all this has been allowed for, he continues, there is an irreducible residuum, an *indefinable* meaning, of ethical terms, which is their most characteristically ethical meaning; and this is 'emotive meaning', and is non-rational. When all the facts have been described, all the reasons exhausted, then 'no *reasoned* solution of any sort is possible',[41] and there remain only 'non-rational methods' of securing ethical agreement.

The most important of the non-rational methods will be called 'persuasive', in a somewhat broadened sense. It depends on the sheer, direct emotional impact of words—on emotive meaning, rhetorical cadence, apt metaphor, stentorian, stimulating, or pleading tones of voice, dramatic gestures, care in establishing rapport with the hearer or audience, and so on.[42]

Coming to a personal moral decision is a quite similar process of self-persuasion or auto-suggestion. Thus we chide our bad self, cheer on our 'true self', conducting

a kind of persuasion in soliloquy which shames certain impulses into quiescence and gives to the others increased activity.

The process resembles 'rationalisation', but, unlike the latter, it does not involve self-deception and does not depend on false beliefs.[43]

The trend of Stevenson's theory forces us to ask, 'What, then, is the difference, if any, between ethical language and rhetoric or propaganda?' Stevenson faces the question, in a chapter entitled, 'Moralists and Propagandists'. 'A moralist . . . is one who endeavours to influence attitudes';[44]—but so do salesmen, advertisers, journalists, novelists, politicians, clergymen . . . ; so do propagandists. How does the moralist differ? The conclusion of this chapter is that it all depends on how we use the words. 'Moralist' is usually a term of respect, 'propagandist' a term

---

40 p. 82. 41 p. 138. 42 pp. 139–40; cf. pp. 115, 152, 156, 159, 234–6. He likens the moralist to the writer of a didactic novel (pp. 144–5). Cf. also 'The Nature of Ethical Disagreement', in *Readings in Philosophical Analysis*, pp. 590–2. 43 *Ethics and Language*, pp. 148–51. 44 p. 243.

carrying a stigma. But if we could 'neutralise' these terms, completely emptying them of emotive content and concentrating only on their descriptive meaning, then we could decide to

> say with tranquillity that all moralists are propagandists or that all propagandists are moralists.[45]

Yet Stevenson sees very well that this will not do, and he is forced to make ethics a special *kind* of propaganda. There is good persuasion and bad persuasion. We must learn which to accept, which to reject; but persuasion is what gives enthusiasm to life, vigour to action, influence to the moral reformer; we cannot banish it from our lives.[46]

Running through all this discussion, however, is a malaise which has troubled all naturalists, and which we have noted in Hume, the logical positivsts, and Ayer, as well as in Stevenson's papers. In order to make it plausible to assimilate ethical judgments to, say, feelings or exclamations, they call ethical judgments *special sorts* of feeling or exclamation. But then, when they have to give content to the word 'special', they come round, in the end, to calling ethical judgments *moral* kinds of feeling or exclamation; and the whole of their naturalist translation has collapsed. Stevenson is exactly in the same dilemma. He wants to assimilate ethical language to emotive and persuasive language; therefore he says ethical terms are one kind of emotive-rhetorical expression of favour or approval for some object. But he has to grant that ethical terms are a *special* kind of emotive expression of a *special* kind of favour: it is when he comes to explain in what ways ethics is 'special' that we find the theory breaking down.

Thus he says, 'morally good'

> refers not to *any* kind of favour that the speaker has, but only to the kind that is marked by a special seriousness or urgency.[47]

He admits that

> 'This is good' is more nearly approximated in its full meaning, by 'This is worthy of approval' than by 'I approve of this'; for 'worthy' has an emotive strength which 'approve' lacks. And 'worthy', like 'good', lends itself to discussions that involve agreement or disagreement in attitude.[48]

We have seen him, in the paper on 'The Emotive Meaning of Ethical Terms', remark that part of the subtle persuasive force of ethical terms is that they centre 'the hearer's attention not on his interests but on the object of interest'.[49] We shall see, in the next two sections, the importance Stevenson now attaches to the fact

---

45 p. 252, and the whole section, pp. 243–52; cf. pp. 162–4.   46 pp. 163–4.   47 p. 90; compare p. 105; ' "Good" is emotively strong in a way that "approve" is not.'   48 p. 107.   49 *Readings is Ethical Theory*, p. 425.

that ethical words demand to be reinforced by 'empirical descriptions' and by reasons. We have noted above that a distinctive character of ethical experience for him is the requirement it contains of seeking to obtain the agreement of others through discussion.

If we put together these various features which Stevenson allows ethical language to have, we shall find that he is admitting by implication that, when one uses ethical terms one presupposes that there are grounds in objective reality, and valid reasons, which make one set of ethical terms or judgments required by a situation and exclude the contrary set; in other words, which make one set right or true and the other wrong or false. One cannot accept or be content to act upon one's moral judgment unless one is convinced that it is true; and equally one cannot help justifying one's moral judgments to others, in other words trying to convince others by argument by their validity or truth. What does all this amount to, except the admission that what is 'special' and 'indefinable' about the 'emotive meaning' of ethics is not emotive meaning at all, but cognitives meaning, propositional form, objective reference, truth-claim. Ethical terms differ from purely emotive terms in just this, that ethical terms are *not* merely emotive but are also rational; and their *rational* character is what makes them 'peculiarly ethical'.

5 THE DESCRIPTIVE ASPECT OF ETHICAL TERMS

Stevenson's book, we have noted, marks, as compared with his earlier papers, a greater awareness of the complexity of ethical language. In particular, he now allows greater importance to the descriptive role of ethical terms and a greater place to definitions in ethics. He shows, however, a remarkable tenacity in interpreting the new data in the light of the original theory.

In order to allow more scope to descriptive meaning he introduces a supplementary 'second pattern of analysis' of ethical terms. This has the general form:

'This is good' has the meaning of 'This has qualities or relations X, Y, Z . . .', except that 'good' has as well a laudatory emotive meaning which permits it to express the speaker's approval, and tends to evoke the approval of the hearer.[50]

The first pattern 'referred to' the speaker's attitudes and 'suggested' certain objective descriptions relevant to them; the second pattern 'refers to' objective descriptions and 'suggests' corresponding attitudes of the speaker, also recommending the latter to the hearer.[51]

We might suppose that Stevenson introduces the new pattern in order consciously

---

50 *Ethics in Language*, pp. 206–7. 51 Op. cit., pp. 206–8; cf. p. 89.

to account for the *prima facie* cognitive, assertive and objective character of ethical language. But he is quick to disabuse us. He remains an unrepentant emotivist.

The great variety of meanings which the second pattern recognises, as compared with the first, and the greater 'content' which it seems to provide, end by making no essential difference to the nature of normative ethics. Ethics becomes neither richer nor poorer by the second pattern, and neither more nor less objective. . . . With increased descriptive meaning, ethical judgments are open to a more direct use of empirical and logical methods, and thus seemingly more amenable to the ordinary considerations of proof and validity. We shall see, however, that this is a wholly unimportant matter, without any results upon the possibility or impossibility of reaching ethical agreement.[52]

Not infrequently, Stevenson speaks of the 'descriptive meaning' of ethical terms as referring to the feelings of the speaker. This is more prominent in the 'first pattern of analysis' than in the second; but it occurs in both.[52a] In either case, it seems a mistaken way of speaking from the point of view of Stevenson's theory. Ayer pointed out that 'evincing my feelings' is 'not at all the same thing as saying that I have them'. He quite rightly contended that to say that ethical judgments refer to or describe my feelings is to turn ethics into psychology.[52b] Stevenson is all the time concerned to avoid just this. It would seem a slip on his part to include the speaker's feelings in the 'descriptive meaning' of ethical expressions.

Most of the time, Stevenson understands by 'descriptive meaning' the reference ethical terms make to objective situations. He speaks of the factual descriptions used in support of ethical judgments as 'definitions', of ethical terms; and his account of the purpose and forces of these definitions is given wholly in terms of his ideas about 'persuasive definitions' as expressed in the paper of that title.

---

52 p. 209; cfr. 235, 237. Cf. pp. 230–1; 'The second pattern, with its more complicated descriptive meaning, does not provide ethics with a richer 'content'. A man who *defines* good with reference to benevolence, honesty, altruism, and so on, may seem to manifest a richer mind than one who defines it in the colder manner of the first pattern. But surely, so long as these characteristics are the object of a man's aspirations and exhortatory aims, it can make no difference whether he indicates this by definition or by some other means. That is, from Stevenson's point of view, very careless language; for science too is an 'object of man's aspirations' and the scientist's desire to diffuse scientific knowledge is part of his 'exhortatory aims', but scientific statements and definitions are not held by Stevenson to be rendered 'emotive' or 'persuasive' thereby. 52a See pp. 22, 85–6, 89–90, 92–7, 102–8, 154, 165–8, 177–8, 209, 228, 230–1. 52b *Language, Truth and Logic*, pp. 109–10. On Stevenson's principles too, of course, describing or referring to attitudes pertains to psychology, not to ethics: see e.g. p. 33, and cf. 'The Emotive Meaning of Ethical Terms', in *Readings in Ethical Theory*, pp. 417–9. Ayer and Stevenson have no place in their theory for meanings other than 'emotive' and 'descriptive'. It was partly to do justice to words which are non-descriptive, yet have a function quite different from 'evincing feelings', that J.L. Austin introduced the concept of 'performatory words', like 'I promise', 'I advise', 'I commend'. These have their proper criteria of validity, their reasons, and can properly be called true or false. See *Other Minds*; also an unpublished paper 'Performatif—constatif', read at Royaumont, March 1958. Cf. H.L.A. Hart, 'The Ascription of Responsibility and Rights', in *Logic and Language*, ed. A. Flew, Second Series (Blackwell, Oxford, (1951) 1952), pp. 157–9). 'I approve' is much more properly treated by this analysis than by saying that it 'refers to' my feelings.

We need not, therefore, dwell further on this topic. Let us only note the nerve with which he persists in maintaining that definitions in ethics are *always* 'persuasive'.[53] This involves him in saying that *no* 'definition' of an ethical term can be given that is not 'persuasive'; that is, no content, no reference, can be given for an ethical term except as part of the process of giving 'emotive praise to whatever the definiens designates'.[54] To define justice is not to *know* something or even, strictly, to *state* something; it is to 'plead a moral cause'. To say of someone that he has a 'low' or a 'high' conception of justice is to say that he

> upholds [or otherwise] ideals which clash or concur with our own—those that we are in the very course of defending.[55]

Stevenson does not, of course, intend or accept the apparently cynical implications of this. He does not see the self-stultifying, truth-destroying character of his theory. He is only, as Wittgenstein would say, being a typical philosopher, unable to take his eyes off a beautiful picture of how things *must be*, in order to look at how things *are*.

Let us note, finally, that Stevenson's 'descriptions' and 'definitions', are all supposed to be 'factual' or 'empirical'. He is repeating the familiar quasi-naturalistic fallacy of deriving a moral judgment from non-moral facts. But, as usual, the 'facts' are morally 'doctored'; they are surreptitiously 'injected' with moral quality first. Stevenson suggests that when a man refers to 'benevolence, honesty, altruism', he is describing facts non-ethically; when he applies the ethical term 'good' to them, he is praising these facts and exhorting others to do so.[56] No error recurs in Anglo-Saxon ethics with more monotonous regularity than this one.

---

53 p. 210: 'Description [in ethics] is usually a secondary consideration. Ethical definitions involve a wedding of descriptive and emotive meaning, and accordingly have a frequent use in redirecting and intensifying attitudes. To choose a definition is to plead a cause, so long as the word defined is strongly emotive. . . . Disagreement in attitude may be debated over the dictionary. . . . In any 'persuasive definition' the term defined is a familiar one, whose meaning is both descriptive and strongly emotive. The purport of the definition is to alter the descriptive meaning of the term, usually by giving it greater precision within the boundaries of its customary vagueness; but the definition does not make any substantial change in the term's emotive meaning. And the definition is used, consciously or unconsciously, in an effort to secure, by this interplay between emotive and descriptive meaning, a redirection of people's attitudes.' Cf. pp. 61, 71–2. 54 pp. 210, 218, 222, 229. 55 p. 223; cf. 234–5, 277–97. On pp. 224–6, he discusses Plato's 'definitions' of the virtues and pronounces them 'a part of a spirited plea for a class system, a beautiful and moving appeal for a special kind of aristocracy.' Plato is attaching 'laudatory titles' to the social structure he wants to promote. Plato's theory of Ideas 'depended on a linguistic resolution. Anything which was not an object of his aspirations was not to be called an Idea.' Alas, poor Pluto, how travestied is your philosophy! 56 See pp. 230–1; cf. 224–5. On p. 272, he contends, as against Moore, that the *descriptive* meaning of ethical terms is 'exhaustively definable in naturalistic terms'; it is the *emotive* meaning alone which is indefinable.

6 REASONS AND PERSUASION

Stevenson's theory of ethics is in great part a reaction against intellectualist theories which over-emphasised the theoretical or cognitive aspect of ethics to the neglect of its practical or dynamic aspects.[57] The danger of reactions is that they go too far in the opposite direction. Stevenson recognised the danger.

> If traditional theory too often lost sight of attitudes in its concern with beliefs, we must not make the opposite error of losing sight of beliefs in our concern with attitudes. The latter error, which would give ethics the appearance of being cut off from reasoned argument and enquiry would be even more serious than the former.[58]

But Stevenson's account of the place of reasons in ethics is vitiated from the start by his definitions of 'reason', 'reasons', and related words; which definitions are the unargued premises of his whole philosophy. These definitions are indistinguishable from the definitions of the logical positivists, so often nowadays proclaimed to be outmoded. 'Reasons', 'proofs', 'facts', belong monopolistically to science. They can affect ethical judgments only extrinsically, indirectly. In ethics as such there are no proofs. There are no *ethical* reasons as such. There are only ethical attitudes to non-ethical facts.[59] The reasons that support ethical judgments are, as a general rule, related to these judgments psychologically rather than logically.[60] They are an extrinsic adjunct to the emotive power of ethical words, and by no means a sign that ethical words are non-emotive.

> *Any* statement about *any* matter of fact which *any* speaker considers likely to alter attitudes may be adduced as a reason for or against an ethical judgment.[61]
>
> The intellectual processes that attend ethical deliberation are all of them concerned with matters of fact. They do not exhibit the exercise of some *sui generis* faculty of 'practical reason', sharply different from some other reasoning faculty. Reasons and reasoning processes become 'practical' or 'ethical' depending upon their psychological milieu; when they direct attitudes they are 'practical'.[62]

In one passage, Stevenson refers to ethical arguments which present 'a whole *body* of beliefs'. This has, both in the past, and again by more recent philosophers, been seen as a characteristically moral type of consideration. Moral decisions involve one's whole 'way of life', one's fundamental philosophy of human existence. But Stevenson attaches no particular importance to the point.[63]

---

57 See pp. 117, 134, 173–4, 307. The same tendency has been encountered above in Reichenbach. Much in contemporary ethics is a reaction against ethical intellectualism or rationalism. 58 p. 23. 59 pp. 21–8, 31, 70–1, 87–8, 138, 152–3. 60 p. 115; cf. 27–8, 112–3, 135. 61 p. 114. Spinoza is quoted as having anticipated this view (p. 115). Cf. Stuart Hampshire, *Spinoza* (Penguin Books, 1951), pp. 121, 139–44, 177–8, 184–9. 62 *Ethics and Language*, p. 133; cf. pp. 131–2, 234–5. 63 p. 129.

He believes that it is both mistaken in theory and retrograde in practice to look for reasons of a strictly ethical kind. Those who do so usually appeal to the notion of 'intrinsic value'. But to speak thus is to commit the error of thinking that disagreements in ethics are disagreements in belief about ends, instead of being disagreements in attitude to ends. Errors of this kind suggest that there is an arm-chair way of obtaining knowledge, by ethical reflections, rather than by scientific research. Such errors

> become particularly misleading when they serve to excuse philosophical moralists for an ignorance of science.[64]

Science must be consulted; for reasons, facts and knowledge must be brought to bear on moral problems and only science can provide them. But it does not follow that, when science has effected accurate knowledge of the empirical facts relevant to moral judgments, 'enlightened moral accord' will necessarily ensue.[65] For moral differences, in what is peculiarly moral in them, are not matters of belief, knowledge, facts or reasons. The last court of appeal in ethics is not reason but persuasion, which is non-rational.[66]

7 VALIDITY AND TRUTH IN ETHICS

This being so, Stevenson has already answered in the negative the question whether ethical judgments can be valid. His chapter on 'Validity' is crucial for the evaluation of his theory. On the first page of it, he writes:

> When ethics uses the methods of logic or science *directly*, the ordinary canons of validity remain in full operation. On the other hand, validity has *nothing* to do with persuasive methods. It is cognitively nonsensical to speak either of 'valid' or of 'invalid' persuasion.[67]

This turns on the distinction between the descriptive and the emotive—persuasive parts of the meaning of ethical terms. The descriptive part includes statements of empirical fact, definitions, logical reasoning. These are relevant to, and are adduced in support of, ethical judgments. But they are not themselves ethical in the *peculiarly ethical* sense of 'ethical'. The latter signifies an attitude taken in face of a situation which is constituted, in itself, of non-ethical elements. The question of validity in ethics is essentially the question of the validity of the step from the 'descriptive' to the 'persuasive' elements in an ethical term. This is the

---

64 p. 177; cf. pp. 178–80, 183–5, 189, 203. 65 pp. 136–7; cf. 204. 66 pp. 138–9. 67 p. 152. The persuasive part of ethics could, he goes on, be no more 'valid' or 'invalid' then 'the emotional impact of a military band' (p. 153).

same as the question of whether 'the inference from a factual reason to an ethical conclusion' can be valid.[68]

This 'inference' clearly neither itself 'exemplifies persuasion' nor 'exemplifies any inductive or deductive procedure'. It cannot therefore be 'valid' in the sense in which the term 'valid' is used in logic or science. Stevenson regards this—and quite rightly—as a 'triviality'; to say that an 'inference' which is neither logical nor scientific cannot be valid by the rules of logic or science, is a mere truism. The interesting question is:

Is there not some *other kind* of validity, peculiar to normative arguments, that deserves equal emphasis?[69]

This question, for Stevenson, must clearly be above all a question of the expediency of a 'persuasive definition' of ethical arguments. To call them 'valid' carries with it an emotive association with 'true'; and this

might foster a misleading ambiguity, and keep people from making the requisite distinctions between reasons in ethics and reasons in logic or science. In the interest of clarity, then, it will be expedient to deny the word any application to the ethical cases in question.[70]

But Stevenson will not have us interpret him as saying, as Carnap and Ayer said, that ethical judgments 'cannot sensibly be called "true" or "false"'.[71] This is to forget that ethical judgments have descriptive meaning as well as emotive meaning. Their descriptive meaning is embodied in statements about facts and about attitudes; and these 'may be true or false in the ordinary way'. It is their emotive meaning which has 'nothing to do with truth or falsity' in the ordinary sense.[72] The result of calling the step from descriptive to emotive meaning 'true' or 'valid' would be to suggest that ethical disagreement is disagreement in belief, to be removed by proof or knowledge; whereas it is disagreement in attitude to be removed by persuasion. To speak of validity or truth in ethics would amount to reducing ethics to science. Hence,

unless 'valid' is to have a misleadingly extended sense, the question 'Does R permit a valid inference to E' [where R is 'a set reasons' and E is 'an ethical

---

68 p. 153. On the same page, he writes: 'If "R" and "E" stand respectively for a set of reasons and an ethical conclusion, related neither deductively nor inductively, then it is of interest to ask whether an inference from R to E is valid.' Cf. p. 156. 69 p. 153. 70 p. 154. 71 Ibid. On p. 267, Stevenson calls the Carnap-Ayer contention that ethical judgments are 'neither true nor false', 'paradoxical' and 'wholly misleading'. 72 This position is not unlike that of C.I. Lewis, who wrote: 'The denial to value-apprehensions in general of the character of truth or falsity and of knowledge . . . is one of the strangest aberrations ever to visit the mind of man'. But Lewis locates truth or falsity in the value-apprehensions part of ethics, which he holds to be empirical; and he denies the application of truth or falsity to the strictly ethical part of ethics, or that concerned with 'right' and 'ought'. See the paper, 'Value and Obligation in Dewey and Lewis', by Morton G. White, first published in *The Philosophical Review*, 1949, and reprinted in *Readings in Ethical Theory*, eds., Sellars and Hospers, p. 338.

conclusion'], is devoid of interest. . . . The notion of validity retains its accustomed application to any aspect of an ethical argument that is concerned wholly with established *beliefs*. . . . But wherever these matters are in questions an ethical argument is factual, its methodology falling within the . . . fields of logic and scientific method. For the steps which go beyond these, and use beliefs in their turn to alter *attitudes*, questions about validity, in any helpful sense of the term, are irrelevant. In short, wherever ethical methodology must be *distinguished* from logic and scientific method, validity presents no problem at all.[73]

Stevenson recognises that a critic will immediately accuse him of giving equal value all methods of 'altering attitudes'. 'So long as one's opponent is impressed, a hasty critic may suppose, one method is as good as another.' But, Stevenson replies, the critic would be confusing two different questions, a question of analysis and a question of moral decision. The question, 'What methods ought to be used in ethics?', is an ethical question. It can be settled only in ethical ways; that is, by factual considerations insofar as these are relevant, and by emotive methods when the factual questions have been fully resolved. But the question, 'What methods *are* used in ethics?' is a question of philosophical analysis. This tells us how we *do* talk and argue and strive for agreement in ethics. It passes no value judgment on the methods of ethical persuasion. It views 'controversy about ethical methods with ethical *neutrality*'. When the moral philosopher says that ethical disagreement

can be resolved by persuasive methods only if the persuasion which people decide to use will be sufficiently moving,

he is simply noting a fact about ethical methods, 'all praise or blame of them being withheld'.[74]

We shall have to return in the next section to this question of the alleged distinction between moral philosophy as neutral analysis of moral language and morals itself as taking sides in moral disputes. For the moment, it is enough to say that in Stevenson's present difficulty, it seems an ingenious rather than a convincing solution. In the first place, no one believes more strongly than Stevenson that the words 'valid', 'invalid' are 'emotive' and that definitions of them are, for that reason, 'persuasive'. To this extent, Stevenson, on his own principles, has been 'taking sides', on the question of validity, for science and against ethics. In this entire discussion, Stevenson has not been 'seeing' how the words valid—invalid, true—false, *are* used, but 'recommending' a use of them. This is not 'analysing' but 'persuading', and indeed 'moralising'. We can put the

---

73 *Ethics and Language*, pp. 155–6; cf. 169–70.   74 Op. cit., pp. 158–60; cf. pp. 164–5, 171.

same point differently by saying that 'analysis' can only be one or other of two things for Stevenson: an investigation of how words are in fact used, or a recommendation as to how they should be used. On the first alternative, philosophy is either lexicography or the psychology and sociology of linguistic habits.[75] On the second, philosophy is non-rational persuasion. His own theory either turns philosophy into science or makes it non-rational.

The dilemma is common to all emotivists. It is clearly a heritage of logical positivism. The most striking thing about the thought of Stevenson is how much it is dominated by the 'dogmatic, restrictive', question—begging definitions of logical positivism. The report of the death of the latter must be judged 'considerably exaggerated'. Stevenson has struggled manfully to allow, in spite of positivistic theory, for the common-sense fact that ethical arguments can rightfully be called valid or invalid. But the theory has a more powerful grip on him than the facts. What he allows to be valid or invalid, true or false, is only what he calls the descriptive or non-moral part of ethics. The moral part of ethics remains as non-rational, non-propositional, and 'not in the literal sense significant' in *Ethics and Language*, as it was in *Language Truth and Logic*. And for the same reasons. The conclusion, in both cases, is 'begged' in the definitions of the operative terms. If 'reason', 'fact', 'proof', 'validity', 'truth', are so defined that they can occur only in science, then obviously ethics, not being science, cannot possess these attributes.

Stevenson has the merit of seeing that ethics must be distinguished both from science and from logic. But positivistic definitions lay it down that science and logic constitute the whole of reasoning. Therefore ethics must lie outside the domain of reasoning. Reasoning can indeed occur in connection with ethics, both in so far as empirical facts are relevant to ethical judgments and in so far as some ethical judgments logically entail others. But there cannot be ethical reasoning. Ethics cannot be rational. Reason cannot be practical. All this, however, is merely, and pejoratively, a matter of definitions. In Stevenson's own words, the whole argument is 'a triviality'.

Stevenson obviously commits a naturalistic fallacy about truth. Truth is established in ethics, on his view, when people have come to 'agree in attitude'; and Stevenson has no criterion for discriminating between agreement in right attitudes and agreement in wrong attitudes, agreement in truth and agreement

---

75 On p. 159, describing the 'neutrality and detachment' of philosophical analysis, he says its business is 'simply to specify the factors which could cause or fail to cause an agreement on ethical methods to come about; it is to view controversy about ethical methods with ethical *neutrality*, studying . . . under what circumstances . . . people will come to approve of the same methods . . . without explicitly trying to alter what ethical methods people may agree to accept.' But this is a description of a typically psychological-sociological investigation into the efficacy of methods of directing attitudes. It is not a philosophical enquiry, either in the analyst's sense or in any sense in which philosophy is distinct from science.

in error, agreement rightfully arrived at and agreement wrongfully induced.[76] Truth is eliminated in philosophy as well as in morals. Both philosophy and ethics are replaced by empirical psychology.

We have spoken so often about this before that we shall here allow two other critics to speak instead. D.J. O'Connor writes:

> There is a clear sense in which we can call on someone to justify his attitudes. We should be asking not indeed that he should show that his *attitude* was true but that he should show that it was well-grounded in being based on true beliefs about the world. . . . Yet it is precisely here that theories [like Ayer's and Stevenson's] seem to fail. . . . The facts that explain or account for a moral attitude are not necessarily regarded as *justifying* the attitude. . . . Common-sense morality at least, though it may be in error on this point, wants to distinguish sharply between causal explanations of attitudes and moral justifications of them. Now Stevenson's theory does show how moral disagreements may be resolved by a combination of language uses. But to show how a dispute in ethics may be brought to an end is not necessarily to show how a moral judgment may be validated. . . . We have to recognise . . . the difference between *persuading* someone to adopt a certain moral point of view and *justifying* that point of view.[77]

G.E. Hughes, in a valuable paper on 'Moral Condemnation', objects to all analyses of ethical judgments in terms of emotive-expressive language, that they cannot account for the *rational* characteristics of ethical judgments. Moral condemnation may indeed be accompanied by an emotion of indignation, and the words and tone in which it is formulated may be in part an expression of emotion. But if moral condemnation were *only* emotive, I could retract it when the emotion had subsided, and justify my retraction by saying that 'I don't happen to feel indignant any longer'. But I cannot do this with a moral judgment. If I do, the 'correct comment . . . ought to be that I was not making a *moral* judgment'. Similarly, moral judgments commit me to *general* judgments about *kinds* of action; whereas emotional attitudes are aroused by particular situations.

> The man who condemns some particular action but who does not regard this condemnation as committing him to condemning any other action . . . is thereby showing that his condemnation is not *moral* condemnation.

---

76 See pp. 157–9. He argues, as we have seen, that discrimination between methods of securing agreement in ethics is itself a matter of ethical attitude, able to be settled, in the last analysis, only by non-rational methods. The circle is complete and is notably vicious. Stevenson never succeeds in finding a criterion for evaluating 'ethical methods', different from 'forensic effectiveness' (p. 157) or the 'sufficiently moving character of the persuasion (p. 158). 77 *An Introduction to the Philosophy of Education* (Routledge, London, 1957), pp. 68–9, and the whole section, pp. 62–71. This criticism is close to that made of Stevenson's theory by Toulmin: see *The Place of Reason in Ethics* (Cambridge, 1950), pp. 37–9.

Moral judgments, Hughes continues, carry with them a demand that we 'should bring a certain *consistency* into [our] system of condemnings and condonings', and to reject this demand is 'tantamount to an admission that [our condemnings and condonings] are not *moral* ones at all'.[78] Moral condemnations commit me, as emotional repugnances do not, to avoiding the actions I condemn, and all actions like them in the relevant respects; and to condemning such actions done by others. The characteristics of ethical judgments underlined by Hughes are clearly rational characteristics. It must be noted that they are intrinsic to moral judgments *qua* moral. Stevenson makes the rational features of ethics extrinsic to the 'peculiarly moral' features, which remain non-rational.

We note one last point, before passing to another topic, namely that Stevenson suggests a wider use of the word 'true' in which ethical judgments could be called 'true'.

> Although . . . reasons are related to the truth of . . . ethical utterances, they are related in a way that makes the use of 'valid' wholly inappropriate. They do not *show* that any ethical utterance *is* true but rather alter attitudes, by means of beliefs, in a way that *makes* the utterance true.[79]

Reasons, supporting emotive—persuasive suggestion, give 'truth' to ethics by bringing it about that people agree in attitudes. The pragmatist resonances of this are obvious, and the suggestion is still permeated with naturalism. But Stevenson was not far from hitting on an important truth about ethical judgments. These are not just facts to be known but ideals to be lived; their truth is not solely a piece of cognitive information; they *are* true, but also they have to be *made* true, by moral effort, in our lives and in society.

8 STEVENSON'S NATURALISM

Stevenson's task, throughout his writings on ethics, is to work out an analysis of ethics which shall distinguish it from science, but shall admit no 'non-natural' qualities and allow no opening to metaphysics. Ethics must neither be a natural science nor a 'non-natural' science. This is what he means when he speaks of

> the constructive aim of this study—that of setting up a practicable analysis of ethics without departing from the world of experience.[80]

These words already show us, encapsulated in definitions, a whole theory

---

78 This paper, with others, all specially written for the volume, is published in *Essays in Moral Philosophy*, ed. A.I. Melden (University of Washington Press, Seattle, 1958), pp. 108–34. 79 *Ethics and Language*, p. 168. 80 Op. cit., p. 147; cf. 276, 321–4. On the need to distinguish ethics from natural science, see pp. 10–11, 13, 16, 20, 325–7.

of metaphysics and experience as mutually incompatible. Stevenson's anti-metaphysical arguments are merely repetitions of these definitions and of others more persuasively 'loaded', more 'forensically effective'. Metaphysics is identified with 'hypostatic obscurantism';[81] it is 'peculiar and occult';[82] 'other-worldly' and unscientific;[83] it is 'mythical thinking' designed to provide 'solace for failure in coping with the environment';[84] it is man's effort to 'conceal his insecurity, from himself as much as from others, by consoling pretences.[85] The Archpriest of metaphysical escapism and anti-humanism was Plato. Stevenson does not spare him even the old and tired libel of the 'noble lie'.[86]

The obvious comment on all this is that it is an excellent illustration of Stevenson's own thesis about the use of definitions as non-rational methods of persuasion. This is propaganda, not philosophy. It expresses Stevenson's emotions, but gives no information about metaphysics. The litany of abuse, for it can only be called that, of what is supposed to be metaphysics and of what is supposed to be Platonian and to be the supreme expression of metaphysics, is common to all varieties of modern naturalistic humanism. We find it alike in British and American liberals, Sartrean existentialists, Marxist intellectuals, not to speak of old-style communist journalists. The flight from metaphysics is a journey liberals make in the company of curious sorts of bed-fellows.

Stevenson's way with metaphysical ethics is the same. This too is other worldly and anti-scientific;[87] mythical, escapist and consolation-seeking.[88] But the chief complaint he has to make about metaphysical ethics is that it confuses knowledge with persuasion, and thus propagates the erroneous belief that there can be truth, demonstrated, final and absolute truth, in ethics. This belief is not merely erroneous but pernicious, for it engenders fanaticism, dogmatism, obscurantism, intolerance. People who *know* the truth in moral matters both refuse to take part in ethical discussion and will do their best to prohibit it, and will resist all moral change and moral progress. Psychologically, this attitude is due to fear, fear of change, fear of personal responsibility and of decision.[89] Philosophically, it rests

---

81 pp. 110; cf. pp. 8, 115; p. 219 speaks of 'hypostatic confusion'. 82 p. 108. 83 pp. 177, 318–19, 336. 84 p. 334. 85 p. 336. 86 p. 137. 'It is even possible that increased knowledge would be hostile to ethical agreement. Plato tacitly assumed so, perhaps, when he urged that the guardians should be taught not the truth about their ancestors, but rather deliberately romanticised untruths.' Commentators more anxious to understand Plato's Greek than to discredit his philosophy are included to translate the words in question as 'magnificent' or 'inspiring myth' and not as 'noble lie'. See T.Q. Sinclair, *A History of Greek Political Thought* (Routledge, London, 1951, p. 149). Cf. pp. 109–10, 224–6. In a footnote on p. 109, he recognises that 'these interpretations [of Plato may be] one-sided—that there is a Plato whose conceptions have a much more scientific cast. . . .' If so, these criticisms should be taken as directed rather against 'misguided Platonists' still too influential in ethics. There is no substitute, however, for *reading* Plato! 87 pp. 319–30: he speaks of the 'other-worldliness of the metaphysical traditions in ethics and their disregard of the sciences', and quotes an attack on them by an American philosopher, Prall. 88 pp. 108, 147, 334–6. 89 pp. 123–5, 133, 157; cf. 98. On the last page of his book, Stevenson writes: 'Ethical theory is given to the age-old quest for ultimate principles, definitively established. This not only hides the full complexity of moral issues, but puts static, other-worldly norms in places of flexible, realistic ones.' To displace 'illusory conceptions of certitude' and 'consoling pretences', by a realistic and humanistic view of ethics has been one of Stevenson's aims in writing his book.

on a confusion between descriptive and emotive language, between beliefs and attitudes. 'Non-natural' ethical entities are only the 'invisible shadow cast by confusion and emotive meaning.'[90]

Against metaphysics and metaphysical ethics, with their super-human mythologism and their anti-humanist absolutism, Stevenson appeals to 'human nature' and to ethics as a 'man-made structure'.[91]

> Those who cherish altruism and look forward to a time when a stable society will be governed by farsighted men, will serve these ideas poorly by turning from present troubles to fancied realms. For these ideals, like all other attitudes, are not imposed upon human nature by esoteric forces; they are a part of human nature itself.[92]

This is part of the familiar oratory of modern liberalism. But the opposition set up between 'human nature' and metaphysics is due to confusion. Genuine metaphysics is through and through an analysis of human experience, a search for an adequate description of human nature. Metaphysics, in Socrates and Plato and Augustine and Aquinas and the whole of its central tradition, has been the defence of humanism against all pretences to reduce man to purely scientific or naturalistic terms. Stevenson himself in part concurs in this; for he agrees that ethics, at least, cannot be reduced to science. His dilemma is that he wants an ethics that shall neither be scientific nor metaphysical. But he does not succeed. We have seen his ethics at every stage collapse into scientific naturalism and become indistinguishable from psychology and sociology. The dilemma is common to him and to the logical positivists. Writing 'ethics' instead of 'science', we can apply to Stevenson the words of Passmore:

> This is the dilemma in which the logical positivists, like Hume before them, constantly found themselves—throw metaphysics into the fire, and [ethics] goes with it, preserve [ethics] from the flames, and metaphysics comes creeping back.[93]

---

90 pp. 108–9 (an 'invisible shadow' seems odd!). When, Stevenson argues, metaphysicians think they are *explaining* ethical judgments, they are, at most, merely intensifying their *emotive* force by surrounding them with 'other-worldly mystery'. Cf. pp. 117, 163. Cf. 'The Nature of Ethical Disagreement', in *Readings in Philosophical Analysis*, eds. Feigl and Sellars, p. 593.   91 p. 110: 'One may recognise a temple as the man-made structure that it is and still see more than the dirt on its floors.' A temple seems a curious illustration for Stevenson to take of a purely man-made structure. Surely the interesting and distinctive thing about a temple is not the banal fact that men built it, but the beliefs about their own nature and origin which made them build it. Stevenson-persuaded men would not build any temples.   92 p. 110; cf. pp. 100, 147, 332; and the denunciations of 'hypostatic psychology' on pp. 8, 115.   93 *A Hundred Years of Philosophy*, p. 392.

9 MORAL PHILOSOPHY AS ANALYSIS OF LANGUAGE

Stevenson's book, we have remarked, was among the first major studies of ethics to be based upon the neo-Wittgensteinian slogan that philosophy is linguistic analysis and moral philosophy the analysis of moral language. Moral judgments, he says, *use* moral terms; moral philosophy talks *about* moral terms.[94] Moral philosophy '*studies* ethical judgments without *making* them.'[95] The work of moral philosophy is therefore wholly a work of clarification.

> [The] first object [of this book] is to clarify the meaning of the ethical terms —such terms as 'good', 'right', 'just', 'ought' and so on.[96]

Analysis 'has the humble function of clarifying muddled thinking'.[97] It is a detached, dispassionate study, neutral in respect of all beliefs, uncommitted with regard to all actual moral judgments.[98] It has nothing to do with the truth or rightness of moral judgments; it only analyses what we mean when we pronounce them. Similarly, it has nothing to say about the validity of methods of ethical argument; it only describes them.[99]

This theory of what philosophy is, is prompted in part by the desire to find a way of distinguishing philosophy from science. We found it already in the logical positivists. In them it was wholly dominated by the view that science alone is fact-finding and informative. Philosophy cannot discover facts or convey information. Hence it can only study the logic or analyse the language which science uses to state facts or convey knowledge.[100] Carnap distinguished between the material and the formal modes of speech. The former is the commonsense use of language to refer to objects, and it is verifiable by reduction to scientific statements about sense experience. The latter is the using of language to talk about words, not about things; it gives us, not object-sentences, but syntactical sentences. This is the philosophical mode of speech.

> The method of logical syntax, that is, the analysis of the formal structure of language as a system of rules, is the only method of philosophy.[101]

---

94 *Ethics and Language*, p. 104. 95 Op. cit., p. 110. 96 p. 1. 'Its second object,' he goes on, 'is to characterise the general methods by which ethical judgments can be proved or supported.' 97 p. 104. On p. 1, he says that it 'has the limited task of sharpening the tools which others employ.' All this is, of course, strongly Moorean. 98 pp. 1, 104, 110, 113, 251. 99 pp. 113, 156–62, 210. 100 What Stevenson says about the relationship of moral philosophy to moral judgments is strikingly similar to what Ayer said, in *Language, Truth and Logic*, about the relationship of philosophy to scientific propositions: 'It is impossible, merely by philosophising, to determine the validity of a coherent system of scientific propositions. For the question of whether such a system is valid is always a question of empirical fact; and, therefore, the propositions of philosophy, since they are purely linguistic propositions, can have no bearing upon it. Thus the philosopher is not, *qua* philosopher, in a position to assess the validity of any scientific theory; his function is simply to elucidate the theory by defining the symbols which occur in it' (p. 152). 101 *Philosophy and Logical Syntax*, pp. 61–79. The quotation is from p. 99.

Stevenson is re-echoing this when he says that ethical philosophy does not use ethical words but talks about them. The whole theory of philosophy as linguistic analysis remains strongly marked by its logical positivist heredity. This is true of contemporary linguistic analysts in general. It is particularly true of Stevenson. Moore's influence is also evident in this theory.

We have observed already that, as an attempt to give philosophy a function and a method distinct from those of science, the theory breaks down. Stevenson's dilemma is inescapable: if moral philosophy simply describes how people *do* use moral language, it is either lexicography or empirical psychology and sociology; if it prescribes how people *ought* to use moral language, it is non-rational persuasion and is itself using moral language or moralising. We have frequently noted the emotive-persuasive character of Stevenson's allegedly neutral 'analysis'.

Stevensons fails, as do the linguistic analysts generally, to find a distinctive method for philosophy or criteria for the assessment of philosophical analyses. In one passage, Stevenson speaks as though its method were purely logical:

> Analysis is a narrow, specialised undertaking, requiring only close distinctions, careful attention to logic, and a sensitivity to the ways of language.[102]

But this will not do, for it merges philosophy into logic, if not making it a purely tautological or lexicographical explicitation of the meanings of words; or else it turns philosophy into an empirical study of linguistic usages. Stevenson's more usual thought is that moral philosophy explains

> how, as a matter of psychological fact, people are . . . led to decide what they will call 'good'; . . . to describe how people make ethical decisions.[103]

But here again, philosophy has been eliminated, its place being taken by empirical psychology. The naturalistic eliminations of both philosophy and ethics is the inexorable fate of Stevenson's theory at every stage.

The linguistic analysis view of philosophy claims the patronage of Wittgenstein. But we feel that few of the would-be disciples have seen the true force of Wittgenstein's appeal to linguistic usage. For Wittgenstein, we shall argue, this was a plea for 'a clear view' of the whole range of language in a given domain, and, through language, of the state of reality in this domain. For Wittgenstein, this was always a remedy, indeed *the* remedy, for the constriction of vision caused by *a priori* philosophical theories. Stevenson has certainly not been returning to ordinary language in Wittgenstein's sense. He has been examining, not the full range of human moral speech, but only the small number of words allowed to be 'moral words' by recent British moral philosophers, particularly 'good', 'right',

---

102 *Ethics and Language*, p. 222. 103 Op. cit., p. 270. Cf. p. 159, examined in 9.7 above.

'ought'.[104] It is a most significant fact that the whole rich vocabulary of the moral virtues has been dropped completely from the discussions of British moral philosophers since Moore. Descriptions of the virtuous life are no longer seen as moral words. They are thought to be non-moral descriptions; and philosophers distress themselves over the problem of how to 'justify' the 'inference' from them to moral judgments, which can be forced only in terms of 'good', 'right' or 'ought'. This is how philosophers are led, like Stevenson, into the absurdity of saying that 'benevolence, honesty, altruism' are not elements in an ethical judgment but reasons supporting ethical judgments.[105] This is precisely the sort of bad philosophical a priorism that Wittgenstein wanted to put 'out of business'.[106]

In this respect, linguistic moral philosophy is *less* linguistically-conscious than, say, Hume. Hume devotes the greater part of his ethics to the analysis of the language of 'the passions' and the virtues and vices.[106a] It often seems as though his contemporary admirers have read only one page of Hume's *Treatise*, that distinguishing 'morality' from 'matter of fact' and 'ought' from 'is'.

Stevenson's theory of analysis is gravely embarrassed by his personal doctrine of persuasive definitions. He does not say that all philosophical definitions are 'persuasive', but as we have pointed out he provides no criterion for distinguishing between those that are 'persuasive' and those that are rational. Now there is a valid and important sense in which philosophy can be said to be concerned with definitions or 'linguistic proposals', or 'redescriptions' of facts; but this is neither a 'merely linguistic' task nor a rhetorical exercise. The search of philosophy is for adequate descriptions of experience, definitions allowing completely for all aspects of the facts. It is a search for *true* descriptions and definitions, in the classic sense of truth, as 'adequacy of concept or speech to reality'. The criteria for philosophical definitions are experiential, factual, rational; but philosophy recognises, with ordinary language, that human experience is wider than empirical facts, that 'facts' are more than the findings of scientific research, and that reason and proof are more than science, deductive logic or mathematics. In all these respects, Wittgenstein was right as against the Wittgensteinians.

---

104 He includes also 'just' in this select list of ethical terms (p. 1); but his analysis throughout the book bears almost exclusively on 'good'. We see no reason to join in the compliments Mary Warnock pays him for having recognised 'that "good" is not the only ethical word in the English language and that words like 'just' merit discussion as well' (*Ethics since 1900*, p. 105). 105 *Ethics and Language*, pp. 230–1. 106 See Dr M. O'C. Drury, in *The Listener*, 28 January 1960. 106a We should rightly reverse, in Hume's favour, what Stevenson says in his Preface: 'Apart from my emphasis on language, my approach is not dissimilar to that of Hume.'

10 FROM MOORE TO STEVENSON

We noted already in the early *Mind* papers how closely Stevenson follows in the footsteps of Moore. He discusses the relationship of his own doctrine to that of Moore in a passage full of significance for the understanding of the evolution of British ethics.[107] He reproaches Moore for not having distinguished, within ethical terms, the descriptive meaning from the emotive meaning. The descriptive meaning he urges, is 'exhaustively definable in naturalistic terms'. It is the emotive meaning which is indefinable. This is the truth in Moore's doctrine of the indefinability of ethical terms. But Moore made the mistake of intellectualising this emotive meaning into an indefinable *quality*. At least this recognised the extra-scientific factor in ethical judgments; though this factor is wrongly described. Moore was right, however, to insist that no normative ethical judgment can ever be analytic. Moore's reason for this assertion was that of any statement of *what* is good, we can always ask, with significance, '*Is* this good?' Stevenson's reason is that

> one can always disagree in attitude with the persuasive definition that *makes* it analytic.

The deeper reason, common to Moore and Stevenson, is that they both separate description from evaluation, and both limit evaluation to expressions using the terms 'good' or 'right' or 'ought'; so that it always remains meaningful to ask, 'Is honesty good?', 'Is murder evil?'

Stevenson goes on:

> almost all those who now emphasise the emotive aspects of ethics (including the present writer) have at one time been greatly under Moore's influence. It is not easy to believe that this is an accident. The parallel between his views and the present ones—which in spite of all the differences remains surprisingly close—will be evident from this observation: Wherever Moore would point to a 'naturalistic fallacy', the present writer . . . would point to a persuasive definition.[108]

In a footnote he remarks:

---

107 *Ethics and Language*, pp. 271–3; cf. pp. 82, 109.   108 p. 272. He means that Moore's theory would exclude as 'naturalistic fallacy' any attempt to translate ethical terms into non-ethical descriptions; and would implicitly exclude, on the same ground, any attempt to give descriptive meaning to ethical terms. Stevenson with his distinction between the descriptive and the emotive meaning of ethical terms can do justice to their descriptive content and can see their 'peculiarly moral' force as being to persuade us to approve of certain described states of affairs. This is acute comment on Moore, for we have argued that Moore's chapter on 'The Ideal' itself commits the 'naturalistic fallacy' he has so much condemned. It is illuminating to see Moore's chapter, in Stevensonian terms, as an attempt to *persuade* us to call 'good' only 'the pleasures of human intercourse and the enjoyment of beautiful objects.'

It is interesting to note that in Moore's most recent publication on ethics, he is himself half-inclined to accept an emotive view. . . .[109] The writer hopes that the present account . . . will help to dispel Moore's lingering doubts.

In the same chapter, Stevenson compares his own position with that of the emotivists, especially Carnap and Ayer. He writes:

The present work finds much more to defend in the analyses of Carnap, Ayer [and other emotivists] than it finds to attack. It seeks only to qualify their views . . . and to free them from any seeming cynicism. It hopes to make clear that 'emotive' need not itself have a derogatory emotive meaning. And in particular, it emphasises the complex descriptive meaning that ethical judgments can have, in addition to their emotive meaning. . . . Such a procedure avoids any dogmatism about 'the' meaning of ethical judgments, and tempers the paradoxical contention that ethical judgments are 'neither true nor false'. This latter remark is wholly misleading. It is more accurate and illuminating to say that an ethical judgment *can* be true or false but to point out that its descriptive truth may be insufficient to support its emotive repercussions.[110]

We can take this as a laudable expression of good intention; our examination has not given us evidence of fulfilment of these intentions. In particular, the distinction between descriptive and emotive meaning provides no criterion for distinguishing between 'true' and 'false' ethical judgments, and indeed no valid sense for 'true' or 'false' in ethics as such. The distinction is only a new name for the old separation between fact and value, nature and morals, cognition and evaluation. The chasm remains unbridged in Stevenson, as it was left by Moore.

11 SOME MERITS OF STEVENSONIANISM

There is, however, a residue of truth in Stevenson's theory. We have ourselves frequently noted in this book the role of 'persuasive definitions' in the history of philosophy. In many moral discussions, in particular, there is an element which is clearly emotive and persuasive, and which frequently merges into mere propaganda. Any of the modern campaigns for 'revision of traditional ethical attitudes' would provide illustration of the point. The literature advocating abortion is a perfect example of propaganda in ethics, through persuasive definitions. The use of the term 'woman's right to choose' has proved a highly persuasive instrument. We have studied the technique extensively elsewhere in connection with the well-known book by Dr Glenville Williams, *The Sanctity of Life and the Criminal*

---

109 He refers to the pages of *The Philosophy of G.E. Moore*, ed. P.A. Schilpp, which we cited in our n. 86 above.   110 *Ethics and Language*, p. 267.

Law.[111] But, as Wittgenstein constantly repeated, illuminating insights can so 'dazzle' vision that they make us blind to discordant facts. Stevenson compromises a valid explanation by pushing it too far. He leaves no place for definitions that are not persuasive, or for rational persuasion; and this sabotages his own, or any, philosophy.

What Stevenson is seeking, and rightly, is a concept of 'practical reason'; but his own definitions make this concept impossible. He should have questioned these definitions, because they are obviously incompatible with plain facts of moral experience, as revealed in ordinary moral language. We acknowledge the existence of practical reason when we speak of morally good reasons for acting; or when we say that actions are *truly* morally right if the state of affairs they affect is *objectively* morally good.

Stevenson has done a service in calling attention to aspects of language hitherto unduly neglected by philosophers, and by none more than by the rationalists and intuitionists in the British ethical tradition. It was important to show the place of exhortation in moral discussion. It is surely unrealistic for philosophers to ignore the part played by preaching, by spiritual direction, by saintly example, in the development of moral insight and moral life. Stevenson, after his fashion, tried to do justice to such factors. His fault was to see in them only non-rational features, emotion, enthusiasm, rhetoric. He did not see that preaching 'moves' only people who believe in sets of propositions asserting the truth of religious facts and events. He did not see that preaching 'moves' by deepening intellectual insight into these propositions, by strengthening the mind's grasp upon these assertions. He, in other words, ignored the whole cognitive, rational content of preaching. The same is true of his view of moral exhortation. This is far more concerned with arguing for beliefs, proving propositions, about the nature of man, his origin and destiny, and the nature of the universe, than it is with appeals to the emotions. Emotion has its place in preaching and in moral exhortation; but it is a subordinate and a severely limited place.

Criticism of Stevenson's error comes from a somewhat unexpected, but all the more welcome, source, namely a remarkable paper by Gilbert Ryle, 'On Forgetting the Difference between Right and Wrong'.[112] Ryle contends that 'the epistemological wheels on which ethical theories are made to run are apt to be wooden and uncircular'. He says the right question for ethical philosophy to ask is, not 'What sort of process can moral awareness be', since it cannot be 'knowing', or 'learning'; but rather:

> What sort of teaching is the teaching of the difference between right and wrong? What sort of learning is the learning of this difference? What kind of knowing is the knowing of it?

111 See *Morals, Law and Life* (Clonmore and Reynolds, Dublin, 1962). 112 Published in *Essays in Moral Philosophy*, ed. A.I. Melden, 1958, pp. 147–59.

He goes on:

> The notions of *learning*, *studying*, *teaching*, and *knowing*, are ampler notions than our academic epistemologies have acknowledged. They are hospitable enough to house under their roofs notions like those of *inspiring*, *kindling*, and *infecting*.

Ryle rejects the notion that, 'learning to admire' is two things; 'coming to know', and then, as a result, 'coming to have an emotional attitude'. 'Coming to know', he points out, can also *be* 'coming to admire'. This is, in fact, the case in morals. Learning in morals is not acquiring details and information which we could subsequently forget. The question Ryle starts from in his paper is whether one can meaningfully say, 'I once learnt the difference between right and wrong, but now I have forgotten it?' Obviously one cannot say this. Moral learning is also *caring*.

> This *caring* is not a special feeling; it covers a variety of feelings, like those that go with being shocked, ashamed, indignant, admiring, emulous, disgusted and enthusiastic; but it also covers a variety of actions, as well as readinesses and pronenesses to do things like apologising, recompensing, scolding, praising, persevering, praying, confessing, and making good resolutions.

These two series of states, 'feelings' and 'dispositions to act', are not separate from one another or from 'knowing' or 'having learnt' the difference between right and wrong.

> *Because* [a man] has learned the difference between right and wrong, he both makes reparations and feels contrite; and the 'because' is the . . . noncausal 'because'.

All of these elements of moral knowing or learning show that it involves the having of principles and the being willing to act on them; it 'includes an inculcated caring, a habit of taking certain sorts of things seriously'.[113]

This is excellent 'linguistic philosophy', it is authentic Wittgensteinianism. It is significant that Ryle says his question has been discussed, so far as he knows, only by one philosopher, namely Aristotle. It will be recalled that Prichard got an 'extreme sense of dissatisfaction' from 'a close reading' of Aristotle's *Ethics*. The references to Aristotle in Stevenson are few and make no impression on this thought. One of the needs of Anglo-American moral philosophy today seems to be a rediscovery of Aristotle. May I, for one, add also a rediscovery of Aquinas?

113 Op. cit., pp. 147, 153–6.

CHAPTER NINE

Ludwig Wittgenstein

It has been said that Wittgenstein 'inspired two important schools of thought [logical positivism and analytic philosophy or linguistic analysis], both of which he repudiated.'[1] He did not work expressly on ethics; yet no account of modern British ethics would be complete or even intelligible without some study of his thought. He is by far the greatest influence British philosophy has known in this century. His general philosophy, in both its phases, but particularly in its second, profoundly affected the course of British moral philosophy. His own rare references to ethics are important in themselves and were influential.

There were two clearly distinct periods in Wittgenstein's thought. The first is marked by the *Tractatus Logico-Philosophicus*, which was written during the First World War, when Wittgenstein was serving as a soldier in the Austrian Army. It was published in 1922.[2] It was strongly marked by the joint influence of Frege and Russell, though their ideas are completely transmuted by the highly original genius of Wittgenstein himself. It is difficult to treat of the *Tractatus* briefly without misrepresenting it. But this must be attempted; for, without the *Tractatus*, the later thought of Wittgenstein is incomprehensible, and the two 'schools of thought' which issued from Wittgenstein's earlier and later work cannot be rightly understood.

1 THE 'TRACTATUS'

The *Tractatus* has been described as 'a synthesis of the theory of truth-functions and the idea that language is a picture of reality'.[3] These two ideas are connected, for the former implies that all propositions can be analysed into elementary propositions which in turn can in principle be analysed into the 'atomic facts' and 'simple objects' which constitute reality; these atomic facts being that which

---

1 G.H. von Wright., in *Ludwig Wittgenstein. A Memoir*, by N. Malcolm (Oxford University Press, 1958), p. 1. 2 With German text and an English translation (recognised to be very defective) by C.K. Ogden, and an Introduction by Bertrand Russell (which greatly displeased Wittgenstein), it was published in the International Library of Psychology, Philosophy and Scientific Method, by Kegan Paul, London. The best commentary in English is Miss G.E.M. Anscombe's *An Introduction to Wittgenstein's Tractatus* (Hutchinson's University Library, 1959). We have made use in what follows of two articles on Wittgenstein which we previously published: 'Logical Positivism, Metaphysics and Ethics; I. Ludwig Wittgenstein', in *Irish Theological Quarterly* (Maynooth) April 1956, pp. 111–49; and 'New Light on Wittgenstein', in *Philosophical Studies* (Maynooth) vol. X, December 1960.

propositions and language 'picture'. When Wittgenstein says that propositions 'picture' facts, he is claiming to present a logical theory of meaning, which prescinds from all epistemological or psychological assumptions about the nature of 'facts' and 'objects'. He disavowed empiricism and held that empirical questions did not concern him as a logician.[4] What the picture theory does declare is that, for a proposition to have meaning, we must know what state of affairs *would* be the case *if* it were true; and what difference as to states of affairs would be made by its being true or false respectively. Proposition pictures represent *possible* states of affairs.

The picture theory requires that there should be a correlation between the elements of the picture (the proposition) and the elements of the reality which is pictured. But not every element of the proposition has a state of affairs corresponding to it. Some elements of the proposition have the function, not of 'representing' or 'picturing' but of being operations we perform with the picture. Such are the 'logical constants', 'is' and 'is not', 'all', 'some', 'if—then', 'implies', 'is related to'. Wittgenstein was convinced that most of metaphysics, and a great deal of classical philosophy generally, arose from the mistake of looking for real correlatives for logical operators or logical constants. It is this mistake which created all the 'Platonic' heavens with their Universals, Negative Facts, Subsistent Relations, etc. A particularly prolific source of metaphysical myth-making had been the word 'is'. All the metaphysics of Being came from a simple mistake, that of thinking that 'is' *represents*, whereas it only serves to connect things that are represented. After having himself passed, under Meinong's influence, through a 'Platonic' period, Russell devised his Theory of Descriptions to 'demythologise' language forever. Wittgenstein's 'picture theory' is strongly influenced by Russell's Theory of Descriptions. His 'Occam's Razor' is contained in the sentence: 'My fundamental thought is that the "logical constants" do not represent.'[5]

A slightly different way of putting the same point is this: concepts corresponding to 'logical constants', such as 'existence', 'identity', 'relation', are 'formal concepts' as distinct from 'proper concepts'. Formal concepts belong to the structure of language, not to its employment; they are shown in speaking about the world, but they are not part of the world or of reality and they cannot be spoken about. If we confuse 'formal concepts' with 'proper concepts', we are at once propelled into a pseudo-space peopled with pseudo-existents such as Being, Truth, Goodness, Identity, Equality, etc. But 'the question about the existence of a formal concept is senseless'.[6] Yet this confusion runs through the whole of the old logic and the whole of traditional philosophy.[7] Hence:

---

3 G.H. von Wright, *Memoir*, p. 8.   4 See von Wright and Malcolm, *Memoir*, pp. 7, 86; Miss Anscombe, op. cit., pp. 19, 44, 91–2.   5 4.0312.   6 4.1274.   7 4.126–7; 3.324.

Most propositions and questions, that have been written about philosophical matters, are not false but senseless (*unsinnig*). We cannot therefore answer questions of this kind at all but only state their senselessness (*Unsinnigkeit*). Most questions and propositions of the philosophers result from the fact that we do not understand the logic of our language. (They are of the same kind as the question whether the Good is more or less identical than the Beautiful.) And so it is not to be wondered at that the deepest problems are really *no* problems.[8]

Here is Wittgenstein's 'elimination of metaphysics', which was to be so eagerly seized upon by the logical positivists and by A.J. Ayer in his early phase. In order to keep metaphysics 'eliminated' Wittgenstein, like Russell, projected the ideal of a perfect logical language, a symbolism which would exclude the philosophical confusions lurking in the 'language of everyday life' by obeying 'the rules of logical grammar—of logical syntax'.[9]

There is another parallel route by which the picture theory leads to the 'elimination of metaphysics'. Let us recall the criterion of meaning which it involves. A proposition is allowed to be meaningful if we understand what state of affairs would correspond to it if it were true; or what factual difference its being true or false would picture or represent. 'States of affairs' or 'factual differences' are, however, matters of contingent fact, not of logic.[10] It follows that there can be no necessary propositions which are in this sense meaningful. 'There is no picture which is *a priori* true.'[11] Analytic propositions are, however, *a priori* true. Wittgenstein classifies these as either contradictions or tautologies. These, he shows, cannot be 'pictures of the reality'. The reason is that their truth makes no factual difference, it is not correlated with any particular state of affairs. What is true for all possible states of affairs cannot be true of any particular state of affairs. Tautology is true in *all* possible circumstances; contradiction is true in *no* possible circumstances; therefore neither tells us anything about any *possible* circumstances. What is unconditionally true has no factual truth-conditions; in other words has no bearing upon existence, tells us nothing about the world.[12] The necessary truth of these propositions is therefore bought at the price of vacuousness.

Necessary propositions are, therefore, 'sense-less' (*sinnloss*). But they are not 'nonsensical' (*unsinnig*). They have meaning but not factual reference. They belong to the structure of language; they are 'part of the symbolism'.[13] But there are propositions which claim to be both necessary and factual, which claim to be both true and true of all possible reality. These are metaphysical propositions; and these are nonsensical (*unsinnig*). We have seen already what features of

---

8 4.003. 9 3.323–5, 4.002, 4.0031. 10 See 1, 1.21, 2.0271–2. 2.04, 2.061–2, 5.634. 11 2.225; cf. 3.04–5. 12 4.46–4.4661; cf. 4.063, 4.466. 13 4.4611.

language trick philosophers into asserting such nonsensical propositions. But there lies a deeper disquietude behind metaphysics: it is the attempt to say the unsayable; to *say* what can only be *shown*; to speak not *in* but *about* the symbolism. Meaningful language, as we have seen, has to refer to actually or possibly existing states of affairs. Therefore there can be no meaningful language about the preconditions of there being states of affairs and of our referring to them.

It is a precondition of meaningful language that there be a logical structure common to language and reality;[14] but this logical structure cannot be spoken about; it shows itself in all speaking. To speak about it, we should have to put ourselves outside language, outside logic, outside the world.[15] A picture can depict a state of affairs; it cannot picture its own picturing of that state of affairs.[16] There must be logic before there can be a language-picturing of the world. But there can be no 'saying' in or about logic. 'All propositions of logic say the same thing. That is, nothing.'[17] There must be logic, as a condition of there being any experience; but this means that there can be no experiencing of logic.[18] 'Logic is transcendental',[19] that is ineffable; the preconditions of thought cannot be thought about.

Before there can be language, there must be a world; but the being of the world cannot be spoken about. Meaningful language refers to facts in the world; but existence is not a fact in the world.[20] It makes no sense to ask: 'What must there *be* in order that everything can be the case?'[21] Before there can be language about the world, there must be a Self using language within the limits of the world. This Self cannot be spoken about; to try to speak about it would be to try to get outside the limits of language and the world.[22] The limits of language are the limits of the world; the Self is the unsayable, 'the metaphysical subject, the limit—not a part of the world'.[23]

All this is for Wittgenstein the sphere of the Mystical, the unsayable; it shows itself, but it cannot be expressed in propositions or spoken about in language.[24] The sin of the metaphysician is to try to turn the mystical into science. But everytime he does so and enunciates a metaphysical 'proposition' we can demonstrate, Wittgenstein claims, that he has 'given no meaning to certain signs in his propositions'.[25] There is a logical mistake underlying all metaphysics. This can be expressed either as the confusing of 'formal concepts' with 'proper concepts'; or as the supposition that there can be propositions which are both about the world and necessarily or universally true; or as the pretension that we can speak in language about that which is the precondition of there being language at all.

There is, however, a profound difference between Wittgenstein's anti-metaphysical philosophy and the banal anti-metaphysics of logical positivism, though

---

14 2.16–8, 4.014, 4.12.   15 4.12, 4.121, 4.1212; cf. 2.172, 2.174.   16 4.12.   17 5.43; cf. 5.551, 6.1222, 6.123–4, 6.126, 6.22.   18 5.552.   19 6.13.   20 3.323–5; cf. 6.432.   21 5.5542.   22 5.621–5.641.   23 5.5571–5.62 and 5.641.   24 We shall point out later the influence of oriental mysticism which came to Wittgenstein through Schopenhauer.   25 6.53.

the latter claimed his patronage. One feels that, for Wittgenstein, it is the Mystical, the *unsayable*, which alone is ultimately important. Even when all that is sayable has been said, when '*all possible* scientific questions [have been] answered, the problems of life have still not been touched at all'.[26] And, of course, as Russell disapprovingly said, in the Introduction which so annoyed Wittgenstein, 'Mr Wittgenstein manages to say a good deal about what cannot be said.'

2 THE 'TRACTATUS' AND ETHICS

It is not hard to see that ethical propositions are excluded on all the counts which disqualify metaphysics. 'Goodness' or 'Value' are 'formal concepts' and therefore cannot be spoken about. Ethical propositions, if there were any such, would have to be necessary; therefore they cannot be about the world. In the world there are only brute facts, of which we can only say that they happen to be as they are; to speak of their significance or their value would be absurd. Value must lie outside the world. It lies in the will in so far as it regards the world as a whole, regarding it consequently from a point of view where action is irrelevant and speech impossible. All this follows from the general theory of the *Tractatus*. We have to see how it is worked out in the passages which treat of the will and of ethics.

The point of departure is that there in no logical connexion between the will and the world,

> The world is independent of my will. Even if everything we wished were to happen this would only be, so to speak, a favour of fate, for there is no *logical* connexion between will and world which would guarantee this, and the assumed physical connexion itself we could not again will.[27]

It follows from this that ethical value cannot reside in my actions or in the world. For ethical value cannot be accidental: whatever is good is necessarily good. But it is accidental that my will should produce this or that effect.[28] It is accidental that the world should have this modification or that.[29] Propositions, in order to be ethical, would have to be necessary; but the only kind of necessity there is is logical;[30] the only necessary propositions are tautologies. Hence there cannot be

---

26 6.52. 27 6.373–4. 28 Its doing so, the connection between will and result, would be a 'mere' fact, an accident pertaining to 'the will as phenomenon (and) of interest only to psychology. (6.423). 29 6.374, cited above. 6.41 In the world,, everything is as it is and happens as it does happen. *In* it there is no value—and if there were, it would be of no value. If there is a value which is of value, it must lie outside all happening and being-so. For all happening and being-so is accidental. The same applies to ethical reward and punishment (6.422). These cannot be 'consequences' or 'events', which, being contingent, can have no ethical relevance. Reward and punishment are necessarily implied by the ethical imperative; they must therefore inhere in the moral will itself—and this has nothing to do with empirical or utilitarian considerations. (6.423). 30 6.375.

ethical propositions.[31] Any attempt to express ethics would fall into senselessness. 'Ethics cannot be expressed.'[32] But ethics shows itself: it is necessary, absolute. Like logic, ethics is transcendental.[33] Like logic, it is not a theory; it does not bear on what there is in the world, nor does it change any state of affairs in the world. As logic is 'a reflexion of the world' as a whole for thought,[34] so ethics is an attitude to the world as a whole on the part of the will. The will which regards the world, and thus is the 'bearer of the ethical'; the 'sense of the world' and 'the sense of life' as regarded, all lie 'outside the world', beyond the domain of question and answer; they are not 'things that can be expressed in language'.[35] Ethics has nothing to do with 'good deeds'.[36] Ethics changes nothing—except the attitude of soul in which we view the world. We can take a large or a small view, a dignified or an ignoble view, of reality and life; and it is in this that morality resides. 'Good or bad willing . . . can change only the limits of the world, not the facts.'[37] Ethics has nothing to do with changing the world, only with contemplating it; and according to the state of our soul, the world for us 'becomes quite other. . . . It waxes or wanes as a whole'. The world is as we view it, and is happy or unhappy according to our attitude; and thus we create our own moral reward or punishment by the equanimity or the baseness with which we view fate.[38] This is an aesthetic view of morality: Wittgenstein says, 'Ethics and aesthetics are one.'[39] It is also a view which has parallels in certain types of Oriental mysticism.[40] But Wittgenstein's mystical ethics seems to have been capable of a development which would have reconciled it with a thomist view of goodness-as-found-in-things, of *ens* as *bonus qua ens*. Miss Anscombe quotes from a lecture on ethics delivered by Wittgenstein 'many years later' than the *Tractatus*.

> If I want to fix my mind on what I mean by absolute or ethical value, it always
> happens that one particular experience presents itself to me which is therefore

31 6.42. 32 6.421. 33 6.421, 6.13. 34 6.13. 35 6.41. The sense of the world must lie outside the world. 6.423. Of the will as the subject of the ethical we cannot speak. 6.432. *How* the world is, is completely indifferent for what is higher. Cf. 6.43, 6.5, 6.52, 6.521. 36 6.4321. The facts all belong only to the task, and not to its performance. (Miss Anscombe points out that *Aufgabe* means school-boy's exercise: she translates: 'The facts all belong to the task set, and not to the solution'. See op. cit., p. 171.) 37 6.43. 38 Ibid. 39 6.421. 40 Hindu and Buddhist mysticism both strive for the annihilation of desire and of activity, for the suppression of thought and of thought-objects: a non-discriminating contemplation, which is really already in eternity, not in time, is the supreme value. See E. Wood, *Yoga* (Penguin Books, 1958), pp. 203ff., 235–9; E. Conze, *Budddhist Scriptures* (Penguin Books, 1959), pp. 103ff.; E.A. Burtt, *The Compassionate Buddha* (Mentor Books, 1948), p. 195ff.; Christmas Humphreys, *Buddhism* (Penguin Books, 1958). Aldous Huxley castigates Christianity for its 'idolatrous preoccupation with events and things in time' (*The Perennial Philosophy*, 1954, p. 62). Wittgenstein too, in the *Tractatus*, thought that to be aware of 'the mystical' was already to 'live eternally'—but he rejected 'the temporal immortality of the human soul, that is to say its eternal survival after death' (6.4312). 'The mystical' is complete escape from temporal experience, from the human condition and from the categories of human thought and language. 'If by eternity is understood, not endless temporal duration, but timelessness, then he lives eternally who lives in the present' (6.4.311). Cf. Aldous Huxley, op, cit., pp. 242, 271: 'Immortality is participation in the eternal now of the divine ground; survival is persistence in one of the forms of time.' 'Personal survival within what is still the temporal order is not the eternal life of timeless union with the Spirit.'

in a sense my experience for excellence . . . the best way of describing it is to say that when I have it *I wonder at the existence of the world.*[41]

But the *Tractatus* ethics as it stands is the very type of acosmic, 'escapist' ethics, which modern liberal—as well as marxist—moralists react against so violently. It is what John Dewey condemns as 'subjectivism': 'this constant throwing of emphasis back upon a change made in ourselves instead of one made in the world in which we live'. But Dewey, and a host of contemporaries, think that this is the morality of the whole metaphysical tradition, and in particular of the 'Aristotelian-medieval' tradition. Of the latter, Dewey says that its morality 'is a doctrine congenial to minds that despair of the effort involved in creation of a better world of daily experience'.[42]

In fact, the ethics of the *Tractatus* goes with a certain acosmic metaphysics, which Wittgenstein later came to see as the great error of his early work. Criticism of this mystical metaphysics was near the heart of Wittgenstein's later thought.

3 THE 'PHILOSOPHICAL INVESTIGATIONS'

It was in keeping with the conclusion of the *Tractatus* that its author should give up philosophy; for there was nothing more to be said. He was, however, sought out in Austria, both by English philosophers and by Schlick and other members of the Vienna Circle. He was eventually persuaded to return to Cambridge and resume philosophy. This he did in 1929. His first philosophical reflections were circulated among small groups of students in the form of type-written notes: these have been published as *The Blue and Brown Books.*[43] The more mature thought of his second period was prepared by him for publication in 1945, but was in fact not published in his life-time. It appeared posthumously in 1953, as *Philosophical Investigations.*[44] A central theme of *The Blue and Brown Books* is that metaphysics is an attempt to say the unsayable; it supposes itself to be a science of the same kind as the natural sciences and purports to discover objects and properties analogous to those of which the sciences treat. But all this is a great confusion. When philosophers ask 'What is the object of a thought', they think that the answer must be like the solution of a problem in physics. Whereas the problem really arises from a confusion over the grammar and logic of words. We are misled by the similarity between 'to say something' and 'to mean something', into thinking that 'meaning' must have a detectable 'object'. This is a 'typically

---

41 Miss Anscombe, op. cit., p. 173. She explains 'my experience for excellence' as Wittgenstein's bad English for: 'The experience which I think of when I want to remind myself what I mean by *excellence.*' 42 'The Construction of Good', a chapter from *The Quest for Certainty* reprinted in *Readings in Ethical Theory*, 1952. See p. 285. 43 Preface by Rush Rhees (Basil Blackwell, Oxford, 1958). 44 Edited by R. Rhees and G.E.M. Anscombe, German text with English translation by G.E.M. Anscombe (Basil Blackwell, Oxford (1953) 1958).

metaphysical' confusion; 'the characteristic of a metaphysical question being that we express an unclarity about the grammar of words in the *form* of a scientific question'.[45] It is typical of philosophers to try to unify to excess the diverse; to force different facts into one explanatory mould; to look for one definition which shall be *the essential* meaning of a term and to refuse to allow any other meanings. Monism is the great disease of philosophers.

Wittgenstein had come to see that the *Tractatus* itself erred precisely through this mania for assimilating the diverse and unifying the multiple.

It did so when it spoke of 'objects' as the ultimate elements of reality—thus assimilating philosophy to science, and confusing the grammars of 'object of thought' and 'fact'.[46] The *Tractatus* erred again in looking for *the* meaning of knowledge, of language, of meaning. This results in our choosing *one* definition of these processes and forcibly assimilating all other uses of the terms to this single use which we have allowed to 'fascinate' us.[47] 'Philosophy', as we use the word, is a fight against the fascination which forms of expression exert upon us.[48] A typical example of this 'fascination' is the tendency of philosophers to take over from mathematics their concepts of 'proof', 'discovery', etc., and imagine there are no other kinds of proof or discovery. [49] In *The Blue Book*, Wittgenstein calls this besetting tendency of philosophers 'the craving for generality'. He also calls it 'the contemptuous attitude towards the particular case'.[50]

The chief remedy against it will be attention to the variety of the ways in which we actually *use* words. This will keep us from monopolistic definitions and from monistic theories. Here is the beginning of the famous appeal to 'ordinary language' as 'all right', and of the slogan, 'don't ask for the meaning, ask for the use'. It is in fact an appeal to return to the facts to which monistic and essentialist abstractions blind us; an invitation to remind ourselves continuously of the multiplicity, complexity and diversity of language and of the real.

The thought of *The Blue and Brown Books* is taken up again in the *Philosophical Investigations* and carried further. The 'picture theory' of language is rejected because it over-simplifies the nature of language. Sentences do not just do one thing—'represent' or 'picture' reality: they do countless things and are of countless kinds.[51] The error of logicians—and of the *Tractatus*—is to privilege the logic and the type of meaningfulness of descriptive or fact-stating sentences, and then try to analyse all other sentences in terms of descriptive sentences.[52] This is part of a wider mistake, that of thinking that ordinary language is respectable in the degree in which it approximates to a calculus, or to an ideal logical language.[53] This in turn is one instance of a deeply ingrained 'twist' in philosophical thinking, by which we are led to merge all philosophy into logic. Wittgenstein calls it 'a tendency to sublime the logic of our language'.[54] This arouses the presumption

45 *The Blue and Brown Books*, pp. 6, 26, 35.   46 Op. cit., pp. 31–2, 64.   47 pp. 26–8.   48 p. 27; cf. pp. 31, 43.   49 pp. 25–6, 28–9.   50 pp. 17–18.   51 *Philosophical Investigations*, 23; cf. 11, 14, 569–70.   52 Op. cit., 23–4, 108, 139.   53 81; cf. 91, 98, 100; II xi.   54 38; cf. 94.

that we can 'understand the basis or essence of everything empirical', penetrate to the '*possibilities* of phenomena', grasp the essences of things, and determine *a priori* the conditions of existence of the world.[55] Philosophers who make logic the essence of philosophy feel that they have grasped the clear, hard, compelling and infallible conditions to which experience and language must conform.[56]

Wittgenstein's words here are a perfect description of the approach to philosophy of the great logico-metaphysicians, particularly Leibniz; of the great logico-empiricists, such as Russell and Carnap; and of the philosophical conclusions usually drawn from the work of the great formalised language constructors, such as Frege. Wittgenstein had himself known the compulsiveness of this requirement for logical clarity and rigour.[57] Now he sees the need to escape from it, and the means of escape. The remedy is to stop prescribing what must be and begin describing what is. Wittgenstein is henceforth suspicious of the 'hardness of the logical must'.[58] He henceforth campaigns against Russell's notion of 'Logic as the Essence of Philosophy'.[59] Frege had wanted to 'break the dominion of the word over human minds'.[60] Wittgenstein wants to return to the word in order to break the dominion of formal logic. For as formal logic turns further and further away from reality and life and language, it becomes more and more empty, incapable of helping us to understand the real, which is the purpose of all thinking. Our thought loses contact with reality; it becomes form without content. We must return to the concrete in its variety, that is to say, to language in its multiplicity. Then our thought shall get its 'grip' again. Wittgenstein speaks of 'turning our whole examination round'. The result will be that, instead of forcing the facts and all sentences into the single mould of a 'preconceived idea of crystalline purity',[61] we shall find our logic in the facts and respect the logic in our sentences. This is the origin of the neo-Wittgensteinian slogan: 'Every sentence has its own logic.'

Wittengenstein retained enough respect for the *Tractatus* to recognise it as an important type of philosophical thinking.[62] Reflection on it would, therefore, give

---

55 89–92, 97. 56 97: 'It is prior to all experience, must run through all experience; no empirical cloudiness or uncertainty can be allowed to affect it.—It must rather be of the clearest crystal. But this crystal [appears] as something concrete, indeed as the most concrete, as it were the hardest thing there is' (Wittgenstein refers to *Tractatus* 5.5563); cf. 437. 57 It is worth noting that Camus felt the same fascination for and the same recoil from rationalism. 'I demand that all shall be explained to me or nothing. And reason is helpless before this cry from the heart. . . . To be able to say, just once, 'That is clear'; then all would be saved. . . . But nothing is clear. . . . One of the only coherent positions in philosophy is revolt. . . . Revolt is the demand for an impossible transparency' (*Le mythe de Sisyphe*, Gallimard, Paris, 1942, pp. 44, 77.) The language is strangely like that of *Investigations*, 106–7. 58 112–4, 295, 352, 437, 599. In 50, he says: 'What looks as if it had to exist, is part of the language . . . a paradigm in our language-game; something with which comparison is made'. 59 The title of one of the chapters of *Our Knowledge of the External World*. 60 W.C. Kneale, Gottlob Frege and Mathematical Logic, in *The Revolution in Philosophy*, ed. Gilbert Ryle (Macmillan, London, 1956), p. 32. 61 *Philosophical Investigations*, pp. 106–8. 62 Malcolm (*Memoir*, p. 69, cited already) quotes Wittgenstein as saying that 'he really thought that in the *Tractatus* he had provided a perfected account of a view that is the only alternative to the viewpoint of his later work'.

insight into the way the minds of philosphers work—and are led astray. Much of the value of the *Investigations* comes from the fact that it is self-examination by a philosopher of the thought processes of philosophers.[63] Philosophers become obsessed with one word, one definition, one function of language, which they separate from its natural use in language and life, which they isolate from its family of related words. Wittgenstein expresses this by two famous similes. 'Philosophical problems arise when language goes on holiday.'[64] 'The confusions which occupy us arise when language is like an engine idling, not when it is doing its work.'[65]

Thus philosophers, as though mesmerised, follow abstractions to a point where they have lost all contact with reality; in the name of the One they deny the Many; in the name of a theory they ignore the facts. The assimilative unifying urge is like a 'bewitchment'; we become 'dazzled', 'fascinated'; we are 'caught' like a fly in a bottle; we are 'calloused', 'cramped', unable to move freely; it is like the compulsive behaviour of someone mentally sick, we are 'tormented' by it.[66] But the malady is not recognised as such: the theories that are its symptoms seem exactly the theories we must and should construct. It is, for Wittgenstein, the very sign of the philosophical *a priori* that 'it is a form of account which is very convincing to us'.[67]

The time-honoured rationalist method of introspecting in order to find out what consciousness or thought are in themselves, apart from their objects, or what the mind is, apart from its acts, is criticised by Wittgenstein right through the *Investigations*. It is an attempt to enter the domain where our thought communes with Thought, becomes Thought itself; where our minds know no limitation or restriction of 'empirical cloudiness or uncertainty',[68] where they no longer have to learn from fact, but dictate to fact; where our minds become Creator and I have become God. But this is an attempt at the impossible, an attempt to get outside thought and language. It defeats itself. When philosophers supposed that they were soaring in the sublime, super-rational realm of pure logic,[69] they were instead stepping off the edge of fact into a giddy void, or floundering in the sub-rational realm of nonsense.[70]

This criticism is obviously directed in part against the *Tractatus*. In the *Tractatus* the metaphysical self had been supposed to 'show itself' at the 'limit of the world'. Indeed 'the feeling of the world as a limited whole' was one and the

63 See op. cit., 295: 'When we look into ourselves as we do philosophy . . .' 64 38. 65 132; cf. 291, 428. 66 See 109: 'Philosophy is a battle against the bewitchment of our intelligence by means of language'; cf. 299. 115: 'A picture held us captive.'; cf. 112–4., 116, 295. 352: 'Our inability to turn our eyes away from this picture.' 100: 'Dazzled by the ideal, we fail to see the actual use.' 309: '[My] aim in philosophy — to show the fly the way out of the fly bottle.' 348: 'Everyone who has not become calloused by doing philosophy notices that there is something wrong here . . .'; cf. 393. 133: 'The real discovery is the one . . . that gives philosophy peace, so that it is no longer tormented . . . cf. 255, 593. 67 158. 68 97. 69 38, 97, 191–2. 70 119, 464, 500, 520, 524. For the 'giddiness' accompanying false abstraction, see 412.

same with the feeling of the Self as part of the Mystical. In this state, Self and World are two poles of one and the same mystic vision. Realism is the view of this whole from the standpoint of the world, so that the I 'shrinks to an extensionless point and there remains the reality coordinated with it'. Solipsism is the view of this same whole from the standpoint of the self, so that the world 'shrinks to an extensionless point, and there remains the I coordinated with it'. But realism and solipsism are ultimately one.[71] Similarly, the *Tractatus* thought of the Will as 'outside the world', incapable of changing the facts in the world; and of value and ethics as 'transcendental' lying 'outside all happening or being so'.[72] There is certainly affinity between the mysticism of the *Tractatus* and Buddhist and Yoga mysticism; and this can be explained in part through the influence of Schopenhauer on the youthful Wittgenstein.[73]

But Wittgenstein has accurately diagnosed here a mentality and a method which have been at the basis of much rationalistic metaphysics and ethics. His critique of it has affinities with the critique which existentialists and phenomenologists make quite independently of rationalism (which they persist in identifying with metaphysics).[74] Wittgenstein's remedy for it is to return to the earth, to facts, to common sense. He summons illuminist philosophers back to 'words and their meanings, knowledge and memory, opinions, comparisons and reasonings'. This is the force of his appeal to 'ordinary language' and ordinary usage.[75] Thus, for example, the temptation to solipsism arises when we isolate the concepts, mind, thought, self, from all contact with things and with the rest of language; when we use these words by themselves, soliloquistically. But the temptation is banished when we recall that mental process words, being part of language, which is necessarily public, are situated from the beginning in an inter-personal and public world.[76]

It cannot be too much emphasised that the return to ordinary language is not 'OED-ism', but a return to reality, to facts. It is the means to getting the 'engine' of thought back in motion again;[77] making the disconnected wheel 'engage' again with the rest of the machinery of experience;[78] getting ourselves 'off the slippery ice', where the conditions looked ideal 'but where also, just because of that, we

---

71 *Tractatus*, 5.5571–5.641, 6.45. 72 Op. cit., 6.4–6.45. 73 See Miss Anscombe, op. cit., pp. 11-12, 168–73; G. von Wright, in *Memoir*, pp. 5, 9. 74 Sartre and Merleau-Ponty, for example, reject both metaphysics and theism because in them the mind has lost all contact with experience and reality and is merely spinning around dizzily in a void. It is interesting that, quite independently, they use the same term as Wittgenstein for this state—'vertige', 'giddiness'. They find its classic example in Descartes' Cogito. Merleau-Ponty describes this as a vain attempt at a 'tête-à-tête of thought with the thought of this thought' (this is exactly Wittgenstein's idea of 'language on holiday', the 'engine idling'); 'whereas they join hands only across the world'. (Wittgenstein's 'language at work', 'engaged cog-wheel'). See *La phenomenologie de la perception*, Gallimard, Paris, 1945, p. 344. Sartre too regards all talk about soul or spirit as Cartesian, and Cartesianism as being essentialism and 'bad faith'. See *Being and Nothingness*, E., trans. by Hazel E. Barnes (Philosophical Library, N.Y., 1956), pp. 35, 438–9, 462ff. 75 *Philosophical Investigations*, 38, 77, 98, 100, 120, 370. 76 Op. cit., 258; cf. 246, 260–3, 286, 290–3, 322, 343, 380, 398. 77 Op. cit., 132. 78 136.

are unable to walk', and 'back to the rough ground' where we have the indispensable 'friction' of hard fact.[79] We must never, Wittgenstein insists, isolate words from 'the stream of life'.[80] Authentic philosophy is wider vision: 'commanding a clear view of the use of our words', and through them, of the state of reality.[81]

Wittgenstein's reaction against mysticism sometimes seems to bring him to the opposite extreme of naturalism. He repeats again and again that language and thought are 'as such a part of our natural history as walking, eating, drinking, playing'.[82] There are many passages in which Wittgenstein seems to pour scorn on all spirit- or soul- or mind-language. He seems to suggest that all talk about 'spirit' is due to failure to find the right 'body'-language, or to understand the 'body-language' we do use. The concepts of 'mind' or 'spirit' seem to be for him typical philosophical illusion, such as arises when language 'goes on holiday'.[83]

But Wittgenstein was no behaviourist. Not everyone who speaks of mental processes, believes in the spiritual; not everyone who rejects a set of concepts of mind is a materialist. We must remember what precisely Wittgenstein is rejecting. And it is precisely a false epistemological and psychological dualism, which is called Cartesian, although Descartes would probably not have recognised it. It is a dualism which separates the spirit from its body, the mind from its objects, the will from its acts; a dualism which ruins both the theory of knowledge, the philosophy of the person and ethics. It is and has ever been, only a stepping stone to some pernicious monism. A spiritual philosophy has nothing to lose, everything to gain, by its elimination.

Wittgenstein was conscious that he would be charged with behaviorism. He denies the charge, and insists that he is rejecting only a wrong way of speaking.[84] What he is destroying is only illusions.[85] What he is rejecting is the Cartesian bifurcation of the person, the Cartesian definition of the 'mind'.[86] What he is

---

79 107. 80 19: 'To imagine a language means to imagine a form of life.' In the summer of 1949, while in America with Malcolm, he used the phrase, which Malcolm thinks summed up a good deal of his philosophy: 'An expression has meaning only in the stream of life' *Memoir*, p. 93. Cf. *The Brown Book*, pp. 102–3. Here he suggests that the point of the William James theory of emotions is that words are not just spoken, they are also felt and lived. 81 122; cf. 125. 82 25, 108, 454, 491. 83 36, 109, 196, 363, 454; cf. *The Blue Book*, p. 47. 84 244 281–3, 307–8, 350, 493ff., 591, 627, II v. II xi (pp. 217–9, 225). In 158, he says that explanations of thinking etc. in terms of 'what goes on in the brain and nervous system' are in fact *a priori*, a typical example of philosopher's reasoning from what must be to what is. We adopt this explanation because 'it is a form of account which is very convincing to us'. In 339, he remarks that we say 'thinking is not an incorporeal process' in order to exclude any ghost—or shadow-conception of thinking. But we may say 'thinking is an incorporeal process' if we 'want to distinguish the grammar of the word "think" from, say, that of the word "eat" '. 'Only that makes the difference between the meanings look too slight.' He means that all talk of thinking as a 'process' is bound to lead us to confuse talk about thinking with talk about physical objects and events. 85 118. 86 Cf. *The Blue Book*, pp. 66–74. He comments on the 'illusion that we use the word "I" to refer to something bodiless, which, however, has its seat in our body. In fact, this seems to be the real ego, the one of which it was said, "Cogito, ergo sum".' (p. 69) . The error he ascribes to the Cogito is fundamentally the same error as that which has led people to think that sense data were 'objects of sense'; it is that of supposing that the 'objects of thinking' are 'thoughts', and that mind is a 'substance whose whole essence or nature consists only in thinking' these thoughts. To reject Descartes is not automatically to become a behaviourist. The last line of *The Blue Book* is 'we can't substitute for "I" a description of a body'. (p. 74).

denying is that a body *has* a soul;[87] instead he affirms: 'the human body is the best picture of the human soul'.[88] What he denies is that I meet other bodies, and infer that inside them there must be other minds; I do not only believe that others are not mere automata; I am not only of the opinion that another has a soul. Souls are not inferred, they are encountered. 'My attitude towards him is an attitude towards a soul.'[89] Just as Wittgenstein's answer to solipsism is that we can only think in words and words are inter-personal, so his answer to behaviourism is the language of personalism, In all these respects, his thought strikingly resembles that of the spiritualistic existentialists and phenomenologists who have reflected on personal encounter. It could have been Marcel, Nedoncelle, Scheler, Buber, who wrote: 'Pity is a form of conviction that someone else [*scil.* not some *body*]' is in pain.'[90]

In all this, there in nothing with which a thomist will quarrel. Aquinas too holds that our mind is known to us only in its activity, which activity is the knowing of the outside world. Wittgenstein's doctrine that mind is known through what we do with language is not essentially different from Aquinas' doctrine that mind is known through its cognitive acts and objects.[91]

4 THE 'INVESTIGATIONS' AND ETHICS

There is no explicit treatment of ethics in the *Philosophical Investigations*, but its lines of thought have obviously an important bearing on ethics. The ethical mysticism of the *Tractatus* stands immediately condemned with the rest of the acosmism of that work. The answer to it is to survey the whole range of our actual language about willing. This shows that willing is not an inner experience, separable from its 'object'. Willing is doing something (even if it be only 'trying') willingly.[92] To put 'willing' in the mind and 'doing' in the world (as the *Tractatus* did) is to make willing inefficacious, the will irresponsible and the world 'independent of my will'. It is to abolish ethics. We must not 'sublime' willing or ethics, any more than logic; that is to say, we must not separate them from experience. The same applies to intention. This is not an interior performance, detachable from its object; but is 'embedded in human customs and institutions'.[93] Intention lies also in what I do.[94] Wittgenstein's escape from acosmism in ethics is via an 'engaged' definition of will and intention which are remarkably like those found in Aquinas. For Aquinas, intention is the willing of an act or situation, and the morality of the will is determined in the first place by the objective goodness or

---

87 283; cf. 284–6. 88 II iv. 89 Ibid., cf. II xi (p. 197). 90 287; cf. 281ff., II xi (pp. 227–8). 91 *S.Theol.* 1.85.2, 1.87. 1–3. 92 611–30; cf. *The Brown Book*, pp. 100–4, 110–16, 150–2. 93 337; cf. 611–20. 94 644: 'I am not ashamed of what I did then, but of the intention which I had.'—And didn't the intention lie also in what I did? What justifies the shame? The whole history of the incident.' Cf. 591–2, 611ff., 620ff., 642–4, II xi (pp. 216–8).

badness of the act or situation which the will embraces.[95]

This critique has obviously application far beyond the ethics of the *Tractatus*. Two of the errors of the intuitionists are immediately exposed: that of supposing that the will can only 'exert itself' to act and cannot be obliged to perform an overt action; and that of holding that motive lies outside the scope of obligation.[96] The deeper reason for these errors is revealed: namely, the isolation of moral predicates from one another, from the whole of language and from life. In this respect, Wittgenstein's thought was partly anticipated by such critics of intuitionism as Joseph and Muirhead. In fact, idealism at its best tried to be this wider vision of reality which Wittgenstein sought. There is more affinity between some idealists (e.g. Bradley) and Wittgenstein than has been usually recognised.

The sole direct reference to ethics in the *Investigations* is, characteristically, equally loaded with consequences for the demolition of bad ethics and the construction of better. It is particularly important for the critique of the rationalist and intuitionist tradition inaugurated by Moore. It is a warning not to 'look for definitions corresponding to our concepts in aesthetics or ethics'; and an adjuration instead to ask: 'How did we *learn* the meaning of this word ('good' for instance)?'—for this will show that 'good' does not mean one *thing*, but 'must have a family of meanings'.[97] Much of the bad English moral philosophy since Moore has been precisely due to the belief that 'good' must mean (i.e. refer to) some *one thing*. Now, the argument went, 'things' *must* be *either* facts or values. Therefore, if 'good' does not refer to an objective 'fact' or 'natural property', then it must refer to an objective 'non-natural property'. But if there are no 'non-natural properties', then there is nothing objective at all for 'good' to refer to. It is, therefore meaningless;—only a substitute for Hurrah! Or else, for the less tough-minded, it is not a statement (since all statements must be descriptive), but a command, a preference, a persuasion, a decision. . . . The development of British ethics in this century provides many confirmations of Wittgenstein's analysis of how philosophers tend to think—and to go wrong. On the other hand, we feel that his view of 'good' as having a 'family of meanings' partly the same and partly different, is reconcilable with the thomist doctrine of the analogical meaning of 'good'.[98]

Our biographical information about Wittgenstein suggests that his practical

---

95 *S. Theol.*, 1–2.9.4; ibid., 12, 1–4, 18 passim, 20 passim. For an excellent study of 'intention' in a Wittgensteinian perspective, see Miss G.E.M. Anscombe, *Intention* (Blackwell, Oxford, 1957), especially pp. 28, 44, 85. 96 In view of what we have said on other pages about the affinity between the mysticism of the *Tractatus* and oriental mysticism, and between certain doctrines of the intuitionists and those of neo-Protestant theologians, it is not without interest to point out that Barth's theology of transcendence has been compared with Vedantic literature because of its insistence on the utter futility of human understanding and activity. See H.D. Lewis, *Morals and Revelation*, pp. 17–19. 97 Philosophical Investigations, 77. 98 In his desire to avoid 'essentialist abstraction', Wittgenstein introduced the notion of 'family resemblances'. Thus: 'These phenomena have no one thing in common which makes us use the same word for all,—. . . but they are *related* to one another in many different ways' (65). 'We see

ethics was of a personalist stamp. He had a profound sense of the dignity of the human person and its right to truth and to love.[99] We have earlier quoted Lord Keynes as saying that Wittgenstein reproached Moore and his young Cambridge friends with 'lacking reverence for everything and everyone'. This accords with what we have said about the personalism of his philosophy of language and of mind.

No subsequent British philosopher could remain indifferent to Wittgenstein. The most influential of them claimed and claim to be his disciples. Wittgenstein has himself put in words what he thought of most of them. He once said despairingly to his students: 'The only seed I am likely to sow is a certain jargon.'[100] And in 1945, the year he wrote the Preface for the *Investigations*, he recorded the anger with which he observed that his 'results (which [he] had communicated in lectures, typescripts and discussions), variously misunderstood, more or less mangled or watered down, were in circulation. Now, fifty years further on, we can better appreciate how much of the better philosophy of post-war Britain has been in fact good Wittgenstein, with source frequently unacknowledged; and how much of the bad philosophy has been pseudo-Wittgenstein frequently claiming his authority. It would be interesting to test this observation by further study of the writings of more recent moral philosophers in the British tradition; but this must be left for other days and perhaps for other hands.

POSTSCRIPT

The present study was meant to be completed by a study of the basic principles of the moral philosophy of Aquinas. This would have explored the ways in which, as we believe, Aquinas escapes the errors which we have criticised in the theories of ethics we have examined, while situating their truths in a more holistic philosophy of the person; and would also have further explored affinities between Aquinas and the later Wittgenstein. This has not proved possible and the work must remain unfinished.[101] A Thomist may perhaps be excused for finding comfort in a phrase from the scholastic tradition: '*Opus philosophiae semper perfectibile*'; 'the work of philosophy is never completed'.

a complicated network of similarities overlapping and criss-crossing . . .' (66–7). We feel that this can be reconciled with Aquinas' doctrine of how analogous terms are predicated: 'not with the same meaning in all cases, as univocal terms are; not yet with totally different meanings, as equivocal terms are; but the meaning varies in the different usages though there is a resemblance, different for each case, connecting together the various uses.' *S.Theol.* 1.13.5; cf. 1.3.4–5; *De Veritate*, 1.1. Aquinas is careful to distinguish his 'metaphysical' abstraction' from mathematical abstraction, and to show that the former is not 'essentialist', in the modern sense. 99 See Malcolm, *Memoir*, pp. 37, 61, 80. 100 Op. cit., p. 63. 101 Some initial contribution to this study was attempted by the present writer in the chapter 'Morality and Being Human', *Law and Morals* (Four Courts Press, Dublin, 1993).

Index